Education, Training and the Future of Work I: Social, Political and Economic Contexts of Policy Development

This book focuses on the recent changes in education and training policy, mainly in the UK. It explores the wider contexts in which such policies have been developed and draws out the connections between changes taking place in work processes and the identities of those who have to prepare for the new flexible work roles required by current labour markets. It also explores the nature of political agency in the development of education and training policy in recent years, and will look at the agendas, strategies and discourses which have underpinned a number of policy changes.

Reader I for the Open University module E837

COMPANION VOLUME

The companion volume in this series is:
Education, Training and the Future of Work II: developments in vocational education and training
Edited by Mike Flude and Sandy Sieminski.

Both of these Readers are part of a course, Education, Training and the Future of Work, that is itself part of the Open University MA Programme.

THE OPEN UNIVERSITY MA IN EDUCATION
The Open University MA in Education is now firmly established as the most popular post-graduate degree for education professionals in Europe, with over 3,500 students registering each year. The MA in Education is designed particularly for those with experience of teaching, the advisory service, educational administration or allied fields.

Structure of the MA
The MA is a modular degree, and students are therefore free to select from a range of options the programme which best fits in with their interests and professional goals. Specialist lines in management, primary education and lifelong learning are also available. Study in the Open University's Advanced Diploma and Certificate Programmes can also be counted towards the MA, and successful study in the MA programme entitles students to apply for entry into the Open University Doctorate in Education programme.

COURSES CURRENTLY AVAILABLE:
- Management
- Child Development
- Primary Education
- Learning, Curriculum, and Assessment
- Inclusive Education
- Language and Literacy
- Mentoring
- Education, Training and Employment
- Gender in Education
- Educational Research
- Science Education
- Adult Learners
- Maths Education
- Guidance and Counselling in Learning

OU supported open learning
The MA in Education programme provides great flexibility. Students study at their own pace, in their own time, anywhere in the European Union. They receive specially prepared study materials, supported by tutorials, thus offering the chance to work with other students.

THE DOCTORATE IN EDUCATION
The Doctorate in Education is a new part-time doctoral degree, combining taught courses, research methods and a dissertation designed to meet the needs of professionals in education and related areas who are seeking to extend and deepen their knowledge and understanding of contemporary educational issues. It should help them to:

•develop appropriate skills in educational research and enquiry
•carry out research in order to contribute to professional knowledge and practice.

The Doctorate in Education builds upon successful study within the Open University MA in Education programme.

How to apply
If you would like to register for this programme, or simply to find out more information, please write for the *Professional Development in Education* prospectus to the Course Reservations Centre, PO Box 724, The Open University, Walton Hall, Milton Keynes, MK7 6ZS, UK (Telephone 0 [0 44] 1908 653231).

Education, Training and the Future of Work I

Social, political and economic contexts of
policy development

Edited by

John Ahier and
Geoff Esland

at The Open University

**London and New York in association
with The Open University**

First published 1999
by Routledge
11 New Fetter Lane, London EC4P 4EE

Simultaneously published in the USA and Canada
by Routledge
29 West 35th Street, New York, NY 10001

© 1999 Compilation, original and editorial matter,
The Open University

Typeset in Garamond by
The Florence Group, Stoodleigh, Devon

Printed and bound in Great Britain by
TJ International Ltd, Padstow, Cornwall

British Library Cataloguing in Publication Data
A catalogue record for this book is available
from the British Library

Library of Congress Cataloging-in-Publication Data
Education, training, and the future of work I: social, political and
economic contexts of policy development/edited by John Ahier and
Geoff Esland.
    p.   cm.
1. Education and state—Great Britain.   2. Occupational
training—Government policy—Great Britain.   3. Vocational
education—Great Britain.   4. Employment forecasting—Great
Britain.   I. Ahier, John.   II. Esland, Geoff.
LC93.G7E376 1999
379.41–dc21   98–40352
                          CIP

ISBN 0–415–20208–6 (hbk)
ISBN 0–415–20209–4 (pbk)

Contents

Figures and tables

Preface

This is the first of two volumes of readings entitled *Education, Training and the Future of Work*. Volume I, edited by John Ahier and Geoff Esland, is organized around the theme of the *social, political and economic contexts* of education and training. Volume II, edited by Mike Flude and Sandy Sieminski, focuses upon the *development of vocational policy*.

Both volumes – which are designed to be complementary – form part of the Open University MA Module, *Education, Training and the Future of Work* (E837). The course itself is based on a Study Guide in which the readings contained in these volumes are integrated within an analysis of a range of themes relating to post-compulsory education and training and the future of work. However, it is our hope that these collections will also appeal to a wider audience with an interest in policy developments in these areas.

Anyone working in this field cannot but be aware that anxieties abound about the future of work. In 1998, after six years of economic growth, and just at the point when it began to stall, the official unemployment level in Britain stood at 1.8 million, having reached well over 3 million during the recession of 1990–92.[1] The significance of these figures is that even when the economic cycle is favourable, unemployment remains at levels which would once have been unthinkable. In his foreword to the report *Unemployment and the Future of Work,* published in 1997 by the Council of Churches for Britain and Ireland, the Bishop of Liverpool, the Rt Revd David Sheppard asked

> Will there ever be enough jobs to go round? . . . New technology brings prosperity for many people, but for many others it means redundancy and unemployment. As the world economy becomes more and more competitive some people are giving up hope that they will ever work again. Is mass unemployment here to stay?

For those in work, there is a widespread sense of insecurity resulting from the growing use by employers of various forms of 'flexibilization': outsourcing, part-time work, short-term contracts and unsocial hours. Long working weeks are also common, particularly in Britain, where survey after survey confirms that on average its workforce has the longest working week in Europe. Evidence of the scale of the problem was provided by a survey of managers published by *Management Today* in June 1998 which reported that

> A massive 84 per cent of the sample [made up of 5,500 responses] admitted to having made important sacrifices in pursuit of their career. The survey asked managers to consider the biggest personal sacrifice they have made in their career. Missing children growing up and letting work intrude on home life head this listing, although answers reveal a wide range of personal regrets – from missing a school event or the birth of a child, to divorce, the postponement of a parent's funeral and not being with a partner during serious illness or even death.

One of our main aims in preparing these readers has been to extend and deepen the debates about post-compulsory education and training (PCET) by situating them in the broader contexts of economic and employment policy, both in the UK and in the field of international political economy. Many of the agendas that underpin PCET are frequently associated with the dynamic of economic globalization, so that ideological pressure is often directed at individuals – and their schools, colleges and universities – to prepare for participation in a competitive global economy. There is a widespread consensus – at least among 'Anglo-Saxon'-style economies – that the new 'post-Fordist' forms of production require increasing degrees of 'flexibility' in employment, so that individuals are exhorted to take responsibility for continually updating their skills in a lifetime of learning. 'Portfolio employment' has become the lodestar for the successful, upwardly mobile professional, who is advised to abandon any vestigial craving for the 'job for life' and the 'psychological contract' which characterized employer–employee relationships in an earlier era. Much, too, is made of the economic 'weightlessness' of large parts of international business and trade, due to the fact that a high proportion of transactions now take place via electronic media. Both the financial markets and the Internet have in their different ways become the symbols of a new global information consumerism, giving credence to the view that the traditional boundaries of the nation state are becoming increasingly irrelevant in the new electronic, 'borderless' world. As a consequence, it is claimed, the new technologies will continue to require appropriately skilled people capable of performing effectively in the 'knowledge-based' economies of the future.

Underlying the techno-utopianism which sometimes characterizes the popular discourse surrounding globalization is a rather more sober reality based on the fact that the main economic principles driving it are derived from the international endorsement of free markets, especially in relation to trade, finance and labour. This has been particularly true of the United

Kingdom, where four successive Conservative administrations were able to establish a deregulated financial system while scaling down the levels of employment protection previously operating in the labour market. In those sectors of the economy which could not be privatized, highly regulated quasi-markets were introduced that had as one of their main objectives the delivery of services on a reducing unit cost basis, so that more was required from fewer employees. The impact of two recessions, a succession of legislative measures designed to weaken the trade unions, and the promotion of enterprise, efficiency and competitiveness in all parts of the economy led to high levels of unemployment and a growing culture of insecurity and long working hours for those in employment. Within less than a generation, the social democratic commitment to state welfare and the promotion of collective responsibility for the alleviation of the grosser forms of inequality and poverty, had been displaced by policies critical of individual and family 'dependency' on the state. The consequence has been that individuals and families have themselves had to bear substantially more of the risks and costs associated with participation in the global labour market. The absence of decently paid jobs for many young people, coupled with rising personal costs of education and training (especially for those entering higher education) has led to growing numbers becoming trapped in a cycle of debt and insecurity as they struggle to find jobs which will enable them to gain financial and personal independence. Unless the deregulated global economy is able to generate a far higher number of skilled jobs than it has hitherto seemed capable of doing, those young people are likely to find that as they repay their student debts, they will also have to find the resources to insure against future insecurity and poverty as well as providing for their own retirement.

For the past two decades, one of the central premises of economic and employment policy in the UK has been that responsibility for generating employment opportunities rests essentially with the individual and those institutions involved in the supply of skills – schools, colleges and universities in particular. According to the 'supply-side' argument, employers are absolved from any moral responsibility for creating the conditions which will generate employment. This has meant, for example, that the role of the City financial institutions, which have been criticized by commentators such as Will Hutton for their negative impact on national investment, have remained largely untouched by the state. Where Conservative governments did become involved in employment generation was in the promotion of inward investment from overseas multinationals, many of which have been prominent in electronics and motor vehicle production. According to a report in *The Observer* (2 August 1998), this policy had by 1998 generated some £160 billion worth of foreign-owned business, but it is becoming apparent that certain of the companies involved have become vulnerable to instabilities in the global market – especially those based in Korea, Taiwan and Japan following the Asian financial crisis of 1997. A particularly high profile example of this vulnerability was the decision in July 1998 by the German electronics company Siemens to close down its semi-conductor production facilities on Tyneside, with the loss of at least 1,500 jobs only fifteen months after it was opened by the Queen amid great local fanfares. The cause of the closure was said to be the collapse in the price of semi-conductors due to over supply and seriously reduced demand, arising in part from the collapse of the East Asian economies. In her report on the closure, *Observer* journalist Joanna Walters, commenting on Britain's reliance on foreign investment, quoted one of her informants as claiming that

> Britain has become as easy to exit as it is to enter because of flexible, insecure labour conditions and lack of pressure on investors to integrate with the local economy, causing the UK to either stand by and watch as foreign firms pull out when the going gets tough or bail out factories to stop them shifting abroad.
>
> ('Global crisis, local tragedy', *The Observer*, 2 August 1998)

As a number of commentators have pointed out, collapses of this kind will become increasingly typical of the inherent instability of free market global capitalism and are likely to generate even greater insecurity, unless and until the main industrial powers decide to address the need for some form of international market regulation – a debate which has yet to take place.

In spite of their acknowledgement of the importance of the global free market and its relevance to education and training provision, policy makers and their advisers have been reluctant to engage publicly with the critical challenges that are being made to the underlying premises of current policy. In its consultation paper, *The Learning Age*, published in 1998, the Department for Education and Employment, for example, makes no reference to the negative impact of globalization on employment opportunities and chooses not to open up the issue as to whether the vocational courses and systems of qualifications adequately prepare individuals for labour markets which, it appears, will largely continue to operate according to the neo-liberal principles put in place by the New Right. To a large extent, the globalization project and its significance for education and training are deemed to be non-negotiable. As disquieting is the fact that with the growing emphasis on highly prescriptive training courses for educational professionals, in which there is little scope for critical reflection on the *contexts* of practice, there is a diminishing space for engagement with issues of the kind we are raising. It is our hope that the collections of readings we have put together will stimulate what we regard as a necessary debate on the terms of current policy.

Geoff Esland.
Chair of Education, Training and the Future of Work Course Team.
August, 1998.

Note

1   These figures need to be interpreted within the context of the many changes
     that have been introduced in the methodology for calculating levels of unem-
     ployment. Under the four Conservative administrations after 1979, the formula
     for calculating unemployment was changed many times. Most of these changes
     had the effect of reducing the total figure. The basis of calculation used by the
     fourth Conservative administration after 1992 was a decision to include only
     those who were claiming benefit. This had the effect of excluding those who
     were out of work and unable to claim benefit (for example, because their partner
     was still in work), and some of those who had left the labour market alto-
     gether. In May 1998, the Labour Government changed the formula again in
     order to bring it into line with that used by the ILO. The new methodology
     employed is based on a sampling of the population. The immediate effect of
     the change was to add an additional 400,000 unemployed to the register,
     bringing the total to 1.8 million, but even this figure understates the true
     position of those who would choose to work if employment were available.

Acknowledgements

The editors would particularly like to thank those who have contributed to the compilation and development of these collections. We are especially grateful to Brenda Jarvis who took responsibility for compiling the manuscripts, and we would also like to thank Margaret Bird and Aileen Cousins for the numerous ways in which they helped in bringing the project to fruition. The Course Team is also grateful to Denis Gleeson and Andrew Pollard who were helpful sources of advice in the preparation of the course materials.

Source acknowledgements

Chapter 1
Council of Churches for Britain and Ireland (1997) 'The changing nature of Work', from *Unemployment and the Future of Work*, London: CCBI, pp. 13–30.

Chapter 2
Brown, P. and Lauder, H. (1996) 'Education, globalization and economic development', *Journal of Educational Policy*, ii(1), pp. 1–25.

Chapter 3
Carnoy, M. (1997) 'The great work dilemma: education, employment and wages in the new global economy', *Economics of Education Review*, 16(3) pp. 247–54.

Chapter 4
Aronwitz, S. and DiFazio, W. (1994) 'The new knowledge work', from *The Jobless Future*, Minneapolis: University of Minnesota Press, pp. 13–23 and 46–56.

Chapter 5
Grieve Smith, J. (1997) 'Jobs and people', ch. 8 from *Full Employment: A Pledge Betrayed*, Basingstoke: Macmillan, pp. 149–67.

Chapter 6
Keep, E. and Mayhew, K. (1996) 'Evaluating the assumptions that underlie training policy', Booth, A. and Snower, D.J. (eds) *Acquiring Skills: Market Failures, their Symptoms and Policy Responses*, Cambridge: Cambridge University Press, pp. 305–34.

Chapter 7
Council of Churches for Britain and Ireland (1997) 'Expanding employment', from *Unemployment and the Future of Work*, London: CCBI, pp. 82–101.

Chapter 8
Esland, G., Esland, K., Murphy, M. and Yarrow, K. 'Managerializing organizational culture: refashioning the human resource in educational institutions'. (Original text.)

Chapter 9
Winter, R. (1995) 'The University of Life plc: the industrialisation of higher education?', from Smyth, J. (ed.) *Academic Work: The Changing Labour Process in Higher Education*, Society for Research into Higher Education/Open University Press, pp. 129–43.

Chapter 10
Robertson Elliot, F. (1996) 'Economic restructuring and unemployment: a crisis for masculinity?', ch. 3 from *Gender, Family and Society* Basingstoke: Macmillan, pp. 75–109.

Chapter 11

Furlong, A. and Cartmel, F. (1997) 'Social change and labour market transitions', ch. 3 from *Young People and Social Change*, Milton Keynes: Open University Press.

Chapter 12

Ahier, J. and Moore, R. 'Big pictures and fine detail: school work experience, policy and the local labour market in the 1990s'. (Original text.)

Introduction

Geoff Esland and John Ahier

Despite the changes that have taken place in the British political context during the 1990s, a number of the issues which continue to dominate debates about education, training and the future of work have changed little over the past two decades. More than twenty years after the event, the criticisms of education and training expressed by James Callaghan in his Ruskin College speech in October 1976 still continue to resonate within official policy discourse. This is especially true of his strictures on school standards and the use of 'progressive' teaching methods, but it also applies to the basic premise of his argument that it is the system of education and training which holds the key to national economic improvement and prosperity. Despite a number of challenges to its validity (see Esland 1996), this view still remains the cornerstone of current policy.

Although the Conservative government which came into office in 1979 built upon and intensified the ideological stance towards education and training which the previous Labour government had taken, it did so from within a very different set of economic and political objectives. Not only were economic and employment issues accorded a higher priority in educational policy, but, in terms of its organization, governance and management, the system itself also underwent a major transformation, first through the reforms introduced by the 1988 Education Reform Act and later by the Further and Higher Education Act of 1992. One of the objectives of the legislation was to bring about a reduction in the discretionary areas of professional practice within education and training institutions while strengthening market and managerial controls over the ways in which teachers performed their jobs.

As some commentators suspected might happen (see Avis *et al.* 1996), the political settlement established by the New Right during its eighteen years in power continued to provide the main parameters of policy for the Labour government after it took office in May 1997. Although there have been changes of emphasis and priority, and some alleviation of the more extreme right wing elements of employment policy, the neo-liberal promotion of free market economic globalization has continued to provide the overarching framework for Britain's political economy as it enters the new millennium.

From this observation, it might be inferred that the political principles established by the New Right during its years in office now form the basis of a 'new consensus'. If the main political parties are divided only over the detail rather than the principle of economic deregulation, and if they share the view that 'supply side' reforms of the education and training system are the primary means of promoting a more 'competitive' economy, then the question arises as to whether there is any basis for an alternative perspective capable of challenging the assumptions that prevail in this new consensus.

The significance of this question becomes greater if we extend it to the international context and include other nation states such as the US, Australia and New Zealand, which have forged a similar political consensus around the neo-liberal principles of economic deregulation, privatization and reduced welfare expenditure. Indeed, according to Grey (1998), the consensus also extends to the main international economic NGOs such as the Organisation for Economic Cooperation and Development (OECD), the World Bank, the IMF and the World Trade Organisation (WTO). These agencies form part of what Grey calls the 'Washington consensus' which collectively provide the main ideological and managerial thrust behind the US pursuit of free market, economic globalization – a goal which he claims to be the ultimate Enlightenment project.

In spite of its dominance, the neo-liberal consensus – particularly as it affects economic, employment and welfare policy – is facing a variety of challenges. Some of these emanate from research and intellectual debate, but there are others which take the form of concerted popular pressure and occasional outbreaks of mass protest at what are perceived as threats to individual survival, social cohesion and environmental integrity. High levels of unemployment across the main industrial economies (not least in the European Union) and the economic and social instability affecting many of the Pacific Rim countries after the financial collapse of 1997 are just two examples of the fault lines which lie beneath the international commitment to economic globalization. These and similar manifestations of instability have led Grey and other critics of the global free market – notably the international financier, George Soros (1996) – to predict that as with nineteenth-century attempts to establish a *laissez-faire* international economy, the current policy will become increasingly difficult to sustain.

At the level of rhetoric, at least, education and training policy continues to play an important role in sustaining the ideological commitment to the neo-liberal concept of globalization, largely because it has now become the default institution for nurturing the psychological conditions necessary for 'competitiveness'. The notion that in order to compete in the global economy, the modern nation state requires a highly trained and 'flexible' workforce, in which 'knowledge- and people-based skills' form the basis of a 'self-perpetuating learning society' (FEFC 1997) has become the *sine qua non* of the age. Under advanced capitalism, symbolic analysis, creation and manipulation are seen as the major new source of commodification, exchange and profit. As technology advances, allowing investment and production to seek out the most profitable locations, the chief source of competitiveness lies in the utilization of symbolic skills – a phenomenon described by one commentator as a characteristic of the 'weightless economy' (Coyle 1998).

There are, however, a number of problems with this formulation. As Ashton and Green (1996: 70) point out 'the remarkable thing about these claims is that they are typically presented with relatively little theoretical grounding and even less of a basis in solid empirical evidence'. We will note here a number of reservations which we have with the globalization argument.

The first problem relates to the structural impact of economic globalization on employment. At the heart of the international neo-liberal project is the priority attached to 'sound finance' as distinct from the securing of 'full employment'. Any nation unable or unwilling to give priority to maintaining low inflation levels is liable to find itself punished by the financial markets (Eatwell 1995), and possibly subjected to the intervention of the IMF in the running of its economy. The inherently deflationary nature of this policy places limits on national growth rates, but also acts as a deterrent on nation states from using public borrowing to stimulate a flagging economy, and therefore to generate jobs. The consequence has been a massive rise in international levels of unemployment, as nation states have struggled to find their 'natural' or 'non-accelerating inflation rate of unemployment' (NAIRU) – the level to which unemployment can be allowed to fall without causing inflation to rise (see this volume, chs 5 and 7).

Alongside the priority attached to low inflation lies the other key principle of the neo-liberal global free market: the promotion of economic deregulation – particularly as far as employment policy is concerned. In Britain and the United States especially, the effect of two decades of neo-liberal employment legislation has been to strengthen the power of employers *vis-à-vis* the interests of the workforce. The consequence has been that in the cause of 'efficiency' and 'greater productivity', employers have demanded increasing 'flexibility' from their employees whether in the form of part-time working, the use of short-term contracts or the demand for individuals to work unsocial hours. In some cases, companies have gone further through the introduction of out-sourcing and the sub-contracting of services which they formerly undertook themselves. The result has been a massive rise in job insecurity, a culture of long working hours, often based on fear, and a growing polarization in pay levels between the high salaries of boardroom members and those of the great majority of workers.

The third problem with the argument that global competitiveness requires increasingly high-level skills is that new technology is as capable of eliminating jobs as it is of creating them. Recent analyses (e.g., Rifkin 1995) have argued that even relatively high levels of skill are being subsumed within the capability of computerized technology. Aronowitz and DiFazio (1994: 3; see also this volume, ch. 4), for example, claim that their research leads them to the conclusion that

> All of the contradictory tendencies involved in the restructuring of global capital and computer-mediated work seem to lead to the same conclusion for workers of all collars – that is, unemployment, under-employment, decreasingly skilled work, and relatively lower wages . . . High technology will destroy more jobs than it creates. The new technology has fewer parts and fewer workers and produces more product.

If in the interests of promoting 'efficiency' private sector companies seek to use technology to substitute for human labour, it is even more likely that the same process will operate within public sector organizations, restricted as they are by the limits imposed on national public expenditure. Despite the high volumes of work that are in need of being carried out in the labour-intensive sectors such as health, education and the social services, the requirement on public sector managers to deploy their human resources within the expenditure limits imposed on them is what gives rise to the work intensification – and sometimes de-skilling – that we referred to earlier. Here more than anywhere in the economy is the clearest example of work organization being driven by cash limited budgets rather than social 'need' (see this volume, ch. 8).

The fourth point we would make is that the emphasis on the importance of 'supply side' reform as the means of generating competitiveness, rests on the assumption that employers are both able and willing to utilize higher levels of skill where they are available. There is evidence to suggest that this may well be true of some sectors but not all, and that many employers are content to compete on price at the lower end of the market. As Keep and Mayhew have argued on a number of occasions, (see this volume, ch. 6), many companies choose to tailor their products to a specific market in which the high-skill, high-tech route is not the only option available to them. The

> alternatives include increasing use of crude work-intensification practices, low pay, insecure and casualised employment, and the sub-contracting of more complex parts of production . . . Producing high-tech, high-quality goods and services that require high levels of skill is not, in itself, intrinsically important to a company. The issue of over-riding concern is whether or not its product market strategy allows it to survive and to make adequate . . . levels of profit. If companies can achieve these ends through the production of low-cost, low-quality, high-volume goods and services that require minimal skill levels, then there is little reason for them to alter their strategies.
>
> (this volume, ch. 6: 118)

Finally, there is the problem of taking at face value the view promulgated by educational policy makers that the new systems of vocational qualifications are the appropriate ones for meeting the 'requirements for a highly skilled workforce in a global economy'. As with the other assumptions contained within this formula, this one, too, requires examination. Although the 1990s saw an increase in participation rates in post-16 education and training, vocational curricula have continued to experience the low status that has traditionally characterized their position in the British education system. In part this is due to the long history of tripartism, but it also has to do with the accumulation of negative perceptions which young people and their families formed about the succession of post-16 schemes from the late 1970s onwards. These training programmes were widely seen to be devoid of content and as having little relevance to the difficult employment situations in which young people found themselves, and they did little to disarm the cynical perception that they were essentially a means of keeping young people out of the labour market (Field 1995: see vol. II, ch. 7). The 1990s have seen a different approach to vocational qualifications in the form of NVQs and GNVQS, but this too has attracted a good deal of critical comment. Although the new qualifications have been perceived as offering wider opportunities for access to training than anything that had previously existed, they have also been criticized for concentrating on the accreditation of low-level skills and for their reliance on a competence-based form of assessment which, in the view of some commentators, has lacked a sufficiently robust knowledge base to meet even current, let alone future, occupational requirements (see vol. II, chs 6 and 7). One of the consequences of this policy has been the creation of a system in which there is polarization between the high-level skills produced by the HE institutions and lower-level skills accredited through the competence-based route.

Despite the vigorous repetition by policy makers and others of the globalization formula, there is little evidence in our view on which to base a challenge to the diagnosis put forward by Finegold and Soskice (1988) that a fundamental problem with the British economy is that it is founded on a 'low-skills equilibrium', and that the education and training system reproduces and reinforces that problem (see also vol. II, ch. 2). Because of the mono-causal nature of explanations of Britain's economic weakness in which education and training are represented as the main source of economic renewal, other more significant factors have been ignored, not least the low levels of investment – both public and private – which could have generated new economic activity (Hutton 1995). Furthermore, as Ashton and Green (1996) have argued, the 'high-skills route' to capital accumulation requires a concerted commitment by both state and employers to provide a generously funded system of education and training, in which employers are committed to the effective utilization of high-level skills. In Britain, that approach has not been forthcoming, for the reason that too small a proportion of its businesses appears to require genuinely high-level skills – a situation reflected in the fact that state and employers have resisted the notion of systemic, long-term investment in post-16 education and training. Furthermore, by leaving the provision of PCET to market forces, the state has produced additional barriers to the creation of a high-skills route. As Esland *et al.* suggest (this volume, ch. 8), when a competitive market is tied to a vigorously applied centralized funding formula based on falling unit costs, there is every inducement for further and higher education institutions to boost student numbers while scaling down curricular content and choice and making reductions in staffing resources – a process which is perceived by some as a serious threat to the quality of learning.

In our view, these collections of readings offer important exploration and analysis of the issues we are raising. A number of them are critical of the moral and intellectual premises of the current globalization orthodoxy and suggest some alternative approaches. It may be thought that they take an unduly pessimistic view of current policies. For this we are unapologetic. Public discussion of education and training policy has, in our view, been too narrowly focused for too long, and has been concerned with confirming rather than questioning the principles on which it is based. One of the reasons why there has been so little change to the parameters which govern the development of policy in post-compulsory education and training is that governments themselves have been reluctant to allow broad-based debate to take place in which practitioners themselves could have a role. In its concern to neutralize the influence of 'producer interests' and its desire to persist with a low-trust relationship with those who are employed in the system, the state has closed off an important area of response and feed back from those most closely involved in the implementation of policy. Our hope is that these collections are able to make a small contribution to the opening up of that process.

This volume begins with a chapter from the report published in 1997 by the Council of Churches for Britain and Ireland entitled *Unemployment and the Future of Work*. In focusing on 'the changing nature of work', it brings together a range of dimensions that are central to the discussion of the future of work – social and moral, as well as political and economic. In outlining the connection between technological change, globalization and employment, the authors of the report are concerned to challenge the presumption that nation states are impotent in the face of increasing global competition. There are, they suggest, legitimate ways in which new – and socially necessary – forms of employment can, and should, be generated. They are also critical of the decline in employment protection and the consequent rise in levels of job insecurity. That and the prevailing long hours culture are seen as having a damaging impact on families and relationships. Although the report adopts an explicitly Christian view of the issues, the values on which its arguments rest are those which could be readily accommodated within a broad ethical humanist position. This is particularly true with regard to its strictures on the dominance of the market, where the authors refer to 'the moral dangers inherent in it', observing that:

> In the last twenty years or so there has grown up a tendency to treat the market as if it were an arbiter of social value . . . We must never venerate the market as if it were some kind of god – or idol.

This passage underlines one of the central issues raised by the chapter, which is the prevailing lack of a *moral* or ethical response to a self-legitimating, amoral economic system. If the political discourse surrounding globalization has effectively excluded any possibility of making ethical judgements about its impact, then, according to the authors of this report, this state of affairs should not be permitted to continue unchallenged.

Chapter 2 by Brown and Lauder also includes a critical analysis of markets within its broad critique of the globalization paradigm and its relationship to education policy. Again there is an implied ethical judgement in their argument that markets tend to magnify and reinforce existing social inequalities between groups and individuals. The authors go on to suggest that within the 'global auction' for investment, technology and jobs, which now characterizes the competitive relationship between nation states, knowledge skills have assumed strategic importance in securing economic advantage – skills which are widely perceived as essential for creating 'magnet' economies capable of attracting inward investment from foreign-owned companies. The authors identify the emergence of two contrasting national strategies in the response to economic globalization: the neo-Fordist approach of the New Right and the post-Fordist approach of the 'left modernizers'. Although the latter – which the authors claim 'informs the direction of Labour Party policy in Britain' rejects the adversarial employment policies of neo-Fordism, it nevertheless shares with it a belief in the importance of 're-skilling the nation' and investing in high-level skills as the main means of securing economic growth. Brown and Lauder are, however, sceptical of the assumptions underlying the left modernizers' position, suggesting, first, that continuing economic deregulation will inhibit the creation of more highly skilled jobs, and second, that as the polarization of income inequalities intensifies, many individuals seeking further education and training will be denied access to what are likely to become increasingly expensive forms of provision.

Carnoy in Chapter 3 also addresses the implications of economic globalization for employment and focuses on the existence of what he describes as a 'work crisis'. This is more than simply the shortage of jobs experienced by the populations of many advanced industrial societies. Carnoy is also concerned that economic deregulation has led to the erosion of earnings and increasing degrees of inequality across many sectors of the labour market, thereby creating a welfare crisis as well. This in turn, he suggests, has led to a 'rapid increase in dysfunctional families, individual stress and deteriorating communities'. According to Carnoy, neither of the two national economic strategies currently on offer has been able to avoid the problems generated by global competition. The US and British model, based as it is on the deregulation of labour markets and the 'flexibilization' of the workforce, has generated high social costs; the European model, which incorporates greater employment protection, has given rise to substantial increases in unemployment. Carnoy is unconvinced that more and better education and training will of themselves reduce either unemployment or wage decline. A prior condition, he believes, will have to be major changes in management–labour relations, part of which will need to contain agreements for joint responsibility to be taken for the development of more flexible systems of education and training.

A similar scepticism towards the idea that education and training provide the key to competitive national advantage forms part of the argument put forward by Aronowitz and DiFazio in Chapter 4. They suggest that in the light of the destruction of many 'good jobs' and their replacement by 'unstable and mediocre' jobs, the promise held out by education and training investment 'might lead nowhere for many who bought the promise'. The authors are particularly concerned at the readiness of many employers to invest in technology – both computerized and computer-controlled technology – in order to displace human labour. They also point out that current management theories actively encourage companies to embark on organizational changes, such as those created by mergers, acquisitions, and decentralization, as part of the strategy to cut labour costs. Another major factor in the downsizing of the labour force has been the increasing confidence of employers in their ability to dismantle the system of collective bargaining that their workforces had taken for granted a decade or so earlier. The consequence has been a growing polarization between a minority of occupations which rely on innovative uses of knowledge and the mass of jobs which are witnessing the de-skilling of their occupants. As with other contributors to this collection, Aronowitz and DiFazio are concerned at the implications of an apparently amoral system which is denying people meaningful work – or indeed, any work at all – while also increasing their dependence on corporately controlled sources of 'simplified' news and information resulting from the market domination of tabloidism.

A rather different perspective on the employment crisis is provided in Chapters 5, 6 and 7, where one of the central issues is the importance of the 'demand' side of the economy. The first of these consists of an extract from John Grieve Smith's book *Full Employment: A Pledge Betrayed*, in which the author puts forward a strongly argued neo-Keynesian critique of the prevailing neo-liberal orthodoxy. A central theme of the book is that the abandonment of 'full employment' – a key principle of the economic policy espoused by Beveridge and Keynes in the post-1945 era – was in itself an act of social injustice, resulting as it has in persistently high levels of unemployment. In this chapter, Grieve Smith criticizes the belief inherent in monetary policy that it is changes to the supply side of the economy (education and training and the cost of labour) that should constitute the main basis of economic management. The problem with this argument, according to the author, is that the emphasis on reducing labour costs and raising skill levels as the means of increasing the number of jobs available is not tenable. In reality, such a policy simply leads to employment insecurity which results in depressed demand and low investment as companies lack confidence in the market. Grieve Smith also takes issue with the notion that education and training can of themselves lead to more employment opportunities. He draws attention to research which shows that, contrary to conventional wisdom, an increasing proportion of the unemployed possess high qualification levels – A levels and degrees – and suggests that the problem is not one of a shortage of skilled people, but of a lack of jobs and inappropriate skill utilization on the part of employers. According to Grieve Smith, the main impact of education and training is that they tend to redistribute individuals within the existing labour market, and he claims that

> There is no reason to think that such programmes by themselves will lead to any increase in jobs . . . Any political platform to reduce unemployment based solely on such measures is guilty of offering a false prospectus.

A similar view is taken by Keep and Mayhew in Chapter 6, where they argue that the problem of economic regeneration is less one of supply side weakness and more one of demand for skills. They suggest that

> Britain's skill problem is at least as much one of low demand for skills as one of inadequate supply. Policy concentrates on enhancing supply in a system which is employer-led and which to a large extent ignores deep-seated reasons for lack of employer demand.

One of the central arguments which the authors put forward is that many companies are reluctant to recruit employees with high-level skills because their market strategy is directed towards the supply of low-cost products or services in which competition on price takes precedence over competition on quality. The production of high-quality, high-cost goods and services is not in itself a significant issue for many companies, so long as their particular market strategy enables them to survive and make a profit. In pursuing this argument, Keep and Mayhew draw attention to the ambiguities in government policies, which, while emphasizing the importance of the high-skills route for the national economy, make a virtue of the fact that Britain is able to offer employers a low-cost, deregulated, flexible workforce. Despite the priority given by Conservative administrations of the 1980s and 1990s to the role of employers in the development and implementation of national training policy, there has been considerable scepticism among some employers about the relevance and appropriateness of the programmes on offer. Some of this scepticism is attributable to intra-organizational factors which deter companies from embarking on a full-scale commitment to upgrading their employees' skills. But employees themselves have to be convinced that investment in training will benefit them. In the light of their analysis, Keep and Mayhew are concerned that policy debate should both recognize and address the problem of employer utilization of skill rather than simply its supply.

Chapter 7, which also focuses on the demand side of the economy, consists of a further extract from the CCBI report, *Unemployment and the Future of Work*. Our decision to include it was influenced by the fact that its authors set out a seriously argued challenge to what they perceive as the prevailing intractable and negative mind-set towards enacting policies for reducing unemployment. In putting forward a programme of tax reforms which they believe would be functional for the generation of more jobs, the authors suggest that on both moral and economic grounds there has to be some reprioritizing within government economic policy, so that the creation of jobs is given as much attention as the need to restrain inflation.

Their proposals include first, making reductions in the costs to employers of employing labour – particularly through changes in tax and insurance contributions – and, second, the expansion of employment in the public sector paid for by gradual increases in taxation. Pointing out that 'compared with the rest of Europe, Britain has a relatively low ratio of taxation to GDP', and rejecting the notion that 'the expansion of employment in the public sector would not be compatible with maintaining financial control and accountability within government', they suggest that modest increases in taxation would be an important first step in repairing the shortfall in public sector investment that has characterized national policy over the past two decades. In proposing the restoration of the state's responsibilities for expanding employment opportunities, the CCBI report is clearly placing itself in the tradition of Beveridge and Keynes who saw 'full employment' as the mark of a humane society.

One of the points made by the CCBI report is that the public sector services are both 'needs-driven' and labour intensive, and – self-evidently in health, education and the social services – highly qualified and trained staff are necessary for dealing with both the complex and diverse problems of 'client management' and the high volumes of case work. Here in these sectors of the economy, above almost all others, is a demonstrable requirement for high-level skills. Yet the policy of the Thatcher and Major governments was to denigrate the public sector as self-serving and inefficient, while subjecting it to long-term resource cuts in the pursuit of the goals of 'economy, efficiency and effectiveness'.

As part of their commitment to supply side reform, the Conservative administrations of the 1980s and 1990s embarked on fundamental changes in the funding, governance and management of public sector education and training institutions. Some of the consequences of these policies form the subject matter of Chapters 8 and 9 where the focus moves to the ways in which British colleges and universities have been required to adapt to the legislative changes in education policy during the 1980s and 1990s. Esland *et al.* in Chapter 8 argue that as a consequence of the Education Reform Act of 1988 and the Further and Higher Education Act of 1992, FHE institutions have been obliged to introduce some form of human resource management (HRM) into their management processes in order to deal with the financial and staffing demands of the new market culture. The authors argue that the compounding of financial, curricular and staffing changes has led many FHE institutions to use HRM as a legitimating means of driving down staffing costs: first by enabling teaching and curricular inputs to the learning process to be redefined as variable costs, and, second, through its utilization as a 'disciplinary' instrument for the identification of employee 'underperformance'. In spite of the emphasis in HRM rhetoric on the importance of organizational 'modernization' and the enhancement of the skills of the employee, the reality for many is that it has been used to justify the de-skilling and in some cases, the redundancy of professional practitioners. The authors conclude that, on the basis of their own and other research, this approach to management–professional relationships raises serious questions as to the quality of learning taking place in some areas of post-compulsory provision.

The impact of marketized managerialism on higher education is the subject of Chapter 9 by Winter. Here the author suggests that the changes imposed on HE institutions can be seen as the ultimate stage in the industrialization of the labour process in which 'knowledge production' itself becomes commoditized, a process which takes place when

> services begin to be incorporated into the relationships of an industrialised market economy when the provision of what is *needed* is converted into the provision of what can be profitably marketed.

Although, universities continue to retain limited elements of their traditional value system, the significance of 'market logic' is that it transmutes the relationship between teacher, student and curriculum into 'a relationship between producer, consumer and commodity'. The force of this process is that the curriculum then becomes redefined according to the demands of the market, which is shaped by student (or consumer) choice. Those areas of knowledge for which there is weak demand are then withdrawn. As Winter points out, the market itself is open to political manipulation, as the state – and other powerful interests – are able to stipulate which forms of training (of teachers and social workers, for example) will receive official sanction. Thus, by means of the market logic, the entire edifice of 'academic freedom' and the right to engage in intellectual enquiry and critique are put at risk. The compounding of managerialism and regulated marketization with which HE institutions have been infused presents a formidable challenge to HE professionals. Winter himself, however, while concerned at the implications of this development, reminds us that coercive management is itself vulnerable to the consequences of its own authoritarianism.

In Chapters 10 and 11 the focus moves to the impact of current employment policies and practices on the family and private life. One important context in which young and not so young people make decisions about their own educational and employment futures is that of their families and private lives. The chapters by Robertson Elliot and Furlong and Cartmel may be used to introduce this different dimension into debates about employment and post-compulsory education. Both together provide some ways into considering how private life has changed with recent developments in employment. The first looks at the research on the private effects of economic restructuring. In particular, it concentrates on how various aspects of family life, such as economic well-being and the sexual division of labour, have been affected by unemployment, underemployment and the growth of certain kinds of work carried out by women. Where some have seen the positive aspects of flexibilization for private life, Robertson Elliot uses the concept of 'casualisation' to draw our attention to some of the problematic effects for people's everyday lives of economic restructuring.

Chapter 11, by Furlong and Cartmel, concentrates on the current conditions under which many young people now negotiate their transition from school to work. Their point is that whilst there has been a growth in the diversity of the routes taken by young people as a whole, class and gender remain crucial in determining young people's experiences of education, training and labour market entry. But, for them, such structuring does not provide any personal experience of predictability or coherence. The rapid changes in the demands for different types of labour, and the related break in the continuity between the generations, have brought new subjective risks and uncertainties to young people.

The difficulties of using broad descriptions of economic change to justify initiatives in educational policy are illustrated in Chapter 12 by Ahier and Moore. This begins with a brief analysis of what they call the 'big pictures' of national and international economic conditions found in publications by government and employers organizations, and used to justify the provision of work experience for young people at school. They then go on to show how the implementation of such a programme always depends upon the concerns of local managers, and the structure of the local youth labour markets, which, in turn, may call into question the original rationales for the policy.

In Volume II, the focus is much more on the construction and implementation of vocational education and training policies and their impact on the experience and opportunities of young people. Particularly important is the nature of the relationship between the political and economic agendas with which this volume has been concerned and the kind of outcomes that have been achieved through the various reforms.

References

Aronowitz, S. and DiFazio, W. (1994) *The Jobless Future*, Minneapolis: University of Minnesota Press.

Ashton, D. and Green, F. (1996) *Education, Training and the Global Economy*, Cheltenham: Edward Elgar.

Avis, J., Bloomer, M., Esland, G., Gleeson, D. and Hodkinson, P. (1996) *Knowledge and Nationhood: Education, Politics and Work*, London: Cassell.

Coyle, D. (1998) 'Jobs in a weightless world', *Economic Report* 12(5), Employment Policy Institute.

Eatwell, J. (1995) 'The international origins of unemployment', in J. Michie and J. Grieve Smith (eds) *Managing the Global Economy*, Oxford: Oxford University Press.

Esland, G.M. (1996) 'Education, training and nation-state capitalism: Britain's failing strategy', in J. Avis *et al.* (eds) *Knowledge and Nationhood: Education, Politics and Work*, London: Cassell.

Field, J. (1995) 'Reality testing in the workplace: are NVQs employment led?', in P. Hodkinson and M. Issit (eds) *The Challenge of Competence: Professionalism Through Vocational Education and Training*, London: Cassell.

Finegold, D. and Soskice, D. (1988) 'The failure of training in Britain: analysis and prescription', *Oxford Review of Economic Policy* 4(3).

Further Education Funding Council (FEFC) (1997) *Learning Works: Widening Participation in Further Education* (Kennedy Report), Coventry: FEFC.

Grey, J. (1998) *False Dawn: The Delusions of Global Capitalism*, London: Granta Books.

Hutton, W. (1995) *The State We're In*, London: Cape.

Rifkin, J. (1995) *The End of Work: The Decline of the Global Labor Force and the Dawn of the Post-market Era*, New York: Putnam.

Soros, G. (1996) 'The capitalist threat', *The Atlantic Monthly*, September.

Chapter 1

The changing nature of work

Council of Churches for Britain and Ireland

Historians looking back to the closing decades of the twentieth century may well identify our own times as the crucial period of a new industrial revolution. Certainly they will identify some profound changes in the nature of work. It is too soon to make such historical judgements, as these changes are still taking place around us now and their full implications are far from clear. But already we can see that there are pervasive effects on economic organisation and living standards, on family and household structure, and on community and social cohesion.

Our way of thinking about work in our society is so conditioned by the modern world as it developed out of the industrial revolution of the late eighteenth century that it is not easy for us to stand back and view it as if from the outside. Yet this is necessary if we are to address the issues, and make the choices, on which depend the character of our society in the future. Our Christian inheritance can be invaluable, stretching back as it does over two thousand years and not a mere two hundred. It is not dependent on the experience of just one form of economic organisation. It gives us a framework of values, or a decisive point of reference, as we try our best to address some important and complex questions about the future of work and of employment.

The issues addressed in this report are of great concern to all sections of society, and they are being actively studied from many different points of view. (. . .) We believe that, as an expert working party set up by the churches, we have an important and distinctive contribution to make to the debate.

We have found it helpful to distinguish three different strands in the web of social change, although they are all closely related and mutually interactive. The *first* is the introduction of new technology, especially in communications and information processing. The *second* is the changing composition of the labour force, with male participation rates falling and female participation growing. This has profound implications for the workplace as well as the home. The *third* is the liberalisation or deregulation of markets resulting in greater intensity of competition both within our countries and internationally. Much else is happening in our society at the same time which could be thought relevant to our enquiry, not least the changes in religious belief and the role of our own churches, but it is on these three trends we will concentrate our attention. We will describe them in a preliminary way in this chapter of our report. Their consequences are the challenge that we see to society today. We have no choice but to enter a new age, with new technology, global markets and increasingly equal opportunities for men and women in employment, but we *do* have a choice about the future of work and of unemployment in that new society.

New technology

We are told that before long the storage and transformation of information in any form will become almost costless, and so will be its communication to anywhere in the world. Once an information system is set up and running there will be almost no need for human beings to be involved in any of these operations anymore. In the past, machines have replaced physical effort and stamina, now they are replacing patience and manual dexterity, knowledge and skill as well. To give just one example we met out of the thousands we might have observed and quoted, computers have now taken over from scientists with PhDs the task of carrying out routine tests on the chemical properties of newly developed medicines. This illustrates the point that it is not only what are conventionally thought of as 'unskilled' jobs which can be made redundant by technical change. Currently, we are advised, it is particularly the skilled or semi-skilled jobs in data processing that are most at risk, not least the new jobs created by earlier generations of computer technology.

On our industrial visits we have been impressed, like any group of relative innocents, by the precision of computer-driven manufacturing machinery, for example in a modern shipbuilding yard. A vast and complex structure can be assembled according to a pre-set design and time schedule with relatively little human effort, because the process is guided by the information which is stored and transmitted very cheaply and accurately in a multitude of computer installations. We may see such processes as humbling or threatening, but we should also celebrate them as magnificent achievements of human ingenuity.

Another, not altogether trivial, example is worth recording. One member of our working party, Kumar Jacob, is a manager in a software company which designs and makes computer games. Some of us visited the firm and were duly impressed by the technology on display. Computer games, of this very sophisticated kind, may suggest lessons to be learnt about the use of computers at work as well as at play. They depend for their fascination on the interaction of human and mechanical abilities. The role of the human mind is active, not passive, requiring imagination and strategic vision very different to that possessed by the machine. We must bear this in mind when futurologists tell us that computers will make all human labour obsolete.

An American book, *The End of Work* by Jeremy Rifkin (1995), begins with a disturbing vision:

> From the beginning, civilisation has been structured, in large part, around the concept of work. From the Palaeolithic hunter/gatherer and Neolithic farmer to the medieval craftsman and assembly line worker of the current century, work has been an integral part of daily existence. Now, for the first time, human labour is being systematically eliminated from the production process.

In another passage he considers the long-term implications of artificial intelligence. 'Nicholas Negroponte of the MIT Media Lab,' he tells us

> envisions a new generation of computers so human in their behaviour and intelligence that they are thought of more as companions and colleagues than mechanical aids.

We need to reflect critically on this 'envisioning'. It raises some deep questions, including some religious questions, about what it means to be human and about how human work differs from the work we can get out of a machine, however intelligent. When we say that human beings are made 'in the image of God' we mean, amongst other things, that they are creative. Much of the work which human beings actually do is not like the work of God at all, because it is repetitive, boring and essentially mechanical. That kind of work could well be mechanised. But the element which we describe as creative is different in kind as well as degree. No machine now in existence is creative in that sense; it is a matter of dispute amongst scientists and philosophers whether a truly creative machine is possible as a matter of principle.

There is, in any case, a great range of tasks which of their very nature only a human being can perform. They involve human relationships. The more obvious examples may come from the caring professions, but a similar point could be made about jobs which involve, persuasion, selling something or public relations, and about jobs which involve aesthetic or moral judgement. It is no accident that careers guidance nowadays puts so much stress on the need for 'interpersonal skills'. A well-drilled computer programme may be able to mimic some such skills, but only as a form of deception. A vast number of jobs require the real thing.

Even if, as we believe, new technology does not exactly spell the end of work, it does nevertheless imply some fundamental changes in its nature. On the whole these changes should be beneficial, as were most of the long-term effects of earlier industrial revolutions. If machines can take over what is mechanical in human work, what is left should be better suited for humans to do. E. F. Schumacher (1980) in *Good Work* described most forms of work, whether manual or white-collared, as 'utterly uninteresting and meaningless'. 'Mechanical, artificial, divorced from nature, utilizing only the smallest part of man's potential capabilities' he described work in an industrial society as 'sentencing the great majority of workers to spending their working lives in a way which contains no worthy challenge, no stimulus to self-perfection, no chance of development, no element of Beauty, Truth, or Goodness'. His son, Christian Schumacher, has developed the concept of 'Whole Work', based on analogies between the structure of human work and Christian theology. He says that every job should involve planning, doing and evaluating; every job should perform some complete transformation, whether of material or of information, for which the workers can take responsibility; workers should be organised into teams whose members are responsible for one another. These ideas also relate well to new styles of management made possible by new technology. People work better when they are treated more as human beings, less as machines. It becomes increasingly possible to do this, as information processing takes over the mechanical parts of human work.

Simone Weil (1952), who described the actual experience of work in very negative terms, wrote in *The Need for Roots* (written in 1943) that liberation would come from new technology. 'A considerable development of the adjustable automatic machine, serving a variety of purposes,' she wrote, 'would go far to satisfy these needs' – that is the need for variety and creativity as well as relative safety and comfort. 'What is essential is the idea itself of posing in technical terms problems concerning the effect of machines upon the moral well-being of the workmen.' Half a century later the need to pose such problems is even more evident, and the potential to solve them greatly enhanced. Technical advance can and should be a liberating and humanising influence on the future of work. Whether it is in fact so depends on the economic system and the choices people make within it.

A textbook on the subject, *The Economic Analysis of Technological Change* by Paul Stoneman (1983), concludes as follows:

> The nature of the development of the economy that is likely to result from this complicated and involved process of technological change is not necessarily going to be ideal. Reductions in price and increases in consumer welfare may result, but these may only be generated at a cost ... Nobody pretends that, in a world where decisions are made on the basis of private costs and benefits, the world will normally behave in a socially optimal way.

When a new product or process is introduced there will always, in a market system, be winners and losers. Some of the winners will be easy to identify because they will be the owners of the innovating firms and those workers who have a stake in them. The other winners will be more difficult to point out because they will be members of the general public who enjoy a better product at a lower price. The losers will of course be the owners of the firms that compete with the innovation and especially the workers who lose their jobs. Typically they will move to much lower paid employment, if indeed they do not remain unemployed. (. . .)

Even at this stage, however, we can make one thing clear. We have not seen or heard anything which convinces us that work has no future. Certainly there are needs to be met and many of those needs can be met only by human effort. It is not only the very clever, well educated or uniquely qualified people whose work is needed. Even a four-year-old child can do some things much more efficiently than the best computers in the world. The problem is one of social organisation. How can we match the potential of the people who want to work with the needs that exist, given the stock of equipment and the resources, and given the state of technical know-how? There is no reason why we should assume that this problem has no feasible solution.

The supply of labour

As our society gets richer one might suppose that people would choose to work less hard. With a larger stock of capital invested in machinery and infrastructure, with increased knowledge and technical efficiency, the same standard of living could be achieved with less human effort. It would be reasonable to expect – indeed it would be a prediction of standard economic theory – that most people would choose to take some of the benefit of higher productivity as increased leisure, or perhaps in undertaking some kind of unpaid work which they enjoyed doing, rather than taking the whole of the benefit as higher income and more consumption of goods and services. Yet looking back over the past generation there has been little change overall to the supply of labour to the market economy. One indicator of this is the proportion of the population aged 15 to 64 who are recorded as being in the labour force, that is to say either in work or actively seeking work. For the advanced industrial countries in aggregate (the OECD area) that proportion was 69.6 per cent in 1960 and 70.8 per cent in 1990. The fall in the male participation rate was almost exactly offset by the increase in the female participation rate. Similarly in Britain between 1985 and 1996 the activity rate overall was unchanged at 62.8 per cent: the rate for men fell from 76.4 to 72.3 per cent whilst the rate for women rose from 50.3 to 53.8 per cent. Figure 1.1 shows the numbers of men and women employed in Britain since the late 1960s.

The fact that women as well as men now expect to take part in paid work is itself a change in the nature of work and for society of immense significance. It is at least as important and as challenging as the development of new technology. We need again to take a long historical perspective and note how the industrial revolution brought about a very sharp distinction

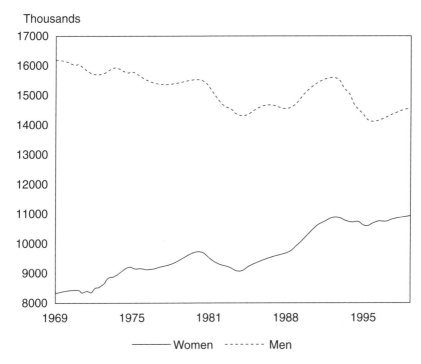

Thousands

Figure 1.1 Employment of males and females (including self employment)

between the work that men and women do. In a pre-industrial society men and women were more often working together and organising their work in similar ways. In a post-industrial society, if that is the right term to describe the pattern of life and work now emerging, men and women may again see their tasks as, in many if not all respects, the same.

The sociologist Anthony Giddens (1994) has described how heavy industry required a division of labour in which men's physical strength and endurance was stretched to the limit. This was possible only if women were able to give them both practical and emotional support:

> Women became 'specialists in love' as men lost touch with the emotional origins of a society in which work was the icon. Seemingly of little importance, because relegated to the private sphere, women's 'labour of love' became as important to productivism as the autonomy of work itself.
> (*Beyond Left and Right*, 1994: 196–7)

In pre-industrial society the family was often the unit of production. Husband and wives, parents and children, worked together at common tasks, typically farming a small plot of land, doing some small-scale manufacturing, or running a small shop. Following the industrial revolution all this changed. By the early twentieth century, work had come to mean quite different things to different members of the family. The husband was the breadwinner, working full time, if he could, from when he left school to when he retired. Typically he worked as part of a large team in a hierarchical organisation with its own sense of community and strong bonds of mutual loyalty. His responsibility was limited to just one function within a larger whole that he did not need to understand. Work was like being in the army. It required discipline, loyalty, stamina and courage. It was a duty you owed to your wife and children. It was your fate, not something to be chosen or changed.

All this is now passing into history. Many of the traditionally male jobs, in mining and manufacturing for example, have disappeared. At the same time traditionally female jobs, in services for example, have increased. These changes in the composition of output are one part of the revolution which is going on, but not the whole of it. Thanks to changing attitudes and legislation women have access to jobs previously closed to them. At the same time some women are obliged to take low-paid jobs to supplement the family income. It is a complex picture. The changing composition of the labour force has effects which interact with the changes that are due to new technology and new approaches to personnel management. The structure of work in most industries is becoming less hierarchical, with more scope for initiative at all levels. Work is still as a rule separated physically from the home, but they are no longer two different worlds. Employers sometimes try to be more 'family-friendly'. Work and family are both having to make compromises. We are in a period of transition, a period of particular stress, as the old patterns conflict with the new. Women are often trying to fulfil the roles of housewife and worker simultaneously, which is a very demanding combination indeed. There will be pressure for further changes both at work and at home.

During our visits we have heard concern expressed that there are now no longer enough jobs for men. Employment is declining in manufacturing, transport, mining and other industries which have in the past been largely male territory, while at the same time employment is expanding in service industries which have been mainly reserved for women. Moreover full-time employment is declining, while part-time employment grows, a trend which obviously suits many women with responsibility for young children.

The participation rate for men is falling – that is to say the proportion of the male population either in work or actively seeking work. It is very difficult to say to what extent this fall is voluntary and how far it is a recognition that good jobs are hard to find. More young men are prolonging their education, in the hope of improving their chances in the labour market. Others seem to have dropped out of the labour force altogether, and may well be involved in unrecorded casual work or in criminal activities. At the other end of the age range early retirement is becoming very common indeed. The typical situation is that men in their fifties or even forties lose one job as a result of closure or redundancy and then cannot find another. There may be work of a kind to be had, but it is low paid, perhaps also seen as low status, may involve long hours and high levels of stress, may involve living away from home or moving to a new part of the country. If many men decide not to take up such work opportunities, it does not necessarily mean that early retirement is really the option that they wanted to take.

The Carnegie Inquiry into the Third Age has investigated in some depth the employment situation for men and women over the age of fifty. They propose a phased transition from work to retirement. The general picture is one of frustration rather than relief at shedding the burdens of work. The section of their report on future prospects concludes: 'In general the position is bleak . . . Labour market pressures in the 1990s are unlikely to be sufficient to force change.' At the conference in 1996, when the third stage of the programme was presented, there was a call from angry members of the audience for legislation that explicitly outlawed employment discrimination by age. Despite all the talk there has been in the past about the coming of the leisure society, what many people still want, it seems, is to continue in paid work for as long as they physically can.

Such, indeed, is the apparent enthusiasm for paid work in our society even today that we shall need in this report to consider what remedies there are to the problems that result from overwork. Many individuals, of course, have no option but to overwork given the job that they are doing and given the attitudes of their employers and colleagues. When trade unions were more powerful they were more effective in limiting hours of work. But looking at society as a whole it is extraordinary how we have come to expect and accept hours of work, and a pace of work, which would have been called intolerable by many of our predecessors say twenty years ago. Perhaps a generation ago some people were inclined to take things too easy, but now the opposite danger is much more in evidence.

In reflecting on these changes in the supply of labour we miss a sense of the proper balance between work and the rest of life. We admire the enterprise, the enthusiasm, the persistence and sheer hard grind on which our collective prosperity is built. Yet we know that human fulfilment also requires periods of rest and recreation, time for family life, for cultural involvement, for prayer and worship. These are social as well as individual needs. In the Old Testament Law the observance of the Sabbath day was both a duty and a right. We need something analogous to that in our own society. If we can no longer observe Sunday as a work-free day for everyone, we can nevertheless reflect in other ways the attitudes that it fostered. Even if, in a post-industrial age, work becomes more creative and more humane, everybody will still need to get away from it from time to time to enjoy or endure all the rest that life has to offer.

Competition and world markets

The third strand we have sought to unravel in the web of social change is the liberalisation of markets and the increased competition that goes with it. The old regulations that kept national markets apart have largely been abolished and within each country many of the rules which limited what firms could do have gone as well. In our own deliberations this is the strand which has caused the most profound concern and aroused the strongest feelings. We have been led into wider issues of the relationship between social justice and the market system, economics and the Christian gospel. What we have to say about unemployment and the future of work necessarily reflects what we believe about these even broader questions.

There is no doubt that economic life everywhere has become more competitive, both within countries and in the world as a whole. International competition owes something to the development of better communications, easing the transfer of information anywhere in the world. Cheaper transport may also be important. But in recent years the most significant change results from the elimination of political barriers to trade and the reduction of regulations limiting access to world markets. This has direct consequences for markets in tradeable goods and services as well as markets for capital. It has important indirect consequences for labour markets as well. Many international firms are in a position to locate their production where labour costs are lowest, pressing wages downwards and worsening conditions of work in relatively rich countries like our own. On the other hand, the expansion of world markets benefits consumers in our countries who get more variety to choose from as well as lower prices for the goods and services they buy. Many firms in Britain and Ireland also benefit from wider markets for their products, as we have observed at first hand on our visits. Some people gain and others lose.

Globalisation and new technology interact powerfully with one another. New technology both destroys and creates jobs, but not necessarily in the same parts of the world. New jobs in data-processing can be created anywhere in the world, provided it is within reach of a telephone. Airline booking, insurance underwriting, software writing, copy editing – the list is endless of the jobs which are now being done wherever it is most convenient and cheap. These are some of the occupations for which demand will be growing fastest, and the rich advanced countries like our own will be too expensive to capture them.

One prominent British politician suggested to us that we should take up the unfashionable cause of protectionism as a means of safeguarding jobs at home. The argument is that Britain could opt out of international competition, so as to preserve our older industries without necessarily losing the opportunities to expand production in some new industries as well. We decline the invitation to support that cause. It does not seem to us plausible that Britain could stand aside from the globalisation of markets, without becoming increasingly isolated and impoverished. It would, of course, be incompatible with many treaty commitments, not least those with the European Union. In fact we see the opening of our markets to international trade as being in the interests of the country as a whole, as well as a means of helping development in some poorer countries. (. . .) It is important to add, however, that the burden of adjustment to global markets is something which should be shared by society as a whole, not just carried by the communities which depend on industries where Britain no longer has a comparative advantage in world trade.

There are further qualifications which must be made to the generally beneficial effects of trade. One is the environmental damage which too often results from the development of products for export in relatively poor countries, the destruction of the tropical rain forests being just one of many such ecological disasters. Another is the over-use of energy resources in transportation. Moreover, countries which consume the products of cheap labour abroad cannot avoid all moral responsibility for the conditions in which those products are made. Increasingly charities are offering the alternative to individual consumers of purchasing goods which are traded on conditions which can be described as fair. This means cutting out unnecessary profit by traders and ensuring that most of the purchase price goes to the people who do most of the work. This is admirable, but our national governments could have far more direct influence on conditions in poor countries if they were prepared to use it. We do not see this as a reason for holding back the development of international trade. On the contrary we see the expansion of trade as the most promising route to the reduction of poverty. However, we deplore some of the effects of unregulated production and employment. In societies which are themselves unjust and uncaring, the opening up of markets for trade can make the working conditions of some very poor people even more intolerable and unfair.

In the sections of an advanced economy like ours which engage in international trade there is no real alternative to pursuing competitiveness and higher productivity. Firms which do not keep their costs under control and keep abreast of new technology will not survive long, as much of British industry has learnt in the past to its cost. The incomes earned from trade by world-class firms and industries can be used in part to generate employment elsewhere in the economy, especially in the service sectors, both public and private.

Typically the future of industry in countries like Britain and Ireland will be in relatively high-technology activities, involving research and development rather than cheap mass production. This puts us in competition with other advanced industrial countries, most of them enjoying living standards as high as our own. We would not want, for several reasons, to see the future as being in competition with industry in the low-wage economies of the so-called Third World. As a strategy for Britain it does not appear likely to succeed, or only at the cost of a sharp fall in the living standards of much of the population. It would also mean trying to prosper at the expense of people in poorer countries whose need is in fact much greater than our own.

Competition within the home economy

Competition within domestic markets has been increased by the deliberate policy of deregulation as well as the backwash of developments in the world at large. In the public sector conditions like those in a market have been created wherever possible, so as to encourage the same motivation and exert the same discipline. The intention has been to promote innovation and efficiency in public services, but on our travels we have met many people who regard these developments with anger or dismay.

The arguments in favour of a market system are well-known. It can allocate economic resources for use where there is most demand for them, without the need for central planning. It leaves people free to make their own choices, within the limits of the economic resources they control. It rewards self-reliance, prudence, thrift, enterprise, diligence and other qualities which promote social as well as individual prosperity. The issue is not whether there should be a market system, but how it should be regulated and what activities should be within its domain. Some economic activities certainly do need regulation and planning, for example traffic in town or fishing in the sea. No one should be seriously advocating a market system with no role for government at all.

Whilst accepting the need for a market system we must also draw attention to the moral dangers inherent in it. In the last twenty years or so there has grown up a tendency to treat the market as if it were an arbiter of social value. It is as if some people thought that the outcome of market forces, the equilibrium between supply and demand, was necessarily right and fair. This is nonsense – no system of exchange will put right an injustice in the initial distribution of the resources which each person brings to the market. We must never venerate the market as if it were some kind of god – or idol. The fact that we have adopted a market system, and not a command economy, does not relieve us, individually and collectively, of all responsibility for the outcome in social as well as economic terms.

Christianity and the market system have never been altogether at ease with one another, and probably never will be. To put it no stronger, the market does not actively encourage the Christian virtues of compassion and generosity; neither does it promote social justice or moderation in the enjoyment of material things. On the contrary it sometimes excuses or even encourages a kind of selfishness and a kind of callousness which would be totally unacceptable if they were shown in relationships face to face. It may also be a vehicle for ambition and greed, or an obsessive need to accumulate wealth. Some of these unattractive features of the market system have been very much in evidence, alongside much that is good, in our society over the last twenty years or so.

Economists draw a distinction between markets in which competition is 'perfect' or 'imperfect'. Under perfect competition individual producers and consumers have no effect on prices, because there are so many other producers and consumers in the market. An individual farmer, for example, has no effect on the market price of potatoes. Under perfect competition 'the market' is an altogether impersonal force, and business is transacted, as it were, at arm's length. Imperfect competition, which in fact characterises many of the most important markets in modern economies, is another matter altogether. Individual producers or purchasers, who are often giant companies, exercise considerable market power. They are very conscious how their behaviour will influence the price of the things that they buy and sell. They have also to calculate how their behaviour will alter the behaviour of their main competitors. Relationships of co-operation, rivalry or outright warfare develop between firms. The smaller players in such a market, the consumers of the final product or the producers of raw material for example, find themselves at a strategic disadvantage. The benefits of the market system in allocating economic resources efficiently can be claimed for perfect competition, but not with such confidence for imperfect. Elements of monopoly power will disturb the action of Adam Smith's 'invisible hand'.

The difference has a moral as well as an economic significance. The successful use of market power often requires a firm to drive others into extinction or to exploit those that are weaker than itself. Such behaviour would be unacceptable in a personal relationship and it cannot be exempt from moral judgement simply because it takes place in a business context.

Our main concern in this enquiry is with the market for labour. As economists and other social scientists recognise, the hiring of labour is seldom a purely market transaction like the idealised process of exchange described in the elementary textbooks. Relationships at work involve commitment and trust, co-operation and a sense of fellowship as well as contracts of employment and competition for the best jobs. Wages reflect conventions, norms and hierarchies as well as supply and demand. They reflect the bargaining strength of employees and the role played by trade unions. But in recent years reality is coming a little closer to the textbooks and labour is being treated more and more like a commodity. This may or may not increase economic efficiency, but in any case it impoverishes human relations. (. . .)

We are not suggesting that the labour market should be abolished. That might be desirable in a small community, in which everyone knows and cares for one another, but not on a national or a global scale. It might be necessary in wartime, but at the cost of restrictions on individual liberty which would be intolerable under any other circumstances. What we are suggesting is that the labour market should be fair, and also that it should be used as a means to achieve social objectives, including the expansion of employment and improved conditions of work. The best guarantee of fairness is likely to be a bargain struck between market participants who are reasonably evenly matched: employees, usually speaking collectively through their representatives, on one side, employers on the other. We cannot separate the growth of unfair employment practice from the decline over the past fifteen years in the membership and power of the trade unions.

This weakening of worker representation results partly from the changing composition of the labour force (more part-timers, more small firms, a smaller public sector) but also from deliberate government policy expressed in new legislation. It is very likely that the decline of unionisation, of itself, has contributed significantly to the growing inequality of pay, especially the increase in the proportion of very low-paid jobs. The effect on unemployment is less easy to assess. Certainly unions have resisted redundancies, and stronger unions could have done so more successfully. It is less clear how they would have affected the expansion of employment in other areas. Some of the countries with a good record of job creation have strong unions, others do not. The relationship is a complex one, not fully understood by economists.

In the 1950s and 1960s trade unions in Britain were generally agreed to have a very important and constructive role to play in both the public and the private sector, at local and national level. In the 1970s however, relations became antagonistic and the behaviour of some unions was perceived as irresponsible. The public sector strikes of the 1978–9 'winter of discontent' remain a particular vivid memory in the minds of politicians of all parties, as well as the general public. George Woodcock, at one time General Secretary of the TUC, uttered the following prophetic warning in 1975:

> The most likely alternative to co-operation is that governments will have to modify or abandon their commitment to maintain a high level of employment, and their consequential responsibilities for economic growth, stable prices and good industrial relations. If this country were to return to the industrial instability and the heavy unemployment of pre-war days, that would certainly not improve the ability of the trade unions collectively to secure greater social justice and fairness for their members.

Trade union influence has been weakened since the 1980s as Woodcock foresaw. These developments are important to our enquiry. The balance of industrial power, which in the 1970s was tipped in favour of the unions, is now too heavily weighted in the opposite direction. As a result many workers are now employed on a 'take-it-or-leave-it' basis. Too often that is the reality behind the comfortable-sounding phrases about 'individual negotiations' and 'individual contracts'.

The powers of the state to regulate, to tax and to spend, should be deployed so that behaviour which supports social objectives, creating new jobs, for example, is encouraged, whilst behaviour which is socially damaging, paying excessively low wages, for example, is discouraged or even prevented.

This puts considerable responsibility and power into the hands of politicians and officials, who will have to decide what the regulations should be, what taxes should go up and how (and where) the money should be spent. We are, of course, aware that such powers can be misused. Individuals pursue their self-interest and exploit others within bureaucracies or voluntary bodies as well as within commercial enterprises. (. . .) We would nevertheless put forward the following simple proposition: when the economy is not producing what justice demands, in particular not producing enough good jobs to go round, then it is right for the government to take action which will make the market work better. These are some very broad generalisations, our reflections on a debate which has been going on since the eighteenth century, if not before. Against that background we can look at the more immediate historical context of the enquiry.

Varieties of the market system

Recent decades have seen the collapse of communism in eastern Europe and the old Soviet Union and the attempt, by no means successful so far, to replace it with a market economy. The command economies proved unsuccessful, especially at adopting new technologies and responding to consumer demand. They also depended on the suppression of democracy and human rights. It was good to see them go. The attempt, however, to move from one extreme to another is now shown to have been misguided. The chaos now emerging in some parts of eastern Europe demonstrates only too clearly how a market system can operate well only in the context of well-designed and enforced regulation. Nearer home we have seen the failure of mixed economies to cope with the various crises that hit them in the 1970s. The trend towards deregulation and greater reliance on market forces results in large part from the recognition of that failure and reaction against the style of economic policy associated with it. We now have a variety of market systems in different parts of the world in which the role of government policies differs quite a lot.

Economic policy and its institutional setting are very different in the United States and in the countries of Continental Europe, although both are examples of the market system. To oversimplify the contrast, the American system makes a virtue of keeping the role of government to a minimum, whilst the European system sees government, industry and workforce representatives as partners in achieving economic and social goals.

In America, social security provision for the unemployed is limited to a short period with no equivalent of means-tested Income Support or Jobseeker's Allowance, except for families with young children. Provision on the Continent varies considerably but in some countries, as also in Ireland, social security benefits are much more generous than in Britain and available for an unlimited period. In America there is a minimum wage, although it is very low; in some European countries there is a national minimum wage which seems very high in comparison with levels of pay now common in Britain. In Ireland there is no national minimum wage, but there is a system similar to the wage council rates which used to operate in Britain. America relies on individual employment rights enforceable in the courts; Europe relies more on collective bargaining and on regulation of employment by law. Most European countries have relatively large public sectors and relatively high rates of taxation. In Ireland also personal taxation is higher than it is in Britain, although company taxation is relatively low. The dispersion of wages in America is wide, and getting wider, whilst in Europe it remains relatively narrow. To oversimplify again, the main labour market problems in America are low pay and non-participation, whilst in Continental Europe the main problem is unemployment and especially long-term unemployment.

Much of the political debate in Britain is about the choice between these two models. Under Conservative governments since 1979 the movement has been generally in the American direction, partly as a result of spontaneous changes in the culture of business and society but also very much as a result of legislation and changes in economic policy. The parties in opposition, both Labour and the Liberal Democrats, as well as the trade union movement, have been much more in sympathy with most aspects of the European model, supporting for example the social chapter of the Maastricht Treaty. Nevertheless it would be a mistake to associate any of the political parties in Britain with just one model of the market economy, since opinion in all of them is divided.

Much Christian opinion in America strongly supports the market economy as it is in that country, with particular emphasis on freedom and the rights of the individual. In 1986 however, the National Conference of US Catholic Bishops in Washington issued a statement called *Economic Justice for All* which was very critical of some trends in that country, especially the neglect of the poor and the lack of social protection. A vigorous debate followed within the American churches, in which some prominent Catholics came out strongly against the views expressed by the Bishops. As the substance of this report will imply, we feel that the American Catholic Bishops made a lot of valid and very telling points.

This does not mean, however, that all is well with the European model. The situation in both France and Germany at the time of writing this report is a cause for grave and increasing concern. Jacques Delors (1996) has written:

Today the problems of unemployment and social exclusion constitute the main challenge to European society as a whole. They are neither marginal nor accidental but threaten the very foundations of the European social model by casting doubt upon it and leading to unbearable personal situations.

(Preface to Uniapac Report: *Committed Entrepreneurial Action Against Unemployment*)

How could we possibly support a model which produces unemployment rates of 12½ per cent in France, 9 per cent in Germany, 10 per cent in Sweden and 22 per cent in Spain? There must be something profoundly wrong with the Irish economy as well since the rate of unemployment is 12½ per cent in that country, substantially higher than it is in Britain. The condition of the unemployed in Continental Europe cries out for justice just as much as the condition of the working poor in America. To put that right will require major reforms to the European model, not just a few 'schemes' which tinker at the edges.

The benefits and the costs of change

We have identified three strands in the fabric of change: the rapid introduction of new technology, the changing role of women in the labour force, and an intensification of competitive pressure throughout the world. Bringing these three together creates a need for flexibility and a general sense of insecurity. Flexibility is not just a word which employers use when they have to cut wages or make staff redundant. It is a quality which our society must have if we are to benefit from change and the opportunities it can bring.

The White Paper of the European Commission, *Growth, Competitiveness and Employment,* published in 1994 distinguishes two different needs for flexibility in the labour market, flexibility which is external to the firm and flexibility which is internal. External flexibility includes movement of labour between geographical regions and between industries or occupations, with the provision for retraining which that implies. It means less emphasis on preserving old jobs and more emphasis on creating new ones. It means better arrangements for matching those who are seeking work with the work that they could do. Internal flexibility concerns the reorganisation of the existing workforce whilst maintaining continuity of employment. 'The aim', according to the White Paper, 'is to adjust the workforce without making people redundant wherever this can be avoided.' These are fine words, but behind them lie some very difficult choices as to who bears most of the cost of adjustment. How much falls on the firm as employers, and hence indirectly on its shareholders and customers? How much falls on individual employees? How much should society as a whole pick up through the mechanism of taxation and public spending? (. . .)

There can be no doubting the increased sense of economic insecurity which is felt by people in all walks of life. It is not in fact easy to find statistics to back up the common perception that job changes are much more frequent now than they were ten or twenty years ago. The data show a mixed picture, in part because people are reluctant to quit a job if they feel that a new job would be even less secure. Undoubtedly many of the new jobs now being created are temporary, and many of the small firms creating them are themselves in a precarious position. Some uncertainty is inseparable from economic enterprise and some people thrive on it. There are others, however, who are especially vulnerable and who have been made to feel increasingly so in recent years.

(. . .)

References

European Commission (1994) *Growth, Competitiveness, Employment: The Challenges and Ways Forward into the 21st Century*, White Paper Brussels, European Commission.

Giddens, A. (1994) *Beyond Left and Right: The Future of Radical Politics*, Cambridge: Polity.

International Labour Office (1997) World Employment: 1996/97, Geneva: ILO.

OECD (1994) *Jobs Study Report*, Paris: OECD.

Rifkin, J. (1995) *The End of Work: The Decline of the Global Labor Force and the Dawn of the Post-market Era*, New York: Putnam.

Schumacher, E. (1980) *Good Work*, Abacus.

Stoneman, P. (1983) *The Economic Analysis of Technological Change*, Oxford: OUP.

UNIAPAC (1996) *Committed Entrepreneurial Action Against Unemployment*.

Weil, S. (1952) *The Need for Roots*, London: Routledge.

Chapter 2

Education, globalization and economic development

Phillip Brown and Hugh Lauder

Introduction

Since the first oil shock in the early 1970s Western societies have experienced a social, political and economic transformation that is yet to reach its conclusion. At its epicentre is the creation of a global economy that has led to an intensification of economic competition between firms, regions and nation-states (Dicken 1992; Michie and Smith 1995). This globalization of economic activity has called into question the future role of the nation-state and how it can secure economic growth and shared prosperity. At first sight this may appear to have little to do with educational policy; however, the quality of a nation's education and training system is seen to hold the key to future economic prosperity. This paper will outline some of the consequences of globalization and why education is crucial to future economic development. It will also show that despite the international consensus concerning the importance of education, strategies for education and economic development can be linked to alternative 'ideal typical' neo-Fordist and post-Fordist routes to economic development which have profoundly different educational implications.

These neo-Fordist and post-Fordist routes can also be connected to alternative political projects. Since the late 1970s the USA and UK have followed a neo-Fordist route in response to economic globalization, which has been shaped by the New Right's enthusiasm for market competition, privatization and competitive individualism. However, with the election of the Democrats in the 1992 American presidential elections and the resurgence of the British Labour Party there is increasing support for a post-Fordist strategy. Although much has already been written about the flaws in the New Right's approach to education and national renewal, far less has yet been written on what we will call the 'left modernizers'. It will be argued that whilst the left modernizers present a promising programme for reform *vis-à-vis* the New Right, their account of education, skill formation and the global economy remains unconvincing. Therefore, an important task of this chapter is to highlight the weaknesses in the left modernizers' account to show that if post-Fordist possibilities are to be realized, it will be essential for those on the left to engage in a more thoroughgoing and politically difficult debate about education, equity and efficiency in late global capitalism.[1]

Globalization and the new rules of economic competition

The significance of globalization to questions of national educational and economic development can be summarized in terms of a change in the rules of eligibility, engagement and wealth creation (Brown and Lauder forthcoming). First, there has been a change in the rules of eligibility. In the same way that sports clubs run 'closed' events where club membership is a condition of entry, they may also run tournaments 'open' to everyone. Likewise there has been a shift away from the closed or walled economies of the postwar period towards an open or global economy. As a result of this change in the rules of eligibility, domestic economies have been exposed to greater foreign competition (Reich 1991; ILO 1995). Changes in the rules of eligibility have also enhanced the power of the multinational corporations (MNCs). The MNCs not only account for a growing proportion of cross-border trade, but are also a major source of new investment in technology, jobs and skills. Since the mid-1970s the MNCs have grown more rapidly than the world economy. In 1975, the 50 largest industrial corporations worldwide had sales of US$540 billion and $25 billion in profits. In 1990, sales figures for the top 50 had climbed to $2.1 trillion and their profits had reached $70 billion. In real terms, whereas the US economy was growing at an annual rate of 2.8% (the OECD average was 2.9%), the MNCs' annual sales growth was in the region of 3.5% during the period between 1975 and 1990 (Carnoy et al. 1993: 49).

Moreover, the old national 'champions' such as Ford, IBM, ICI and Mercedes Benz have tried to break free of their national roots, creating a *global auction* for investment, technology and jobs. As capital has become footloose, the mass production of standardized goods and services has been located in countries, regions or communities which offer low wage costs, light labour market legislation, weak trade unions and 'sweeteners' including 'tax holidays' and cheap rents. Such investment has significantly increased in the new industrial countries (NICs) such as in Singapore, Taiwan, China and Brazil (Cowling and Sugden 1994). It is estimated that in the 1980s some 700 US companies employed more than 350,000 workers in Singapore, Mexico and Taiwan alone and that 40% of the jobs created by British MNCs were overseas (Marginson 1994: 64).

In reality, the global auction operates like a Dutch auction. In a Dutch auction corporate investors are able to play off nations, communities and workers as a way of increasing their profit margins, bidding spirals downwards impoverishing local communities and workers by forcing concessions on wage levels, rents and taxes in exchange for investment in local jobs. In order to persuade Mercedes to set up a plant in Alabama, the company received an initial $253 million, with tax breaks over 25 years which have been estimated to be worth an extra $230m. The Swiss Bank Corporation will receive some $120m of incentives over the next 10 years from Connecticut, for moving its US headquarters from Manhattan to the city of Stamford.[2]

In the USA and UK the creation of a global auction has also been linked to the breakdown of the Fordist rules of engagement between government, employers and workers. Although some writers have restricted their definition of Fordism to refer exclusively to the system of mass production, Fordism is a label that can equally be applied to Keynesian demand management in the postwar period referring to the expansion of mass consumption as well as mass production (Lipietz 1987; Harvey 1989). The rapid improvement in economic efficiency which accompanied the introduction of mass production techniques necessitated the creation of mass markets for consumer durables, including radios, refrigerators, television sets and motor cars. In order for economic growth to be maintained, national governments had to regulate profits and wage levels to sustain the conditions upon which economic growth depended. Hence, the development of the welfare state in Western industrial societies was seen to reflect efforts on the part of national governments to maintain the Fordist compromise between employers and organized labour. The combination of increased welfare state protection for workers, coupled with full employment and a degree of social mobility, temporarily 'solved' the problem of distribution (Hirsch 1977) under Fordism. The problem of distribution is that of determining how opportunities and income are to be apportioned. Under capitalism this is an ever-present problem because it is a system which is inherently unequal in its distribution of rewards and opportunities. However, during the Fordist era the combination of the rewards of economic growth being evenly spread across income levels, increasing social security, occupational and social mobility according to ostensibly meritocratic criteria generated a high degree of social solidarity. However, over the last 20 years the USA and UK have introduced 'market' rules of engagement. Here the nation-state is charged with the role of creating the conditions in which the market can operate 'freely'. Therefore, rather than trying to engineer a compromise between employers and the trade unions the state must prevent the unions from using their 'monopoly' powers to bid-up wages which are not necessarily reflected in productivity gains. Hence, according to the market rules of engagement the prosperity of workers will depend on an ability to trade their skills, knowledge and entrepreneurial acumen in an unfettered global market-place.

Finally, the transformation in Western capitalism has entailed new rules of wealth creation. These have undermined the viability of building national prosperity on the Fordist mass production of standardized goods and services.[3]

Fordist mass production was based on the standardization of products and their component parts. Many of the tasks previously undertaken by skilled craftsmen, such as making door panels or parts of the car's engine 'by hand', were mechanized by designing jigs, presses and machines able to perform the same operations hundreds, if not thousands of times a day, with the use of a semi-skilled operative. The Fordist production line was characterized by a moving assembly line, where the product passes the workers along a conveyor, rather than the worker having to move to the product as in nodal production. A further feature of Fordism was a detailed division of labour, within which the job tasks of shop floor workers were reduced to their most elementary form in order to maximize both efficiency and managerial control over the labour process. Hence, Fordism was based on many of the principles of 'scientific management' outlined by Frederick Taylor who offered a 'scientific' justification for the separation of *conception* from *execution,* where managers monopolized knowledge of the labour process, and controlled every step of production.

However, in the new rules of wealth creation economic prosperity will depend on nations and companies being able to exploit the skills, knowledge and insights of workers in ways which can no longer be delivered according to Fordist principles. Enterprises which can deliver a living wage to workers now depend on the quality as much as the price of goods and services, and on finding new sources of productivity and investment. Such 'value added' enterprise is most likely to be found in companies offering 'customized' goods and services in microelectronics, telecommunications, biotechnology, financial services, consultancy, advertising, marketing and the media.[4]

In response to these new rules all Western nations, in their domestic economies and foreign affairs, have had to look to their own social institutions and human resources to meet the global challenges they confront (OECD 1989). Lessons learnt from Japan and the Asian Tigers suggest that the 'human side of enterprise' is now a crucial factor in winning a competitive advantage in the global economy. Advantage is therefore seen to depend upon raising the quality and productivity of human capital. Knowledge, learning, information and technical competence are the new raw materials of international commerce:

> Knowledge itself, therefore, turns out to be not only the source of the highest-quality power, but also the most important ingredient of force and wealth. Put differently, knowledge has gone from being an adjunct of money power and muscle power, to being the very essence. It is, in fact, the ultimate amplifier. This is the key to the power shift that lies ahead, and it explains why the battle for control of knowledge and the means of communication is heating up all over the world.
>
> (Toffler 1990: 18)

Although such statements greatly exaggerate the importance of knowledge in advanced capitalist economies, without exception, national governments of all political persuasions have declared that it is the quality of their education and training systems which will decisively shape the international division of labour and national prosperity. Therefore the diminished power of nation-states to control economic competition has forced them to compete in what we call the global *knowledge wars*. In Britain, for instance, the National Commission of Education suggests that:

> For us, knowledge and skills will be central. In an area of world-wide competition and low-cost global communications, no country like ours will be able to maintain its standard of living, let alone improve it, on the basis of cheap labour and low-tech products and services. There will be too many millions of workers and too many employers in too many countries who will be able and willing to do that kind of work fully as well as we or people in any other developed country could do it – and at a fraction of the cost.
>
> (1993: 33)

But how the problem of education and training policies is understood and how the demand for skilled workers is increased is subject to contestation and political struggle. There is no doubt, for instance, that the introduction of new technologies has expanded the range of strategic choice available to employers and managers. However, this has exposed increasing differences, rather than similarities, in organizational cultures, job design and training regimes (Lane 1989, Green and Steedman 1993). There are few guarantees that employers will successfully exploit the potential for 'efficiency', precisely because they may fail to break free of conventional assumptions about the role of management and workers, and cling to the established hierarchy of authority, status and power. As Harvey (1989) has recognized, new technologies and coordinating forms of organization have permitted the revival of domestic, familial and paternalistic labour systems given that, 'The same shirt designs can be reproduced by large-scale factories in India, cooperative production in the "Third Italy", sweatshops in New York and London, or family labour systems in Hong Kong' (p. 187). This should alert us to the fact that the demise of Fordism in the West does not necessarily mean that the majority of workers will find jobs which exercise the range of their human capabilities. The interests of employers seeking to maximize profits and workers seeking to enhance the quality of working life and wages remain an important source of cleavage given that it is still possible for companies to 'profit' from low-tech, low-wage operations. There is no hidden-hand or post-industrial logic which will lead nations to respond to the global economy in the same way, despite the fact that their fates are inextricably connected. Indeed, we would suggest that the universal consensus highlighting education and training systems as holding the key to future prosperity has obscured fundamental differences in the way nations are responding to the global economy.

Therefore, while recognizing that some of the key elements of Fordism in Western nations are being transformed in the global economy, it is important not to prejudge the direction of these changes which must remain a question of detailed empirical investigation (see Block 1990). For analytical purposes it is useful to distinguish two 'ideal typical' models of national economic development in terms of neo-Fordism and post-Fordism (see table 2.1). Neo-Fordism can be characterized in terms of creating greater market flexibility through a reduction in social overheads and the power of trade unions, the privatization of public utilities and the welfare state, as well as a celebration of competitive individualism. Alternative, post-Fordism can be defined in terms of the development of the state as a 'strategic trader' shaping the direction of the national economy through investment in key economic sectors and in the development of human capital. Therefore, post-Fordism is based on a shift to 'high value' customized production and services using multi-skilled workers (see also Allen 1992).

In the 'real' world the relationship between education and economic development reveals examples of contradiction as much as correspondence. Moreover, although it is true to say that countries such as Germany, Japan and Singapore come closer to the model of post-Fordism, and the USA and UK approximate neo-Fordist solutions, we should not ignore clear examples of 'uneven' and contradictory developments within the same region or country. It also highlights the fact that there are important differences in the way nation-states may move towards a post-Fordist economy with far-reaching implications for democracy and social justice.

Nevertheless, these models represent clear differences in policy orientations in terms of the dominant economic ideas which inform them and underlying cultural assumptions about the role of skill formation in economic and social development (Thurow 1993). First we will assess the New Right's interpretation of education as part of a neo-Fordist strategy, before undertaking a detailed account of the left modernizers' vision of a post-Fordist, high-skill, high-wage economy.

The New Right: education in a neo-Fordist 'market' economy

The New Right interpretation of the Fordist 'crisis' is based on what we call the welfare shackle thesis. In the 19th century it was the aristocracy and the *ancien régime* in Europe who were blamed for 'shackling' the market and free enterprise. In the late 20th century it is the welfare state.[5] The New Right argue that the problem confronting Western nations today can only be understood in light of profound changes in the role of government

Table 2.1 Post-Fordist possibilities: alternative models of national development

Fordism	Neo-Fordism	Post-Fordism
Protected national markets	Global competition through: productivity gains, cost-cutting (overheads, wages)	Global competition through: innovation, quality, value-added goods and services
	Inward investment attracted by 'market flexibility' (reduce the social cost of labour, trade union power)	Inward investment attracted by highly skilled labour force engaged in 'value added' production/services
	Adversarial market orientation: remove impediments to market competition. Create 'enterprise culture'. Privatization of the welfare state	Consensus-based objectives: corporatist 'industrial policy'. Cooperation between government, employers and trade unions
Mass production of standardized products/low skill, high wage	Mass production of standardized products/low skill, low wage 'flexible' production and sweatshops	Flexible production systems/small batch/niche markets; shift to high-wage, high-skilled jobs
Bureaucratic hierarchical organizations	Leaner organizations with emphasis on 'numerical' flexibility	Leaner organizations with emphasis on 'functional' flexibility
Fragmented and standardized work tasks	Reduce trade union job demarcation	Flexible specialization/ multi-skilled workers
Mass standardized (male) employment	Fragmentation/polarization of labour force, Professional 'core' and 'flexible' workforce (i.e. part-time, temps, contract, portfolio careers)	Maintain good conditions for all employees. Non 'core' workers receive training, fringe benefits, comparable wages, proper representation
Divisions between managers and workers/low trust relations/collective bargaining	Emphasis on 'managers' right to manage'. Industrial relations based on low-trust relations	Industrial relations based on high trust, high discretion, collective participation
Little 'on the job' training for most workers	Training 'demand' led/little use of industrial training policies	Training as a national investment/state acts as strategic trainer

during the third quarter of the 20th century. They assert it is no coincidence that at the same time western governments were significantly increasing expenditure on social welfare programmes, there was high inflation, rising unemployment and economic stagnation (Murray 1984). Western societies have run into trouble because of the extensive and unwarranted interference by the state. Inflation, high unemployment, economic recession and urban unrest all stem from the legacy of Keynesian economics and an egalitarian ideology which promoted economic redistribution, equality of opportunity and welfare rights for all. Hence, the overriding problem confronting Western capitalist nations is to reimpose the disciplines of the market.

According to the New Right the route to national salvation in the context of global knowledge wars is through the survival of the fittest, based on an extension of parental choice in a market of competing schools, colleges and universities (Ball 1993). In the case of education, where funding, at least during the compulsory school years, will come from the public purse, the idea is to create a quasi-market within which schools will compete (Lauder 1991). This approximation to the operation of a market is achieved by seeking to create a variety of schools in a mixed economy of public and private institutions. In some cases they will aim at different client groups such as the ethnic minorities, religious sects, or 'high flyers'. This 'variety', it is argued, will provide parents with a genuine choice of different products (Boyd and Cibulka 1989; Halstead 1994). Choice of product (type of school) is seen to be sufficient to raise the standards for all, because if schools cannot sell enough desk space to be economically viable, they risk going out of business. Moreover, the economic needs of the nation will be met through the market, because when people have to pay for education they are more likely to make investment decisions which will realize an economic return. This will lead consumers to pick subjects and courses where there is a demand for labour, subsequently overcoming the problem of skill shortages. Equally, there will be a tendency for employment training to be 'demand led' in response to changing market conditions (Deakin and Wilkinson 1991).

Critics of the marketization of education therefore argue that the introduction of choice and competition provides a mechanism by which the middle classes can more securely gain an advantage in the competition for credentials (Brown 1995). This is because not all social groups come to an educational market as equals (Collins 1979). Cultural and material capital are distributed unequally between classes and ethnic groups. In particular, it is the middle classes which are more likely to have the cultural capital to make educational choices which best advantage their children (Brown 1990; Brown and Lauder 1992). In consequence, the introduction of parental choice and competition between schools will amount to a covert system of educational selection according to social class as middle-class children exit schools with significant numbers of working-class children. The consequence will be that the school system will become polarized in terms of social class and ethnic segregation and in terms of resources. As middle-class students exit from schools with working-class children they will also take much needed resources from those schools and effectively add to already well-off middle-class schools.

What evidence there is about the workings of educational markets suggests that they are far more complex than their critics suggest (Lauder *et al.* 1994). Nevertheless, the evidence so far confirms the prediction that choice and competition tend to lead to social class and ethnic polarization in schools (Willms and Echols 1992; Lauder *et al.* 1994). In nations such as the USA and UK, the overall effect will be to segregate students in different types of school on the basis of social class, ethnicity and religion. The net result will again be a massive wastage of talent as able working-class students once more find themselves trapped in schools which do not give them the opportunity of going to university (Halsey *et al.* 1980). If this is the overall effect then it can be argued that the marketization of education, while appearing to offer efficiency and flexibility of the kind demanded in the post-Fordist era, will in fact school the majority of children for a neo-Fordist economy which requires a low level of talent and skill.

The marketization of education will inevitably have an inverse effect on the ability of nation-states to compete in the global auction for quality inward investment, technology and jobs. Although multinational organizations are always on the lookout to reduce their overheads, including labour costs, investment in 'high-value' products and services crucially depends upon the quality, commitment and insights of the workforce, for which they are prepared to pay high salaries. The problem that nation-states now confront is one of how to balance commercial pressures to reduce labour costs and other overheads whilst mobilizing an educated labour force, and maintaining a sophisticated social, financial and communications infrastructure. This problem has been exacerbated by the fact that the low-skill, high-wage jobs associated with Fordism in North America and Europe are being transplanted to the NICs where labour costs are much lower, leading to a significant deterioration in working conditions in the low-skill jobs remaining in the West (Wood 1994).

In the context of the global auction, the market reforms in education are likely to leave a large majority of the future working population without the human resources to flourish in the global economy. Here the link between market reforms and neo-Fordism is barely disguised in countries which were dominated by New Right governments in the 1980s. The principal objective of economic policy is to improve the competitiveness of workers by increasing labour market flexibility by restricting the power of trade unions, especially in order to bring wages into line with their 'market' value. This philosophy led Britain to reject the Social Chapter of the Maastricht Treaty which provided legislative support for workers, because it was argued that it would undermine Britain's competitiveness in attracting inward investment, despite the poor work conditions this would inflict on employees. In contradistinction, market reforms in education and the economy have ensured the conditions in which highly paid middle-class professionals and elite groups are able to give their children an 'excellent' (*sic*) education in preparation for their bid to join the ranks of Reich's (1991) 'symbolic analysts'.

A different critique, albeit coming to the same conclusions, can be mounted against the introduction of market mechanisms in post-compulsory education and training. A key area of the post-compulsory sector for a post-Fordist economy is that concerned with the education of skilled tradespeople and technicians (Streeck 1989). The New Right has argued that the introduction of market mechanisms into this area will ensure a closer matching of supply and demand for trained labour and hence greater efficiency in the allocation of skilled labour. The argument rests on the assumptions that individuals and employers should bear the cost and responsibility for training. It is assumed that individuals gain most of the benefits from such a training and that they should therefore bear much of the cost (Lauder 1987). Moreover, since they are paying substantially for their training they will choose to train in an area in which there is market demand. In so far as employers should help bear the cost of training and the responsibility for the type of training offered, it is argued that employers are in the best position to assess the numbers of skilled workers required and the kind of skills they should possess. Underlying this observation is an appreciation of employers' short-term interests. Given the assumption that they 'know best' what the levels and nature of skilled labour should be, it follows that they will be reluctant to pay taxes or levies for training undertaken by a third party, such as the state.

While this view, as with other New Right views, is plausible, it has come in for sustained criticism. One of the most cogent is that of Streeck (1989, 1992). He argues that under a free labour contract of the kind found in liberal capitalist societies which gives workers the right to move from one firm to another, skills become a collective good in the eyes of employers. This is because the rewards of training individuals can easily be 'socialized' by the expedient of trained workers moving to another job while the costs of training remain with the original employer. Since employers face a clear risk in losing their investment they are unlikely to invest heavily in training. Streeck argues that, as a result, Western economies are likely to face a chronic skill shortage unless the state intervenes to ensure that adequate training occurs.

Moreover, unless there is state intervention employers will reduce the training programmes they do have when placed under intense competitive pressure and/or during a recession. Streeck (1989) notes that in the prolonged economic crisis of the 1970s, Western economies, with the exception of Germany, reduced their apprenticeship programmes. In Germany, government and trade union pressure ensured that the apprenticeship programme was extended. Two consequences followed: the apprenticeship system helped to alleviate youth unemployment and it contributed to the technical and economic advantage enjoyed by German industry in the early 1980s.

There are further criticisms that can be made of a market-determined training system. From the standpoint of the individual, it is unlikely that those who would potentially enter a skilled trade or technical training, working- and lower middle-class school leavers, could either afford the costs of such a training or take the risks involved. The risks are twofold: first, given the time lag between entering a training programme and completing it, market demand for a particular type of training may have changed with a resulting lack of jobs. In the competitive global market, such an outcome is all too likely. If the training received were of a sufficiently general nature to produce a flexible worker that might be less of a problem. However, in an employer-led training system the pressure will always exist for training to meet employers' specific and immediate needs. The consequence is that such a training system is likely to be too narrowly focused to meet rapidly changing demand conditions. Second, a further point follows from this, namely that the industries of today are likely to be tomorrow's dinosaurs. As a result, employer-led training schemes may not contain the vision and practice required in order to maintain the high skill base necessary for a post-Fordist economy. Clearly the structure of Germany's training system offers an example of an alternative which can begin to meet the requirements of a post-Fordist economy. This, as Streeck (1992) notes, involves a partnership between the state, employers and trade unions. It is a system which ensures that employers' immediate interests are subsumed within a system concerned with medium and longer term outcomes. Therefore the outcome of the reassertion of market discipline in social and economic institutions has been the development of a neo-Fordist economy characterized by insecurity and the creation of large numbers of temporary, low-skilled and low-waged jobs. We have also argued that the appeal to 'self-interest' and 'free enterprise' serves to mask the political interests of the most privileged sections of society. Indeed, the very notion of a national system of education is called into question as professional and elite groups secede from their commitment to public education and the ideology of meritocracy upon which public education in the 20th century has been founded.

Left modernizers: education in a post-Fordist 'magnet' economy

Over the last decade a new centre-left project has emerged in response to the ascendancy of the New Right. These 'left modernizers' reject much that was previously taken for granted amongst their socialist predecessors, contending that the transformation of capitalism at the end of the 20th century had significantly changed the strategies that the left needs to adopt in its pursuit of social justice *and* economic efficiency. This involves a recognition that the left must develop a credible response to the global economy, which will include economic policy and management as well as dealing with issues of distribution, equity and social policy (Rogers and Streeck 1994: 138). At the top of their agenda is a commitment to investment in human capital and strategic investment in the economy as a way of moving towards a high-skilled, high-waged 'magnet' economy. Underlying these economic forms of investment is a vision of a society permeated by a culture of learning for it is the knowledge, skills and insights of the population that provide the key to future prosperity. The ideas of the 'left modernizers' are to be found in books such as Reich (1991) and Thurow (1993) in the USA, the Commission on Social Justice (1994) and Brown (1994) in the UK. The ideas represented in these works are also consistent with Democratic politics in the USA and have informed the direction of Labour Party policy in Britain.[6]

The modernizers' account of how to create a post-Fordist economy can be summarized in the following way. It begins with a recognition that it is impossible to deliver widespread prosperity by trying to compete on price rather than the quality of goods and services. They therefore advocate a change in policy relating to investment in both physical and human capital. They advocate what has become known as producer capitalism (Dore 1987; Thurow 1993; Hutton 1995) in which low-cost, long-term investment is linked to the development of human capital. Producer capitalism stands in stark contrast with market capitalism in which price and short-term profit are the key criteria for enterprises. Not surprisingly, they reject the assertion made by the acolytes of market capitalism that the only route to prosperity is through the creation of greater market 'flexibility' by lowering labour costs or by repealing labour protection laws. The modernizers see that in the new economic competition making those at the bottom end of the labour market more insecure and powerless against exploitative employers is not the way for workers and nations to confront the challenge of the global auction. They recognize that the provision of a floor of protective rights, entitlements and conditions for workers in the context of the global auction is both socially desirable and economically essential. In practice what this means is reinforcing labour laws against the worst excesses of unscrupulous employers and the vagaries of the global auction. This will include a minimum wage and various forms of government intervention to get the long-term unemployed back to work. For modernizers, this is part of building a new high-trust partnership between government, employers and workers. For they argue that it is only through such a partnership that a high-skill, high-wage economy can be created. The role of the state in such a partnership is that of a 'strategic trader' (Krugman 1993) selecting 'winners' or guiding industrial development where appropriate and, most importantly, providing the infrastructure for economic development. Here the development of a highly educated workforce is seen as a priority.

The importance the modernizers attach to education stems from a belief that the increasing wage inequalities in the USA and UK over the last decade are a reflection of the returns to skill in a global auction for jobs and wages. The essence of this idea was captured by Bill Clinton in a major address on education:

The key to our economic strength in America today is productivity growth . . . In the 1990s and beyond, the universal spread of education, computers and high speed communications means that what we earn will depend on what we can learn and how well we can apply what we learn to the workplaces of America. That's why, as we know, a college graduate this year will earn 70 per cent more than a high school graduate in the first year of work. That's why the earnings of younger workers who dropped out of high school, or who finished but received no further education or training, dropped by more than 20 per cent over the last ten years alone.[7]

Hence, for all Western societies the route to prosperity is through the creation of a 'magnet' economy capable of attracting high-skilled, high-waged employment within an increasingly global labour market. This is to be achieved through sustained investment in the national economic infra-structure including transportation, telecommunications, R&D, etc. alongside investment in education and training systems. In the modernizers' account it is nevertheless acknowledged that there are unlikely to be enough skilled and well-paid jobs for everyone. However, flexible work patterns are assumed to lead to greater occupational mobility permitting people to move from low-skilled jobs when in full-time study, to high-skilled jobs in mid-career back to low-skilled jobs as retirement age approaches. Of course, such a view depends on substantial mobility in both an upwards and downwards direction (Esping-Andersen 1994). Therefore, in the same way that unemployment is tolerable if it only lasts for a few months, being in a low-skilled, poorly paid job is also tolerable as long as it offers progression into something better.

Education and training opportunities are thus pivotal to this vision of a competitive and just society. For not only can education deliver a high value-added 'magnet' economy but it can also solve the problem of unemployment. However, it is a mistake for nation-states to 'guarantee' employment because this harbours the same kind of vestigial thinking that led to previous attempts to protect uncompetitive firms from international competition: they simply become even less competitive. The only way forward is to invest in education and training to enable workers to become fully employable. In this account, social justice inheres in providing all individuals with the opportunity to gain access to an education that qualifies them for a job. Clearly there is a tension here between the idea of flexibility and the need to guarantee a minimum wage, so protecting labour from exploitation. All the indications are that the modernizers will err on the side of caution and provide what could only be described as minimal protection. In the end, the difference between the modernizers and the New Right on this issue may be marginal although, as we shall see, there are good economic reasons why adequate social protection is desirable.

There are several features of the modernizers' account with which we concur, including the need to introduce a version of 'producer' capitalism, but as a strategic policy for education and economic development it is flawed. Our purpose in exposing these flaws is to set the scene for a more radical and thoroughgoing debate about education, economy and society in the early decades of the 21st century. Our criticisms cluster around four related problems: first, the idea of a high-skilled, high-wage magnet economy; second, whether reskilling the nation can solve the problem of unemployment; third, whether it is correct to assume that income polarization is a true reflection of the 'value' of skills in the global labour market; and finally, the problem of how the modernizers propose upgrading the quality of human resources so all are granted an equal opportunity to fulfil their human potential.

How can a high-skilled, high-wage 'magnet' economy be created?

Their view that the future wealth of nations will depend on the exploitation of leading-edge technologies, corporate innovation and the upgrading of the quality of human resources can hardly be quarrelled with. Nations will clearly need to have a competitive advantage in at least some of the major industrial sectors, such as telecommunications, electronics, pharmaceuticals, chemicals and automobiles (Porter 1990; Thurow 1993). There is also little doubt that this will create a significant minority of jobs requiring highly skilled workers. However, the problem with the modernizers' account is that they assume that highly skilled and well-paid jobs will become available to all for at least a period of their working lives. Indeed, this is an essential tenet of their argument given that they suggest that widening inequalities can be overcome through upskilling the nation and that full employment remains a realistic goal. In other words, the modernizers continue to believe that the labour market can act as a legitimate mechanism (through the occupational division of labour) for resolving the distributional question in advanced capitalist societies.

The plausibility of this account hangs on the idea that the global auction for jobs and enterprise offers the potential for Western nations to create 'magnet' economies of highly skilled and well-paid jobs. This is an idea which has obvious appeal to a broad political constituency. It serves to replenish the spirits of those who see the USA following the UK in a spiral of economic decline after a period of global dominance. We are presented with the comforting picture of a global economy which, although no longer likely to be dominated by American and European companies, is characterized by prosperous Western workers making good incomes through the use of their skills, knowledge and insights. In reality, however, this characterization represents an imperialist throw-back to the idea that innovative ideas remain the preserve of the advanced Western nations, with the possible exception of Japan. Reich, for example, assumes that as low-skilled work moves into the NICs and Third World economies, the USA, the European EU countries and Japan will be left to fight amongst themselves for the high value-added jobs. The problem with this view is that it completely misunderstands the nature of the economic strategies now being implemented by the Asian Tigers, who have already developed economic and human capital infrastructures which are superior to those of many Western countries (Ashton and Sung 1994). This is partly reflected in the international convergence in education systems, at least in terms of expanding their tertiary sectors. Therefore, whilst we should not rule out the possibility that MNCs, when making inward and outward investment decisions, will judge the quality of human resources to be superior in particular countries, it is extremely unlikely that a small number of nations will become 'magnets' for high-skilled, high-waged work.

They have also overestimated the extent to which even the most successful modern economies depend on the mass employment of highly skilled workers. Indeed, an unintended consequence of the massive expansion of tertiary education may be to create a substantial wastage of talent amongst college and university graduates unable to find a demand for their skills, knowledge and insights. This new 'wastage of talent' is likely to be especially acute in countries which have pursued the neo-Fordist trajectory of labour market deregulation, corporate down-sizing and growth of temporary, casual and insecure work – conditions which are hardly conducive to the production of high-quality jobs distinguished by worker autonomy and cognitive complexity.

The difficulty for the modernizers is that by concentrating on the question of skill formation rather than on the way skills are linked to the trajectory of economic development, they obscure some of the fundamental problems, relating to educated labour, that need to be confronted. Piore (1990) has, for example, argued that where labour market regulation is weak, there is no incentive for employers to invest and use the new technology in a way which raises the value added and the quality of work. Rather, weak labour market regulations leads to a vicious circle whereby profit is extracted through sweatshop labour, low wages and low productivity. In effect, what regulated labour markets do is to create an incentive for entrepreneurs to invest in capital-intensive forms of production in order to generate the high value added to pay for the wage levels set by regulated labour markets (Sengenberger and Wilkinson 1995). If Piore is correct then we would expect the patterns of future work to develop along different trajectories depending on the degree to which their labour markets are regulated. While projections of labour supply and occupational change need to be viewed with some scepticism the recent OECD (1994) report on this subject certainly supports Piore's position when the USA is compared with Holland.

On all indices of social protection and labour-market regulation Holland provides an example of far greater social protection for workers, yet the vast majority of new jobs being created could be classified as 'skilled' (OECD 1994). In the USA approximately half the jobs being created were in service occupations requiring little formal training. The lesson here is obvious: the route to a high value-added economy must involve an analysis of factors affecting the demand for educated labour. The implicit assumption, harboured by the modernizers, that through investing in the employability of workers, employers will automatically recognize this potential and invest in upgrading the quality of their human resources is clearly naive.[8] The historical record in both the USA and the UK shows that while there are firms that recognize investment in people to be vital to the medium-term success of their companies, there are many others who equally recognize that fat profits can still be made off the backs of semi-skilled and unskilled, low-waged workers. Equally, the idea that Western nations can compensate for the failings of local employers by attracting inward investment from blue-chip MNCs is clearly not going to be sufficient to move from a neo-Fordist to a post-Fordist economy. Therefore, there seems little doubt that although in some important respects the modernizers will succeed in producing some improvement in the quality of employment opportunities, they will not achieve the goals of post-Fordist development because investment in education and training as the focal point of their policy will not lead to the creation of a high-skill, high-wage economy.

Can reskilling the nation solve the problem of unemployment?

The focus on employability rather than employment also leaves the modernizers accused of failing to offer a realistic return to full employment. Indeed, the high-skill, high-wage route may be pursued at the price of high unemployment. This is because neo-classical economists argue that labour market deregulation is the only way to solve unemployment. The theory is that the regulation of the labour market favoured by the modernizers bids up the price of those in work and discourages employers from taking on more workers. With deregulation the price of labour would fall and employers would 'buy' more workers. The debate over labour-market deregulation has given rise to the view that all advanced societies are now on the horns of a dilemma in terms of unemployment. Either labour markets are deregulated as in the USA, where official unemployment is below 5%, but where there is extensive poverty because wages at the bottom end of the labour market are insufficient to live off, or they are more regulated as in the producer capitalist route pursued by Germany, but unemployment is higher – as is the compensation paid to the unemployed (Commission of the European Communities 1993, Freeman 1995). The problem this poses to the modernizers is that on the one hand a majority of workers can expect good quality jobs and a reasonable standard of living but the polarization of market incomes avoided by the producer capitalist route is reproduced between those in work and those unemployed. The divisions in society remain but the source is different.

Unemployment, at the low levels achieved during the postwar period, was historically unique, depending on a contingent set of circumstances (Ormerod 1994). Attempting to create similar circumstances for the early part of the 21st century is likely to prove elusive and in political terms something of a hoax perpetrated by political parties who promise it or something close to it. It is, perhaps, for this reason that the modernizers translate full employment into full employability, thereby throwing the onus on the individual to find a job.

If we examine the profiles of several OECD countries, there are two striking observations that can be made. First, GDP has been divorced from employment in the past 20 years, just as growth has not led to a shared prosperity during the same period. In Spain the economy grew by 93% between 1970 and 1992 and *lost* 2% of its jobs (*Financial Times* 2 October 1993). This is in stark contrast with the postwar period when both incomes and jobs were linked to economic growth. Growth delivered an even rise in income for all occupational groups. Second, the trajectories taken by OECD countries in terms of their main indicators – inflation, growth and balance of payments – vary dramatically, yet unemployment remains around or above 7%, in terms of the official statistics, for every country with the exception of the USA and Japan. This includes countries with high levels of growth such as Canada, New Zealand and Australia.[9]

What appears to have happened in the past 25 years is that a set of economic and social forces has pushed the lower limit of unemployment up substantially from an OECD average well below 5% in the postwar period to an average well above 7%. Clearly the oil price hikes of the early 1970s had much to do with the initial jump in unemployment but since then a series of contingent factors have conspired to lock unemployment in at this high level. The introduction of new technology, which has enabled machines to replace workers, could have had a significant impact on unemployment for both blue- and white-collar workers as the jobless growth in Spain suggests. Similarly the number of blue-collar jobs lost to the developing nations has added to the problem (Wood 1994). However, these factors have to be placed within the wider context of economic regulation in relation to the global economy. It is worth noting that current economic orthodoxy ensures that interest rates rise with economic growth, thereby potentially choking off further investment in productive capacity and hence employment. It may also reduce demand, especially in countries such as the USA and UK with a high proportion of families with mortgages.

There are two mutually consistent explanations for the link between rising interest rates and growth. The first is that in a deregulated global finance market there is a shortage of investment funds, especially at times of growth. After all, with the potential to invest in developing nations, as well as the developed nations, the competition for investment has increased dramatically. Moreover, in a global economy the business cycles of the developed and developing nations are likely to be more synchronized so that an upturn in the global economy is likely to be met by a global demand for increased investment (Rowthorn 1995). The second is that, within nations, the key instrument for the control of inflation is interest rates. As economies overheat, interest rates are raised by central banks to choke off demand. The use of interest rates to control inflation is claimed to be successful in a way in which other measures tried in the 1970s and 1980s, incomes policies and control of money supply, were not. Again, however, we should note the role of the new global economy in defining the control of inflation as a key element in any successful national competitive strategy. If inflation in any one country rises to appreciably higher levels than in competitor countries, its goods are likely to be priced out of the market. Hence the significance accorded to the control of inflation in a global economy. But the cost of using interest rates to this end is that economies are permanently run under capacity (ILO 1995: 163). The rise in interest rates simply chokes off demand before it can appreciably affect unemployment levels.

More recently, studies have argued that it is declining economic growth and hence demand, among the OECD countries, since 1973 which is the fundamental cause of unemployment (Eatwell 1995; ILO 1995). While the trend in economic growth in all OECD countries has declined (ILO 1995: 133) it is unclear whether raising levels to those in the period between 1960 to 1973 would have the same impact on unemployment now as it did then, as the examples of Australia and Canada show. The problem is that in a global economy, growth may be achieved through exports and the benefits of growth spent on imports rather than home-produced goods. Whereas in the postwar Fordist economies a rise in demand would percolate through the economy, thereby creating jobs, a rise in demand now may simply create jobs in some other part of the world. This may be especially so in countries where increases in incomes are accruing to the wealthy who spend their money on luxury goods from overseas.

The alternative to this macro-analysis of the causes of unemployment is the micro-analysis of some neo-classical economists, who argue that it is labour-market rigidities, of the kind discussed above, especially the power of trade unions and highly regulated labour markets, which cause unemployment and sustain inflation. There are two elements to their explanation. The first is that these rigidities bid up the price of labour and maintain it at a level higher than desirable to clear the labour market of unemployed. The second is that these rigidities allow the 'insiders' who are employed to bid up their wages even when others are unemployed (Lindbeck and Snower 1986). There are two problems with this theory. First, there appears to be no strong relationship between the degree of social protection, labour market regulation and unemployment, with the exception of the USA (although see Freeman 1995). Historically the lowest levels of unemployment, from 1950–73, have been associated with the highest levels of social protection and labour market regulation, while the present period represents one of the lowest levels of protection and regulation and the highest levels of unemployment. Moreover, even during the period under review (1994–5) differences between nations relating to regulation, protection and economic performance hardly bear out this thesis. For example, the UK has one of the lowest levels of labour protection in the OECD and an unemployment rate of 8.4% (OECD 1994: 155). In contrast, Holland, which has an above-average level of protection and regulation, has an unemployment rate of 7.3%. Moreover, their inflation rates are not substantially different. Britain had an annual rate of 2.4% in 1995 and Holland 3%. Second, where labour markets have been deregulated they have not brought about a substantial reduction in unemployment. This is certainly the case in the UK and in New Zealand where unemployment is still about 7%.

Overall, it seems extremely unlikely that the problem of unemployment can be solved by any of the conventional remedies and to pretend otherwise merely holds out false promises to a generation of unemployed. The New Right solution was to price people back into jobs. The modernizers' solution is to create a high-skill, high-wage 'magnet' economy. Neither solution is adequate. The New Right solution manifestly has not worked and it threatens a new cycle of low-wage job creation. The modernizers, whilst having a more sustainable approach to global economic competition, have no answer to unemployment. Therefore, the most important conclusion to be drawn from this discussion is that the modernizers lack an adequate account of how all will share in the future prosperity accrued from the investment in education and national economic growth. Unemployment will remain a structural feature of Western societies and the 'distributional' question (Hirsch 1977), temporarily solved under Fordism through full employment and the even spread of the fruits of growth across the occupational structure, must now be addressed by the modernizers. Consequently, we argue elsewhere (Brown and Lauder forthcoming) that the distributional problem can only be remedied by the introduction of a 'social wage' and that occupational opportunities will have to be shared. Moreover, the question of unemployment is not only one about social justice, but also one of economic efficiency. If the economic fate of nations increasingly depends upon the quality of their human resources, it will not be possible to write off a large minority of the population to an 'underclass' existence. Indeed, the issue of long-term unemployment is part of a wider problem of social and economic polarization. Therefore, we need to examine the modernizers' account of skill and income polarization before asking how those people living in poverty are going to acquire the appropriate skills to get high-skilled, high-waged jobs, when research has demonstrated that social deprivation has a profoundly negative impact on academic performance.

Does income polarization reflect the 'value' of skills knowledge and insights in the global labour market?

Considerable doubt must be cast on the way the modernizers have understood the 'high skill = high wage' equation This is important to our discussion because growing income inequalities are seen to reflect individual differences in the quality of their 'human capital'. Here their argument is based on trend data which show a widening of income inequalities. There has been a dramatic increase in income inequalities in both the USA and the UK since the late 1970s. Such evidence is taken to reflect the relative abilities of workers to trade their knowledge, skills and insights on the global labour market. According to the modernizers, as low-skilled jobs have been lost to developing economies with cheaper labour, the wages of less skilled workers in the West have declined. By the same token, in the new competitive conditions described above, those workers who have the skills, knowledge and insights that can contribute to 'value-added' research, production, consultancy or service delivery in the global labour market have witnessed an increase in their remuneration. Hence analysis and remedy are closely related in the modernizers' account: if the reason so many workers are in low-paying jobs, or worse, unemployed, is that they lack skills, the solution is to give them the skills. It is an appealing analysis but at best it is based on a partial truth.

If increasing income polarization was a consequence of the neutral operation of the global economy we should find the same trend in all the advanced economies. However, the evidence suggests that the increasing polarization in income is far more pronounced in the USA and UK than in any other OECD country (Gardiner 1993: 14; Hills 1995). In Germany there has actually been a decline in income differentials (OECD 1993)!

It could also be expected that if the increased dispersion of income was a result of the changing cognitive and skill demands of work, then nations with the highest levels of technology and investment in research and development would lead the table of income inequalities. Yet, the evidence that does exist suggests quite the opposite. Wood (1994) notes that, 'Japan and Sweden are leaders in applying new technology, while the USA and UK are laggards' (p. 281). He also notes that the work of Patel and Pavitt (1991) suggests that civilian research and development, as a proportion of GDP in the 1980s, was higher in Sweden and Japan than in the USA and UK. Equally, in terms of patenting in the USA, Germany, which experienced declining inequalities of income during this period, greatly outperformed the UK.

One conclusion to be drawn from these considerations is that rather than the returns to skill becoming more responsive to the operation of the global auction, the relationship between skill and income is less direct than the modernizers assume, the reason being that the relationship between income and skills is always mediated by cultural, political and societal factors. This is of course obvious when unpaid child care, undertaken primarily by women, is taken into consideration. Moreover, despite the way skill is used in the current debate about income inequalities and economic performance, it has proved extremely difficult to arrive at an agreed definition of skill, which explains why studies comparing labour markets in neighbouring countries such as Germany and France show that the process of training, career progression and reward for skills is intricate, subtle and substantially different in the two countries (Maurice *et al.* 1986). Another study (Dore 1987) has highlighted differences in the way rewards are distributed for work in the USA as opposed to Japan. In the USA it is assumed by neo-classical economists that there is a direct relationship between skill and income. However, Japanese industry, the exemplar of producer capitalism, has not organized the relationship between skill and income in this way. Rather, it has based income on loyalty to the company and length of service, rather than 'skill' in any pristine sense. As Dore has noted, in Japan there is a remarkable 'lack of consciousness of the market price of a skill' (p. 30). This being the case it could be expected that even if the polarization of income in the USA was a response to the changing demand for skill, this would not be the case in Japan. A further glance at the OECD (1993) data also tells us that while there has been some widening of income differentials in Japan, it does not reflect the polarization characteristic of the USA and UK.

What this evidence suggests is that the modernizers' assumption that by raising skill levels there will be a commensurate increase in income regulated through the global labour market is clearly incorrect. The answer is to be found not in the neutral operation of the global labour market as Reich and others have suggested, but in the way the USA and UK have *responded* to global economic conditions. This response, like the global economy itself, has been shaped by the New Right political projects of Reagan and Thatcher (Marchak 1991). Although the debate about what is distinctive about the USA and UK takes us beyond the confines of this chapter, the polarization in income can be explained more convincingly in terms of differences in labour market power rather than returns to skills (although they are not mutually exclusive). A major consequence of market deregulation has been to enhance the power of 'core' workers in down-sized organizations. This is supported by the fact that the most dramatic changes in income distribution are to be found at either end of the income parade. What income polarization in the USA and UK also reveals is the way in which the 'casino' economies of these countries in the 1980s enabled company executives and senior managers, along with those who worked in the financial markets, to engage in 'wealth extraction' rather than the development of sustainable forms of 'wealth creation' (Lazonick 1993). This largely explains why a study reported by Bound and Johnson (1995) found that in the USA a large part of the increase in the returns to a university degree was due to an increased premium when put to use in the business and law fields. The wages of computer specialists and engineers actually *fell* relative to those of high school graduates.

But if the rising incomes of the work rich are explicable in terms of 'paper entrepreneurialism' (Reich 1984) and corporate restructuring, can the decline in the wages of the unskilled be explained in terms of the neutral operation of the global economy? In addressing this question there is the problem of measuring the extent to which semi- and unskilled work has been transplanted to the developing nations. One estimate is that up to 1990 changes in trade with the South has reduced the demand for unskilled relative to skilled labour in the North by approximately 20% (Wood 1994: 11). However, it is not only that industrial blue-collar jobs were lost, but the perennial threat of relocation to developing world countries which ensured that wages were depressed for remaining unskilled workers. It is, of course, hard to measure the degree to which this threat has been material in keeping down wages. Nevertheless, it is worth noting that there is little correlation between manufacturing competitiveness and low wages. In the most successful industrial economies, Germany and Japan, manufacturing wages are higher than anywhere else. However, New Right governments in the USA and UK took the 'lesson' to heart and helped to drive down wages by labour market deregulation. Estimates for the UK (Gosling and Machin 1993) and the USA (Blackburn *et al.* 1990), for instance, calculate that the decline in unionization in the 1980s accounts for 20% of the increase in wage inequality. In addition, making it easier to hire and fire workers enabled companies to achieve numerical flexibility in terms of their wages bills (Atkinson 1985). At times of economic boom workers could be hired while in times of downturn they could be fired. In Britain, for example, in the last three months of 1994, 74,120 full-time jobs disappeared and 173,941 part-time jobs were created. This is a clear example of how to organize a labour market for short-term expedience, but it also suggests that companies have not only externalized the risks associated with unstable market conditions but also their labour costs, especially among low-skilled workers. In such circumstances it is difficult to see how the modernizers can resolve the problem of widening income inequalities when they are judged to reflect the neutral operation of the global economy.

Indeed, high levels of income inequalities are interpreted by the modernizers as a reflection of educational and corporate inefficiency in a global labour market which can only be narrowed through investment in education and training. If inequalities persist it is because the latter are failing to upgrade the quality of human resources. With respect to national systems of education, inequalities become a useful measure of their effectiveness. However, this raises a set of questions and problems for the modernizers with respect to the social conditions under which education can achieve greater equality of opportunity and higher levels of educational achievement for all. It is to this, fourth, problem that we now turn.

How can the quality of human resources be upgraded where all are granted an equal opportunity to fulfil their human potential?

In answering this question the modernizers recognize that the wealth of nations depends upon upgrading the quality of human resources. They recognize that ways must be found to develop the full potential of a much larger proportion of the population than prevailed in the Fordist era. They point to the need to widen access to tertiary education and to create the institutional framework necessary to offer lifelong learning to all. They also recognize a need to improve overall educational standards as US and UK students appear to be falling behind in international comparative tests. A national commitment to investment in the 'employability' of present and future workers is understood by the modernizers to represent a new social contract between the individual and the state, given that such investment is viewed as a condition for economic efficiency and social justice. However, their interpretation of how equity and efficiency are to be achieved in the global economy is politically impoverished. In part, this is because the question of equity has been subsumed within a debate about how to upgrade the overall quality of education and training systems based on an assumption that domestic inequalities of opportunity are largely irrelevant if a nation can win a competitive advantage in the global knowledge wars, permitting all to compete for high-skilled, high-waged jobs. Therefore, the old national competition for a livelihood, based on the principles of meritocratic competition, is of far less importance than that of how to upgrade the quality of the education system as a whole. Again we find the idea of a high-skill, high-wage magnet economy used to extract the political sting from questions of social and educational inequalities.

The reality is that questions of social justice cannot be resolved through the operation of the global labour market. Indeed, if the creation of a post-Fordist economy depends on a general upgrading of the skills of the labour force, tackling the problem of domestic inequalities in income and opportunities has become *more* rather than less important with economic globalization. There are at least two related reasons for this. First, the use of education and training institutions to raise technical standards for all does not resolve the question of 'positional' advantage (Hirsch 1977). In other words, access to elite schools, colleges and universities, along with the credentials they bestow, remains a key factor in determining labour market power. In addition, if our analysis of income inequalities is correct, labour market power has, if anything, become more important as a result of corporate restructuring and the decline of graduate careers (Brown and Scase 1994). Therefore, the question of social justice will continue to depend on how individual nation states frame the competition for a livelihood.

The question of positional competition has also become more important because there has been a change in the nature of educational selection. Today the institutional expression of a commitment to meritocratic competition in education has been suffocated under the grip of the New Right. A commitment to a unified system of schooling within which students will be educated according to ability and effort has been abandoned in favour of consumer sovereignty based on parental 'choice' and a system of education based on market principles. A consequence of this change in the organization of educational selection from that based on 'merit' to the 'market' (Brown 1995) is, as argued above, that it serves to encourage the creation of underfunded sink schools for the poor and havens of 'excellence' for the rich. Therefore, the school system in both the USA and UK no longer reflects a commitment to open competition but gross inequalities in educational provision, opportunities and life chances. In Washington, DC the wealthy are queuing up to pay as much as $12,000 a year to send their five-year-old children to private schools, while the city is virtually bankrupt and severe cuts to the educational budget are inevitable.[10]

Therefore, although equality of opportunity is recognized as a condition of economic efficiency, the modernizers have effectively avoided perhaps the most important question to confront the left at the end of the 20th century, that is, how to organize the competition for a livelihood in such a way that a genuinely equal opportunity is available to all. Avoiding the positional problem by appeals to the need to raise educational standards for all in the global market not only fails to address this question but also offers little insight into how the foundations for social solidarity, upon which the institutional expression of meritocratic competition rests, are to be rebuilt. Indeed, their focus on increasing the 'employability' of workers reinforces a sense of the insecure nature of work at the end of the 20th century (Newman 1993; Peterson 1994). It encourages people to watch their backs constantly and to put their child first in the educational and labour market jungle. Without an adequate foundation for material and social security the emphasis on enhanced employability within a culture of competitive individualism becomes translated into the Hobbesian condition of 'all against all'. When education becomes a positional good and where the stakes are forever increasing in terms of income, life-chances and social status, powerful individuals and groups will seek to maximize their resources to ensure that they have a stake in the game by whatever means.[11] Therefore, how the state intervenes to regulate this competition in a way which reduces the inequalities of those trapped in lower socioeconomic groups must be addressed, not only as a matter of economic efficiency but also for reasons of social justice in a post-Fordist economy.

The relationship between equity and efficiency at the end of the 20th century does not only rest on the reassertion of meritocratic competition in education, but also on a recognition that the wealth of the nation's human resources is *inversely* related to social inequalities, especially in income and opportunity. Therefore, narrowing such inequalities is likely to be a cost-effective way of investing in human capital, which in turn should lead to improvements in economic efficiency. Hence, we would predict that the polarization of income in nations such as the USA and UK during the 1980s will have led to a wider dispersal of educational achievement than in nations with little or no widening of incomes. We are currently analysing the comparative evidence in order to examine the hypothesis that relative deprivation has an absolute effect on the quality of a nation's human resources (Wilkinson 1994). If our hypothesis proves to be supported by the empirical evidence, it will come as little surprise to sociologists who have consistently found a close relationship between inequality and academic performance.[12] The fact that at least a fifth of children in both the USA and UK now live in poverty is inevitably going to have a detrimental impact on the ability of these children to respond to educational opportunities and to recognize the relevance of formal study when living in neighbourhoods with high unemployment, crime and deprivation. Indeed, the importance of equity to the question of social learning is graphically illustrated in Julius Wilson's (1987) study of the urban underclass in America. He suggests that 'a perceptive ghetto youngster in a neighbourhood that includes a good number of working and professional families may observe increasing joblessness and idleness but he [*sic*] may also witness many individuals going to and from work; he may sense an increase in school dropouts but he can also see a connection between education and meaningful employment' (1987: 56). He goes on to argue that the exodus of 'respectable' middle- and working-class families from the inner-city neighbourhoods in the 1970s and 1980s removed an important 'social buffer' that could deflect the full impact of prolonged and increasing joblessness, given that the basic institutions in the area (churches, schools, stores, recreational facilities, etc.) were viable so long as more economically stable and secure families remained. Hence, the more social groups become isolated from one another the fewer opportunities exist for the kind of social learning which, even in the deprived neighbourhoods of US and UK cities, could offer role models to children other than those which now exist due to the 'political economy of crack' (Davis 1990).

Moreover, the impact of widening social inequalities is not restricted to children from ghetto or poor backgrounds; it also infects the social learning of the wealthier sections of the population. In a characteristically perceptive discussion John Dewey noted that every expansive period of social history is marked by social trends which serve to 'eliminate distance between peoples and classes previously hemmed off from one another' (1966: 100). At times where the opposite happens it narrows the range of contacts, ideas, interests and role models. The culture of the privileged tends to become 'sterile, to be turned back to feed on itself; their art becomes a showy display and artificial; their wealth luxurious; their knowledge over-specialised; their manners fastidious rather than human' (Dewey 1966: 98).

Hence the view which the modernizers take in assuming that inequalities will narrow once there is proper investment in education and training fails to recognize that the future wealth of nations depends upon a fundamental challenge to inequalities in both income and opportunities. Therefore, the role of the nation-state must increasingly become one of balancing the internal competition for a livelihood with a strategy geared towards upgrading the quality of education for all through a reduction in relative inequalities. Moreover, a commitment to equality of opportunity is not only vital to the life-blood of a high-skill economic strategy, but it also provides a clear message to all sections of society that they are of equal worth and deserve genuine opportunities to fulfil their human potential.

Conclusion

The increasing importance attached to education in the global economy is not misplaced in the sense that nations will increasingly have to define the wealth of nations in terms of the quality of human resources among the population. The creation of a post-Fordist economy will depend upon an active state involved in investment, regulation and strategic planning in the economic infrastructure alongside a commitment to skill formation through education and training. We have argued that such an economic strategy is necessary because it is the best way of creating a social dividend which can be used to fund a 'social wage' for all given that the 'distributional' problem can no longer be solved through employment within the division of labour. A social wage which delivers families from poverty thereby becomes an important foundation of a learning society, designed to follow the post-Fordist trajectory to a globally competitive economy and to a socially just society (see Brown and Lauder forthcoming). Hence, if the potential and limitations of educational reform in the creation of post-Fordist economy are to be adequately addressed by the modernizers, there is an urgent need for those on the left to grapple with the issues explored in this paper.

Notes

1 This paper develops a number of themes outlined in earlier papers (Brown and Lauder 1992, Brown 1995). It also serves to clarify our interpretation of the relationship between education and post-Fordism which has been criticized by Avis (1993) and Jones and Hatcher (1994).

2 Figures from *Financial Times* Survey 'North American Business Location' 19 October 1994.

3 Antonio Gramsci (1971) used the term Fordism to describe a new system of

mass production introduced by the American car manufacturer Henry Ford. Gramsci recognized that the introduction of mass production also required a new mode of social regulation 'suited to the new type of work and productive process' (p. 286). Ford's rise to prominence at the time stemmed from the market success of the Model T motor car which was launched in 1916. The system of mass production enabled him to capture 55% of the US market in the early 1920s by selling the Model T at a tenth of the price of a craft-built car (Braverman 1974; Murray 1989).

4 As it is more difficult for competitors to mass produce the same goods or to offer customers tailored services (see Schumpeter 1961; Collins 1986; Blackwell and Eilon 1991). In such companies improvements in productivity depend upon the 'organic' integration of applied science, technological innovation, free-flow information networks, and high-trust relations between management and multi-skilled workers. The increasing costs of errors, demand for quality control, and for multi-skilled workers with a conceptual grasp of a large section of the production process or office activities has made the specialized division of labour in Fordism a source of organizational inefficiency.

5 The idea of a 'Feudal' shackle is discussed by Hirschman (1986).

6 Given such a diverse range of publications there will inevitably be differences in focus and policy emphasis. The extent to which the Clinton administration in America has attempted to introduce a viable industrial policy has been clearly limited; see Shoch, J. (1994) 'The politics of the US industrial policy debate, 1981–1984 (with a note on Bill Clinton's 'industrial policy')', in D. Kotz, T. McDonough and M. Reich (eds) *Social Structures of Accumulation* (Cambridge: Cambridge University Press).

7. 'They are all our children' speech delivered at East Los Angeles College, Los Angeles, 14 May 1992. The modernizers' view contrasts with the rhetoric, if not the practice, of the New Right. There is clearly a tension between New Right views regarding the expansion of tertiary education and the practice of the Conservative Party in the UK, where there has been a rapid expansion of tertiary provision despite the views of influential theorists and journalists such as Friedman, Hayek and Rees-Mogg, suggesting that it is only an élite that needs a university education. It is also worth noting that, in terms of imagery, the New Right do not present the future in terms of a 'learning society' but an enterprise culture, in which a few outstanding captains of industry and commerce, the Bill Gates and Richard Bransons of this world, are fêted as the leaders of an economic renaissance.

8 The floor of protective rights for workers as envisaged by the modernizers is, for example, likely to be too weak to act as an incentive to employers to upgrade the quality of work opportunities. Moreover, see Kuttner's response to Rogers and Streeck (1994).

9 Data compiled from the *Independent on Sunday*'s economic indicators 1994–95.

10 The question of equality of opportunity needs to be addressed head on as it is not only essential to economic efficiency, but also to the legitimization of a system of educational and occupational selection which is inherently stratified in terms of income, status, work styles and lifestyles. In postwar Western societies the reason why a menial labourer is paid $17,000 and a private sector manager $85,000 was legitimized in terms of the outcome of a meritocratic competition based on individual ability and effort. The commitment to open competition found expression in the idea of the socially-mixed-ability high or comprehensive school. Yes, there remained deprived inner-city districts where children, especially from African–American and Hispanic backgrounds, were

clearly not getting equality of opportunity but even here 'head start' programmes were launched to try to create a level playing field.

11 Moreover, for those in lower socioeconomic circumstances their exclusion from decent academic provision is compounded by deindustrialization, which has created a rust belt across the heartlands of both the USA and UK, sometimes destroying vibrant communities (Bluestone and Harrison 1982). Therefore, although the modernizers assume greater flexibility in the occupational structure as a response to the employment needs of men and women at different stages of their lives, the reality seems more likely to lead to intensive competition and highly restricted opportunities to enter the professional core and a constant flux restricted to jobs which are low-skilled, low-waged and inherently insecure. This outcome may well be reinforced by the fact that as employers place a premium on employees with the appropriate social and interpersonal skills alongside their technical know-how, the cultural capital of job-seekers assumes greater importance. Without the financial and social resources required to invest in cultural capital, those from poorer backgrounds who are more likely to attend less prestigious halls of learning will be at a distinct disadvantage (Brown and Scase 1994).

12 For a discussion of the definition of relative deprivation and poverty see Townsend, P. (1993) *The International Analysis of Poverty* (New York: Harvester Wheatsheaf).

References

Allen, J. (1992) 'Post-industrialism and Post-Fordism'. In S. Hall *et al.* (eds), *Modernity and its Futures* (Cambridge: Polity).

Ashton, D. N. and Sung, J. (1994) *The State, Economic Development and Skill Formation: A New Asian Model,* Working Paper No. 3 (Leicester: Centre for Labour Market Studies, University of Leicester).

Atkinson, J. (1985) 'The changing corporation'. In D. Clutterbuck (ed.), *New Patterns of Work* (Aldershot: Gower).

Avis, J. (1993) 'A new orthodoxy, old problems: post-16 reforms'. *British Journal of Sociology of Education*, 14, 245–260.

Ball. S. (1993) 'Education markets, choice and social class: the market as a class strategy in the UK and the USA'. *British Journal of Sociology of Education,* 14(1), 3–19.

Blackburn, M., Bloom, D. and Freeman, R. (1990) 'The declining economic position of less skilled American men'. In G. Burtless (ed.), *A Future Of Lousy Jobs?* (Washington DC: Brookings Institute).

Blackwell, B. and Eilon, S. (1991) *The Global Challenge of Innovation* (Oxford: Butterworth-Heinemann).

Block, F. (1990) *Postindustrial Possibilities: A Critique of Economic Discourse* (Berkeley: University of California Press).

Bluestone, B. and Harrison, B. (1982) *The Deindustrialization of America* (New York: Basic Books).

Bound, J. and Johnson, G. (1995) 'What are the causes of rising wage inequality in the United States?' *Economic Policy Review,* Federal Reserve Bank of New York, 1(1), 9–17.

Boyd, W. and Cibulka, J. (eds) (1989) *Private Schools and Public Policy* (London: Falmer Press).

Braverman, H. (1974) *Labour and Monopoly Capital* (London: Jessica Kingsley).

Brown, G. (1994) 'The politics of potential: a new agenda for Labour'. In D. Miliband (ed.), *Reinventing the Left* (Cambridge: Polity).

Brown, P. (1990) 'The "Third Wave": education and the ideology of parentocracy'. *British Journal of Sociology of Education,* 11, 65–85.

Brown, P. (1995) 'Cultural capital and social exclusion: some observations on recent trends in education, employment and the labour market'. *Work Employment and Society,* 9(1), 29–51.

Brown, P. and Lauder, H. (1992) 'Education, economy and society: an introduction to a new agenda'. In P. Brown and H. Lauder (eds), *Education for Economic Survival: From Fordism to Post-Fordism?* (London: Routledge).

Brown, P. and Lauder H. (forthcoming) *Collective Intelligence: The Future of Society in a Global Age.*

Brown, P. and Scase, R. (1994) *Higher Education and Corporate Realities* (London: UCL Press).

Carnoy, M., Castells, M., Cohen, S. and Cardoso, F. H. (1993) *The Global Economy in the Information Age* (Pennsylvania: Penn State University).

Collins, R. (1979) *The Credential Society* (New York: Academic Press).

Collins, R. (1986) *Weberian Sociological Theory* (New York: Cambridge University Press).

Commission of the European Communities (1993) *Growth, Competitiveness, Employ-ment: The Challenges and Ways Forward into the 21st Century* White Paper, Bulletin of the European Communities 6/93.

Commission on Social Justice (1994) *Social Justice: Strategies for National Renewal* (London: Vintage).

Cowling, K. and Sugden, R. (1994) *Beyond Capitalism: Towards a New World Economic Order* (London: Pinter).

Davis, M. (1990) *City of Quartz* (New York: Verso).

Deakin, S. and Wilkinson, F. (1991) 'Social policy and economic efficiency: the deregulation of the labour market in Britain'. *Critical Social Policy,* 11(3), 40–61.

Dewey, J. (1966) *Democracy and Education* (New York, Free Press).

Dicken, P. (1992) *Global Shift: The Internationalisation of Economic Activity* (London: Paul Chapman).

Dore, R. (1987) *Taking Japan Seriously* (London: Athlone Press).

Eatwell, J. (1995) 'The international origins of unemployment'. In J. Michie and J.G. Smith (eds), *Managing the Global Economy* (Oxford: Oxford University Press).

Esping-Andersen, G. (1994) 'Equity and work in the post-industrial life-cycle'. In D. Miliband (ed.), *Reinventing the Left* (Cambridge: Polity).

Freeman, R. (1995) 'The limits of wage flexibility to curing unemployment'. *Oxford Review of Economic Policy,* 11(1), 63–72.

Gamble, A. (1988) *The Free Market and the Strong State* (London: Macmillan).

Gardiner, K. (1993) A Survey of Income Inequality Over the Last Twenty Years – How Does the UK Compare?, Welfare State Programme No. 100 (London: Centre for Economics and Related Disciplines, London School of Economics).

Gosling A. and Machin, S. (1993) *Trade Unions and the Dispersion of Earnings in UK Establishments 1980–90,* Centre for Economic Performance Discussion Paper No. 140 (London: London School of Economics).

Gramsci, A. (1971) *Selections from Prison Notebooks* (London: Lawrence & Wishart).

Green, A. and Steedman, H. (1993) *Education Provision, Education Attainment and the Needs of Identity: A Review of Research for Germany, France, Japan, the USA and Britain* (London: NIESR).

Halsey, A. H., Heath, A. and Ridge, J. (1980) *Origins and Destinations* (Oxford: Clarendon).

Halstead, M. (ed.) (1994) *Parental Choice and Education* (London: Kogan Page).

Harvey, D. (1989) *The Conditions of Postmodernity* (Oxford: Blackwell).

Henderson, A. and Parsons, T. (eds) (1974) *Max Weber: The Theory of Social and Economic Organisation* (New York: Oxford University Press).

Hills, J. (1995) *Income and Wealth, Vol. 2: A Summary of the Evidence* (York: Joseph Rowntree Foundation).

Hirsch, F. (1977) *Social Limits to Growth* (London: Routledge).

Hirschmann, A. (1986) *Rival Views of Market Society and Other Essays* (London: Viking).

Hutton, W. (1995) *The State We're In* (London: Jonathan Cape).

International Labour Organisation (ILO) (1995) *World Employment* (Geneva: ILO).

Jones, K. and Hatcher, R. (1994) 'Education, progress and economic change: notes on some recent proposals'. *British Journal of Educational Studies*, 42, 245–260.

Krugman, P. (1993) *Peddling Prosperity: Economic Sense and Nonsense in the Age of Diminished Expectations* (New York: W.W. Norton).

Lane, C. (1989) *Management and Labour in Europe* (Aldershot: Edward Elgar).

Lauder, H. (1987) 'The New Right and educational policy in New Zealand'. *New Zealand Journal of Educational Studies,* 22, 3–23.

Lauder, H. (1991) 'Education, democracy and the economy'. *British Journal of Sociology of Education,* 12, 417–431.

Lauder, H. and Hughes, D. (1990) 'Social inequalities and differences in school outcomes'. *New Zealand Journal of Educational Studies,* 23, 37–60.

Lauder, H. *et al.* (1994) *The Creation of Market Competition for Education in New Zealand* (Wellington: Ministry of Education).

Lazonick, W. (1993) 'Industry clusters versus global webs: organisational capabilities in the American economy'. *Industrial and Corporate Change,* 2, 1–24.

Lindbeck, A. and Snower, D. (1986) 'Wage setting, unemployment and insider-outsider relations'. *American Economic Review,* 76, 235–239.

Lipietz, A. (1987) *Mirages and Miracles: The Crises of Global Fordism* (London: Verso).

Marchak, M. P. (1991) *The Integrated Circus: The New Right and the Restructuring of Global Markets* (Montreal: McGill-Queen's University Press).

Marginson, P. (1994) 'Multinational Britain: employment and work in an internationalised economy'. *Human Resource Management Journal,* 4(4), 63–80.

Maurice, M., Sellier, F. and Silvestre, J. (1986) *The Social Foundations of Industrial Power* (Cambridge, MA: MIT Press).

McGregor, D. (1960) *The Human Side of Enterprise* (New York: McGraw-Hill).

Michie, J. and Smith, J. G. (eds) (1995) *Managing the Global Economy* (Oxford: Oxford University Press).

Murray, C. (1984) *Losing Ground: American Social Policy 1950–1980* (New York: Basic Books).

Murray, R. (1989) 'Fordism and post-Fordism'. In S. Hall and M. Jacques (eds), *New Times* (London: Lawrence & Wishart).

National Commission on Education (1993) *Learning to Succeed* (London: Heinemann).

Newman, K. (1993) *Declining Fortunes* (New York: Basic Books).

OECD (1989) *Education and the Economy in a Changing World* (Paris: OECD).

OECD (1993) *Employment Outlook* (Paris: OECD).

OECD (1994) *Employment Outlook* (Paris: OECD).

Ormerod, P. (1994) *The Death of Economics* (London: Faber & Faber).

Parkin, F. (1979) *Marxism and Class Theory: A Bourgeois Critique* (London: Tavistock).

Patel, P. and Pavitt, K. (1991) 'Europe's technological performance'. In C. Freeman, M. Sharp and W. Walker (eds), *Technology and the Future of Europe* (London: Pinter).

Peterson, W. (1994) *Silent Depression: The Fate of the American Dream* (New York: W. W. Norton).

Piore, M. (1990) 'Labor standards and business strategies'. In S. Herzenberg and J. Perez-Lopez (eds), *Labor Standards and Development in the Global Economy* (Washington DC: US Department of Labor).

Piore, M. and Sable, C. (1984) *The Second Industrial Divide: Possibilities for Prosperity* (New York: Basic Books).

Porter, M. (1990) *The Competitive Advantage of Nations* (London: Macmillan).

Reich, R. (1984) *The Next American Frontier* (Harmondsworth: Penguin).

Reich, R. (1991) *The Work of Nations* (London: Simon & Schuster).

Rogers J. and Streeck, W. (1994) 'Productive solidarities: economic strategy and left politics'. In D. Miliband (ed.), *Reinventing the Left* (Cambridge: Polity).

Rowthorn, R. (1995) 'Capital formation and unemployment'. *Oxford Review of Economic Policy*, 11(1), 26–39.

Sabel, C. F. (1982) *Work and Politics* (Cambridge: Cambridge University Press).

Schumpeter, J. (1961) *The Theory of Economic Development* (New York: Oxford University Press).

Sengenberger, W. and Wilkinson, F. (1995) 'Globalization and labour standards'. In J. Michie and J. G. Smith (eds), *Managing the Global Economy* (Oxford: Oxford University Press).

Snower, D. (1995) 'Evaluating unemployment policies: what do the underlying theories tell us?' *Oxford Review of Economic Policy*, 11, 110–135.

Streeck, W. (1989) 'Skills and the limits of neo-liberalism: the enterprise of the future as a place of learning'. *Work Employment and Society*, 3, 90–104.

Streeck, W. (1992) *Social Institutions and Economic Performance* (London: Sage).

Thurow, L. (1993) *Head to Head: The Coming Economic Battle Among Japan, Europe and America* (London: Nicholas Brealey).

Toffler, A. (1990) *Powershift* (New York: Bantam).

Wilkinson, R. (1994) *Unfair Shares: The Effect of Widening Income Differences on the Welfare of the Young* (Ilford: Barnardo's Publication).

Willms, J. and Echols, F. (1992) 'Alert and inert clients: the Scottish experience of parental choice of schools'. *Economics of Education Review*, 11, 339–350.

Wilson, W. (1987) *The Truly Disadvantaged* (Chicago: University of Chicago Press).

Wood, A. (1994) *North-South Trade, Employment and Inequality: Changing Fortunes in a Skill-Driven World* (Oxford: Clarendon).

Chapter 3

The great work dilemma

Education, employment, and wages in the new global economy

Martin Carnoy

I Introduction

Advanced industrial economies in the 1990s face a work crisis that goes far beyond the crisis in creating wage employment or the crisis of more unequal wage distribution in a changing job market. This crisis resides not just in national labor markets, where an increasingly well-educated labor force is facing increasing difficulties finding steady employment at decent wages and less-educated labor is increasingly marginalized. The crisis is also political, with reactions to the core concept of the welfare state threatening to undermine nations' underlying social institutions – family, community, and public education – just as they come under new pressures from labor markets going through radical change.[1] The highly popular policy focus on more and better education as a solution to the crisis cannot be conceptually separated from this larger politics which surrounds it.

Such a broader view of what is normally seen as "just" a jobs problem makes policy interventions much more problematic than simply "getting prices right" through greater labor market flexibility. Deregulating markets is widely supported by conservatives as a solution to the European Economic Communities' drastic problem of high unemployment and failure to create jobs during the 1980s (Figure 3.1). Europe has had only a 10% increase in jobs since 1960, but was able to keep wages for those who had jobs rising faster than inflation. Unemployment never dipped below 8% in the EEC after 1983, and was 12% in the early 1990s. One attractive alternative, then, is to emulate the United States, with its low minimum wages and much lower levels of labor market regulation. But the U.S. deregulatory "solution" to the jobs problem in the late 1970s and 1980s has a serious downside: real wages even for highly educated men remained constant and declined sharply for both women and men with high school education or less (Bluestone, 1990, 1995). This has put pressure on women to work full time, and for men to work longer hours or hold more than one job. Low minimum wages, which allegedly promote greater youth employment, are increasingly earned by adults living at the edge of poverty (Card and

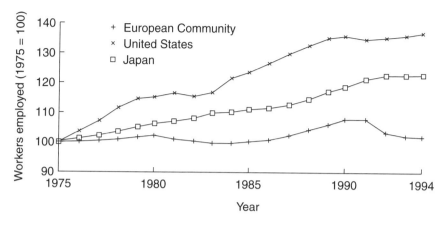

Figure 3.1 Index of employment growth by region, 1975–1994 (1975 = 100). *Source:* Carnoy and Castells (1995); Freeman and Soete (1994: Figure 4.1)

Krueger, 1995).[2] Overall, an argument could be made that the U.S. job creation machine has also created a rapid increase in dysfunctional families, individual stress, and deteriorating communities. It (and similar policies in the U.K.) has been associated with high and increasing income inequality (Table 3.1), which in and of itself has negative consequences for consensual democratic politics.

Many economists do not believe that the deregulation approach to markets is socially optimal (for example, Summers and Blanchard, 1990), and according to them, reduced interest rates and currency devaluation – a more expansionary domestic macroeconomic policy – could alleviate much of the unemployment problem without necessarily lowering real wages or introducing some of the worst effects of the United States model. However, there is a serious question whether a politically acceptable macroeconomic policy alone would increase job creation enough in the 1990s. Competition in international markets is increasing, not decreasing, putting even more pressure on firms to reduce labor costs or to move to lower cost labor environments. Such pressures could require even more domestic expansion than in the 1980s in order to reduce unemployment significantly, especially if policy makers are thinking in traditional definitions of full-time, full-year, "permanent" jobs. Since rapid economic expansion conjures up rapid inflation in inflation-sensitive societies such as Germany that dominate European economic policy, it is unlikely that Europe will risk the kind of "inflationary" macroeconomic policy required to make a big dent in unemployment. In addition, the welfare state policies that form the basis of safety net support for European family and community are less and less sustainable in the present economic environment.

Table 3.1 Trends in the index of Gini Coefficients of income inequality in OECD countries, 1970–1993 (figures represent indices of income inequality in each country over time)

Year	Japan	U.K.	U.S.	France	Germany	Italy	Sweden
1970		98		109			
1971		101					
1972		102					
1973		98					
1974		95					
1975		92		105			112
1976		92					109
1977		90				114	107
1978		91				109	105
1979		96	101	100		110	103
1980		98	100			102	102
1981	100	100	103			100	100
1982		102	107			94	102
1983		103	109		100	95	102
1984	109	108	110	102		98	107
1985		111	110		104		107
1986		117	110			99	112
1987	108	124	110		101	104	107
1988		125	112				107
1989		130	113	102		97	110
1990	113	130	114		104		123
1991			113			95	129
1992			115				
1993			117				

Source: Gottschalk and Smeeding (1995) Cross National Comparisons of Levels and Trends in Inequality, March 3, (mimeo). The indices shown use different measures of income or earnings in each country, but generally employ disposable family income.

Japan has been highly successful in achieving rapid economic growth with full employment and low inflation by means of a "corporatist" macro-economic policy that brings labor and large industries together to agree on wage and price increases. But even Japan has now suffered several years of recession, rising unemployment, and increased competition from other Asian exporters with lower labor costs.

This leaves both the United States and Europe in a conundrum as global competition continues to increase: the U.S., because its flexible labor market policies are generating very high social costs for a large fraction of those who are employed; Europe, because its labor market "inflexibilities", built on the greater effectiveness of labor organizations to regulate employer–employee relations, have protected the traditional European family and communities against the massive changes in capitalist development of the past 25 years but at the expense of leaving an increasing fraction of family members desiring jobs (particularly young people) without work altogether.[3]

In both cases, the costs of the employment "solutions" are politically difficult to sustain.

The most comfortable strategy in attacking the wage crisis for both the U.S. and European policy makers has been educational and training reform and improvement. With all signs pointing to increasing demand for high-skilled labor that has concomitantly lower unemployment rates and increasingly higher wages than less skilled workers (particularly in the U.S. and the U.K.), a human resource strategy seems to have broad political appeal and some promise of making things better. Despite these appeals, I argue in this chapter that the strategy does not work well in the context of a deregulation-oriented political economy – precisely the context in which it is most likely to be applied in both the United States and Europe. Employment and wage policies are nested in larger political philosophies which produce "packages" of policies that inherently influence education and training responses. In a deregulated market economy, employers are less likely to provide general training to workers and the public sector is less likely to invest increasing amounts of funds in public education. The result – increased inequality of access to high quality education and on-the-job training – is exactly the opposite of what the policies claim to want to deliver.

2 Dimensions of the crisis

The work crisis we have just described has two principal dimensions. First, competition has intensified not just among the advanced economies, but also from "late" developers in Asia and Latin America able to produce sophisticated products with highly productive and lower cost labor (see Amsden, 1989). This competition has been spurred by the rapid globalization of economic units and the technological revolution in information and telecommunications accompanying it. Advanced countries have advantages in this competition, especially in the skills of their highly educated labor and in access to capital. But they also have disadvantages, including the relatively high cost of labor and the political power of labor and environmental groups.

Second, although capital is now organized on a worldwide basis, labor is constrained largely within national boundaries by language, culture, and migration barriers. It therefore depends mainly on *national* policies for its welfare. In formulating such policies, family and community have always been relied on to bear a significant part of the social cost of private production, in supplying skills, in tolerating unhealthy environmental conditions at work and at home, and accepting the anxiety of potential work loss and involuntary relocation inherent in "flexible" labor markets. In the United States, a "tradition" of free markets, individual autonomy, and labor mobility has made it possible to get labor to accept a much higher proportion of these social costs than in Europe. In Europe, firms have been made to bear a higher proportion of social costs, particularly those of guaranteeing employment once hired, paying the costs of health and pension benefits to employees, providing workers training, and contributing to child care and generous unemployment insurance.

The payoff to these costs in the past was a rapidly increasing "quality of life" in Europe and the U.S. On average, families and communities on both continents found themselves wealthier, more educated, and with more leisure time. Under conditions of increasing real wages *and* more jobs, families and communities changed their character, but employees got steadily higher-paying jobs, and parents and children were generally healthier, did better and went farther in school, and had more secure lives.

But the intensification of worldwide competition, demographic changes, and the very expectation of an ever-continuing rise in the standard of living have transformed this process in the advanced countries.[4] It has necessarily made firms operating there seek ways to reduce costs, putting increased strain on families in bearing these costs. These strains threaten the underlying fabric of advanced industrial society.

From the early 1970s – when the new competitive era began – until now, strategies of employment creation in the three main advanced economies of the United States, Western Europe, and Japan, differed significantly. Through its less regulated labor markets and more liberal immigration policies, the U.S. economy was able to create large numbers of new jobs, mainly in high- and low-level services, and in much greater proportion for women than for men, but at lower real wages than for men, hence lower average real wages for the labor force as a whole. Productivity in the U.S. grew relatively slowly in this period. The European response created relatively few jobs, but relatively rapid increases in productivity were matched by relatively solid increases in real wages. The Japanese response was most "successful", with solid increases in productivity and wages, and high levels of job creation (Figure 3.2).

No matter how successful each of these models was, by the 1990s each one's disadvantages were accentuated by increased international competition.[5] U.S. economic recovery has created new employment in 1993–1996 but at a much slower pace than in the 1980s or 1970s.[6] Average wages for men and women did not rise in 1989–1994 even though their average education and productivity did (Bradsher, 1995).[7] Furthermore, real earnings even for higher educated men and women have not been increasing in this past recovery, reversing this positive feature of the 1980s employment expansion (Table 3.2). Crime and the decline of family values (the absent family) were producing a true crisis of reproduction, putting ever more pressure on government to improve education and other interventions.

In the 1990s, European unemployment rates rose to record levels and real wages fell. For the first time since World War II, governments proposed

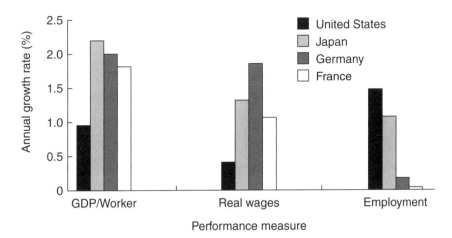

Figure 3.2 Economic performance by country, 1980–1994. *Source*: OECD (1995)
Annex Tables

Table 3.2 Real median annual earnings, by age group and level of education, non-Hispanic white males and females, full-time workers, 1969–1994 (1995 dollars)

	1969	1979	1989	1991	1994
Males					
16–24-yr-old HS grads	21972	21973	18542	17273	16530
16–24-yr-old some college	20656	23258	20097	17242	16411
25–34-yr-old HS grads	31627	31045	27792	25552	24436
25–34-yr-old some college	34486	33861	31756	30278	26722
25–34-yr-old college grad	41435	38506	39019	37451	34907
Females					
16–24-yr-old HS grads	16190	16220	14793	14266	13175
16–24-yr-old some college	18076	18085	16999	16086	14650
25–34-yr-old HS grads	20114	19936	19334	19221	18002
25–34-yr-old some college	21744	22720	23245	22968	21022
25–34-yr-old college grad	24887	26059	30355	29128	28634

Sources: U.S. Department of Commerce, Bureau of the Census, 1/1000 U.S. Census Sample, 1970, 1980, 1990; Current Population Survey, March Sample, 1992, 1995.

reducing the high benefits they provided to workers (at a correspondingly high cost to firms) in order to stimulate employment. In essence, Europe was being urged – at least by its conservative political parties – to "learn from Washington" by cutting government regulation (and spending), privatizing social costs, reducing labor costs, and reducing the costs of hiring and firing workers in order to become more competitive. The depth of Japan's recession has not only affected overall employment, but is also causing firms to rethink

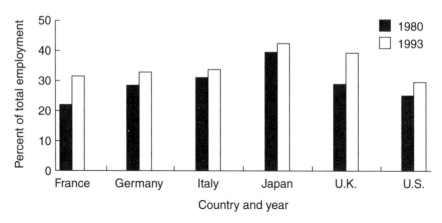

Figure 3.3 Part-time, self-employed and temporary workers as percentage of total employment, OECD area, 1980–1993. *Source:* Carnoy and Castells (1995)

their policy of guaranteed jobs. Japan's employment policy, however, must be put in perspective. Only 40% of Japanese workers are in "permanent", protected jobs, and many of those who are not are part-time or temporary workers, the highest proportion among advanced, industrialized countries (Figure 3.3). In both Europe and Japan, the trend toward less permanent, more contingent jobs is increasing even faster than in the U.S., in part probably because U.S. core workers are more mobile in any case, making the U.S. labor market more inherently flexible without alternative arrangements.[8]

3 The role of education in increasing employment with higher wages and reduced income inequality

Given the growing spread in incomes (in the U.S. and the U.K.) and youth unemployment rates (in Europe) between higher and less-educated labor, policy makers have logically called for improving the quality of education and increasing the proportion of youth who complete higher levels of schooling as one major way out of the work crisis (for example, Reich, 1991; OECD, 1994; Commission of the European Communities, 1993).

There is every reason to believe that a better trained workforce has a greater potential to increase productivity. Major changes in the world economy have now placed a premium on speedy decision making, high-quality output, and the ability to adapt rapidly to change. In addition, production of goods and services seems to require a much broader range of skills even among semi-skilled workers – at least in the eyes of employers trying to meet increasing competition in fast-changing markets. Economies with well-developed education and training systems, such as Japan and

Germany, appear to have done much better, growth-wise and improving the average standard of living. Their firms, it seems, are accustomed to invest regularly in worker training and they consider their workers as sources of innovation and improved productivity. Moreover, there exists in these countries a close relationship at the macro level between the public and private sector and between workers and employers.

It is also likely that reducing minimum wages, barriers to labor mobility, social charges borne by employers, government-imposed constraints on labor, and particularly product market "flexibility", including the growth of part-time labor, will, even in the absence of training programs, increase employment in the short- and medium-run. However, beyond emphasizing this combination of a better trained workforce and a more flexible employment system as the keys to expanded employment, these policies also implicitly assume that serious unemployment and relative wage decline are in large part a result of a rapidly rising, new technology-driven, demand for highly skilled workers and the continued increase of young workers without college education entering a labor market that needs them less and less. This "skills mismatch" drives down wages or increases unemployment especially for less-educated younger workers (Bound and Johnson, 1992; Murphy and Welch, 1993; Katz and Murphy, 1992).[9] The proposed policies suggest that improved education and training will solve these problems even as minimum wages are reduced and labor markets made more "flexible" (Europe), and even as labor markets continue to be governed by policies that focus on keeping wages low (U.S., U.K.).

Yet, despite evidence that such a skills mismatch exists, there is also a great deal of evidence that institutional factors explain changes in the wage distribution in the U.S. or the maintenance of much more equal wage distributions in Europe and Japan. Mishel and Teixeira (1993), Howell and Wolff (1991), and Howell (1994) all provide strong arguments to show that wage gaps in the United States have widened much more than changes in skill distributions can explain. Card and Lemieux (1993) use inter-age and education group wage differences by ethnicity and gender to show that although the return to college education increased for both men and women and blacks and whites in the 1980s, skill differences could not explain why less-educated women's wages fell much less than men's, and the wages of young college educated black males rose much more slowly than college-educated whites. Fortin and Lemieux (1995) show that holding the minimum wage constant in nominal terms from 1981 to 1990 had a major impact on low-end wages in the 1980s.

So wage erosion has come from a combination of factors, such as trade shifts, concession bargaining, downsizing, an increase in part-time and temporary workers substituting for full-time workers, firm relocation to low-wage areas, maintenance of low minimum wages, deunionization, and massive immigration. All of these factors have contributed to the deinstitutionalization of the

U.S. labor market, hurting those with the least bargaining power and therefore lowering the wages of low-wage workers relative to high-wage workers. Further, Freeman and Needels' research on Canada (Freeman and Needels, 1991), and comparisons by Blau and Kahn (1994) and Freeman and Katz (1995) between the U.S. and other developed countries show that institutional differences between countries go far to explain wide differences in the way wage distributions change so differently over time.

It therefore is far from evident that the cause of unemployment in Europe and the declining incomes of workers with less than university degrees in the U.S. is due only to or even mainly to less skills available in the labor force than employers currently demand. Moreover, training programs for the "low-educated" and less-skilled have, in the past, not been particularly successful in getting them jobs and higher incomes (Grubb, 1995). When the training programs do get them jobs, it is often at the expense of other disadvantaged workers. The core "supply side" concept of the deregulation model that more education leads to higher productivity, which then leads to higher income, while persuasive at one level, is suspect at another. Recent data in the U.S. show steadily declining earnings in the 1990s in the face of rising productivity, rising profits, and rising levels of education in the labor force (see Table 3.2). Improved education and more training is not a proven recipe for overcoming serious unemployment or wage decline. Touting them as such distracts from finding real solutions to these problems.

Does that mean that we need less education and training? Not at all. Better education and training should lead to higher productivity, employment, and rising *average* income in the long run. The fact that such generally positive effects may also result in widely varying distributive outcomes suggests that the way in which education and training are conceived and provided and *the macroeconomic policy context in which they are improved have an important impact on workers and firms, and thus, on society as a whole.*

More training and better training are less likely to occur in economies with highly "flexible" labor markets. Firms in the U.S. and U.K. are less willing to provide on-the-job training, claiming that governments should make workers "job ready". Exceptionally, they might provide for highly firm-specific skills; i.e., for training which is least useful to workers should they be displaced or wish to move to other firms. In flexible labor markets, firms are also less likely to provide training that increases long-run productivity based on worker innovation, since such training is generally tied to job security and worker participation (Brown *et al.,* 1993).

Education systems, many now agree, must be built around the concept of recurrent, or lifelong, education and training (Carnoy and Castells, 1995). Individual workers should expect to need retraining several times in their work lives. By anticipating such needs, a recurrent training system could greatly reduce the cost to individuals and society of rapid technological and economic changes. Under the best of conditions, a well-organized, lifelong education system would not only increase economic growth, but also assure that such growth would be distributed in an equitable manner among a nation's workers. Rather than having just one portion of the workforce able to profit from new forms of work organization and technological change, most could be made ready for jobs that might be developed if highly skilled, flexible workers could be there to fill them. That ideal, however, is likely to be in constant conflict with employer demands for labor market deregulation. With deregulated markets high levels of firm "flexibility" would probably mean little, if any, recurrent worker training supplied by firms; and without a high degree of employer cooperation, recurrent training off-the-job provided by governments is likely to be expensive and not particularly effective (Grubb, 1995). Again, in highly deregulated markets, there would be little incentive for employers to bear the "cooperation costs" of training.

The bottom line, then, is that for education and training to result in more and better employment opportunities with equity, the very notion of labor market "flexibility" has to be separated from "deregulation". Calls for reducing unemployment in Europe currrently emphasize reducing minimum wages and barriers for firing redundant workers as well as providing improved education and training. In this notion of "flexibility", the deregulation of labor markets plays the dominant role, and governments hope to correct the resultant increase in wage inequality through providing more skills or convincing employers to increase training. All the evidence suggests that while this model of deregulation-dominated flexibility may improve the employment situation somewhat, it also hinders an increase in training or a reduction in wage inequality. What is needed to improve employability is to start with a notion of flexibility that focuses on *flexible education and training systems and management–labor relations* rather than on lower wages. Advanced economies need education and training systems that respond flexibly to ever-changing skill demands in rapidly changing product and labor markets. For this training to be translated into higher productivity, more employment, and higher wages, management–labor relations need to be reorganized around worker incentives, such as worker participation in profits from productivity gains and worker-initiated cost savings, and guarantees for job security when profits are maintained – not around high worker turnover and downward pressure on wages. This type of work organization should be associated with less, not greater wage inequality.

Simple as this proposition may seem, it does require a political context very different from the one that now dominates in the United States and much of Europe. If education, training, and labor-management relations are to be flexible, that system will require an activist state cooperating with employers willing to bear part of the social responsibility for improving labor skills, participation, and the rewards for higher productivity. Ironically, the United States has one of the most flexible educational systems in the world, well suited for the new flexible labor market environment, and for lifelong education. Europe, on the other hand, has private employers who are much more comfortable with an activist state and a cooperative, regulated work environment, lacking in the U.S. But many of Europe's educational systems are more rigid than U.S. education, especially in terms of when and where young people attend higher education and the ability to change career studies and careers. The enormous number of women more than 30 years old taking degrees in U.S. universities transformed the labor market in the 1980s. Yet, it may well be easier for Europe to make its educational system more flexible than for the United States to make its employers more socially conscious. Educational reforms in Britain and initiatives now being proposed for second chance and lifelong education in the European Union suggest that profound educational changes may indeed occur, and that this may create a flexibility based on higher skills *and* higher wages. That is, unless Europe moves too far down the road to deregulation.

Acknowledgment – This paper was written while the author was a fellow at the Center for Advanced Studies in the Behavioral Sciences, Stanford, California, under a grant from the National Science Foundation.

Notes

1 Manuel Castells and I analyzed these radical changes in the workplace and concurrent changes in the welfare state, family, and community in Carnoy and Castells (1995).
2 If the U.S. minimum wage was raised to US$5.15 from US$4.25 (the current proposed legislation), it would affect over 20% of all wage earners, and only one-fourth would be teenagers. Of those now earning less than US$5.15, over 50% come from the poorest 20% of families (Rothstein, 1996).
3 Nevertheless, the number of such families may, in fact, be lower than is usually imagined, and this may explain why there has been less than expected political reaction to high unemployment rates. For example, in Spain, which reports official unemployment rates well over 20%, the number of families with no one employed is well below 10%, and very high youth unemployment throughout Europe is partly "absorbed" by youth living at home until their late twenties.
4 It may also put the "good life" or even the prospects for employment out of reach of those workers living in developing countries that are not able to orga- nize themselves to gain from the new kinds of work being created by growth in the developed and newly industrializing countries. See for example, Barnett (1993).
5 Even greater challenges are on the horizon: new, large economic competitors are entering global competition. China, with its very low cost labor and poten- tial for adopting new technology and mobilizing the huge amount of overseas Chinese capital, will be increasingly important in buying sophisticated products but also selling much higher quality, low-end manufactured goods and entering high technology markets with cheap, high-skilled labor. India, too, may be right around the corner as a major economic player. This is "good" for the

advanced country multinational corporations, as new markets open up for their products, and for many workers in the developing countries who get jobs and higher pay in the new industries, but perhaps not so good in the short-run for all but the most technically trained advanced country workers, as the lower-educated work to produce those products is dispersed worldwide. In the longer run, as younger advanced country workers take more education than their parents, it is likely that they will move into new jobs created by increasing demand for products in countries such as India and China. That is, unless India and China are themselves increasingly able to produce more advanced products at lower wages.

6 U.S. civilian employment grew at a 2.36% annual rate between 1970 and 1980, 1.73% annually in 1980–1990. and at a 1.1% rate in 1990–1996. The rate of growth in 1992–1996 was 1.76% annually, compared to a 2.79% growth rate in 1982–1989, the previous recovery.

7 The only group to record higher real wages per hour from 1989 to 1995 were women with higher education degrees, and this gain was very small (Mishel and Bernstein, 1996).

8 Robert Hall's (Hall, 1982) study of worker turnover in 1979 showed that U.S. workers change jobs an average of 8–9 times in their working life, even though about one-half of male workers end up working in a single job for 15–20 years. Farber's (Farber, 1993) and others' recent work shows that this combination of enormous mobility among young workers and later stability among older workers had not changed significantly by the 1990s, although other analysts, such as Belous (1989) and Tilly (1996) disagree, arguing that temporary work and involuntary part-time employment have increased rapidly in the past 10 years.

9 The argument is based on empirical evidence in the U.S. suggesting that a significant portion of the change in wages for different skill levels is to be explained through difficult-to-measure within-industry changes in demand for high- and low-skilled employees due mainly to technological change, and that this demand increase has left the economy with a "skills mismatch". The labor force is underskilled in relation to the economy's changing demands. For example, Murphy and Welch (1993) conclude that sectoral shifts do not sufficiently explain the increase in inequality. Rather, they see that "Changes in the returns to skill and skill intensity resulted largely from changes within even narrowly defined industries" (p. 131).

References

Amsden, A. (1989) *Asia's Next Giant*. Oxford University Press, New York.
Barnett, R. (1993) The end of jobs. *Harper's* 298, 47–52.
Belous, R.S. (1989) *The Contingent Economy: The Growth of the Temporary, Part-Time, and Subcontracted Workforce*. National Planning Association, Washington, DC.
Blau, F.D. and Kahn, L.M. (1994) *International Differences in Male Wage Inequality: Institutions versus Market Forces*. Working Paper No. 4678 (March). National Bureau of Economic Research, Cambridge, MA.
Bluestone, B. (1990) The impact of schooling and industrial restructuring on recent trends in wage inequality in the United States. *American Economic Review (Papers and Proceedings)* 80, 303–307.
Bluestone, B. (1995) The inequality express. *The American Prospect* No. 21 (winter), 81–93.

Bound, J. and Johnson, G. (1992) Changes in the structure of wages in the 1980's: An evaluation of alternative explanations. *American Economic Review* 82, 371–392.

Bradsher, K. (1995) Productivity is all, but it doesn't pay well. *The New York Times,* June 25, Section 4 (News of the Week in Review) p. 4.

Brown, C., Reich, M. and Stern, D. (1993) Becoming a high performance organization: The role of security, employee involvement, and training. *International Journal of Human Resource Management* 4, 247–275.

Card, D. and Lemieux, T. (1993) *Wage Dispersion, Returns to Skill, and Black-White Wage Differentials,* Working Paper 4365 (May). National Bureau of Economic Research, Cambridge, MA.

Card, D. and Krueger, A. (1995) *Myth and Measurement.* Princeton University Press, Princeton, NJ.

Carnoy, M. and Castells, M. (1995) Sustaining flexibility. Stanford University and University of California at Berkeley (mimeo).

Commission of the European Communities (1993) Growth, competitiveness and employment: The challenges and ways forward into the 21st Century – White paper. *Bulletin of the European Communities,* Supplement, June.

Farber, H.S. (1993) The incidence of job loss: 1982–1991. In *Brookings Papers on Economic Activity: Microeconomics,* pp. 73–132. The Brookings Institution, Washington, DC.

Fortin, N. and Lemieux, T. (1995). Labor market institutions and gender differences in wage inequality. Economics Department, University of Montreal, Canada (mimeo).

Freeman, C. and Soete, L. (1994). *Work for All or Mass Unemployment.* Pinter, London.

Freeman, R. and Needels, K. (1991). *Skill Differentials in Canada in an Era of Rising Labor Market Inequality.* Working Paper No. 3827. National Bureau of Economic Research, Cambridge, MA.

Freeman, R. and Katz, L. (1995) Rising wage inequality: The United States vs. other advanced countries. In *Differences and Changes in Wage Structures,* eds R. Freeman and L. Katz. University of Chicago Press and NBER, Chicago.

Grubb, W.N. (1995) *Evaluating Job Training Programs in the United States: Evidence and Explanations.* International Labour Office, Training Policy and Program Development Branch, Geneva.

Hall, R. (1982) The importance of lifetime jobs in the U.S. economy. *American Economic Review* 72, 716–724.

Howell, D.R. and Wolff, E.N. (1991) Trends in the growth and distribution of skills in the U.S. workplace, 1960–1985. *Industrial and Labor Relations Review* 44 486–502.

Howell, D. (1994) The skills myth. *The American Prospect* 18, 81–90.

Katz, L.F. and Murphy, K.M. (1992) Changes in relative wages, 1963–1987: Supply and demand factors. *The Quarterly Journal of Economics* 107, 35–78.

Mishel, L. and Teixeira, R.A. (1993) *The Myth of the Coming Labor Shortage: Jobs, Skills, and Incomes Of America's Workforce 2000.* Economic Policy Institute, Washington, DC.

Mishel, L. and Bernstein, J. (1996) *The State of Working America.* Economic Policy Institute, Washington, DC.

Murphy, K.M. and Welch, F. (1993) Industrial change and the rising importance of skill. In *Uneven Tides,* eds S. Danziger and P. Gottschalk. Russell Sage, New York.

Organization for Economic Cooperation and Development (1994) *Employment/ Unemployment Study Policy Report.* May 24 (C/MIN(94)4). OECD, Paris.

Organization for Economic Cooperation and Development (1995) *OECD Economic Outlook,* No. 56 (December). OECD, Paris.

Reich, R.B. (1991) *The Work of Nations: Preparing Ourselves for 21st Century Capitalism.* Alfred A. Knopf, New York.

Rothstein, R. (1996) Minimum wage debates. Economic Policy Institute, Washington, DC (mimeo).

Summers, L. and Blanchard, O. (1990) Hysteresis and the European unemployment problem. In *Understanding Unemployment,* ed. L. Summers, pp. 227–285. MIT Press, Cambridge, MA.

Tilly, C. (1996) *Half A Job: Bad and Good Part-Time Jobs in A Changing Labor Market.* Temple University Press, Philadelphia.

Chapter 4

The new knowledge work

Stanley Aronowitz and William DiFazio

Overview

In 1992 the long-term shifts in the nature of paid work became painfully visible not only to industrial workers and those with technical, professional, and managerial credentials and job experience but also to the public. During the year "corporate giants like General Motors and IBM announced plans to shed tens of thousands of workers".[1] General Motors, which at first said it would close twenty-one U.S. plants by 1995, soon disclaimed any definite limit to the number of either plant closings or firings and admitted the numbers of jobs lost might climb above the predicted 70,000, even if the recession led to increased car sales. IBM, which initially shaved about 25,000 blue- and white-collar employees, soon increased its estimates to possibly 60,000, in effect reversing the company's historic policy of no layoffs. Citing economic conditions, Boeing, the world's largest airplane producer, and Hughes Aircraft, a major parts manufacturer, were poised for substantial cuts in their well-paid workforces. In 1991 and 1992 major retailers, including Sears, either shut down stores or drastically cut the number of employees; in late January 1993, Sears announced it was letting about 50,000 employees go. The examples could be multiplied. Millions, worldwide, were losing their jobs in the industrialized West and Asia. Homelessness was and is growing.

Also in 1992, twelve years of a Republican national administration came to an end. Presidential candidate Bill Clinton successfully made the economy the central issue, eradicating the seemingly unassailable popularity President George Bush won during the brief Gulf War of the previous year. Among the keystones of his campaign, Clinton promised federal action to create new jobs through both direct investment in roads and mass transit and a tax credit to encourage business to invest in machinery and plants. Did this signal a return to presumably antiquated Keynesian policies and fiscal policies to encourage private investment? An important part of Clinton's approach to recovery was more money for education and stepped-up training and retraining programs, the assumption of which is that development of "human capital" was a long ignored but important component of the growth of a technologically advanced economy.[2] According to this argument, a poor educational system and inadequate apprenticeship and retraining programs would inevitably result in a competitive disadvantage for the United States in an increasingly competitive global economy.

The peculiar feature of the latest economic recovery is that while the economic indicators were turning up, prospects for good jobs were turning down. Even before Clinton took office, the trend toward more low-paid, temporary, benefit-free blue- and white-collar jobs and fewer decent *permanent* factory and office jobs called into question many of the underlying assumptions of his campaign. For if good jobs were disappearing as fast as "unstable and mediocre"[3] jobs were being created, more education and training geared to a shrinking market for professional and technical labor might lead nowhere for many who bought the promise. As in many manufacturing sectors, labor-displacing technological change has reached the construction industry. Unless public and private investment is specifically geared to hiring labor rather than purchasing giant earth-moving machines, for example – which would imply changing a tax structure that permits write-offs for technology investments – it seems dubious that Clinton's plan to plow $20 billion a year into infra-structure could result in a significant net employment gain even as it generated orders for more labor-saving equipment. Machine tool and electrical equipment industries are leaders in the use of computer-mediated labor processes. Labor-saving technologies combined with organizational changes (such as mergers, acquisitions, divestitures, and consolidation of production in fewer plants, a cost saving made possible by the technology) yield few new jobs.

Our central contention lies somewhere between common sense and new knowledge. We discuss what should already be evident to all but those either suffering the political constraints of policy or still in the thrall of the American ideology and blind belief in the ineluctability of social mobility and prosperity in the American system. The two are linked: no politician who aspires to power may violate the unwritten rule that the United States is the Great Exception to the general law that class and other forms of social mobility are restricted for the overwhelming majority of the population. Our first argument – that the Western dream of upward mobility has died and it is time to give it a respectful funeral – may have at long last seeped into the bones of most Americans, even the most optimistic economist.

The dream has died because the scientific–technological revolution of our time, which is not confined to new electronic processes but also affects organizational changes in the structure of corporations, has fundamentally altered the forms of work, skill, and occupation. The whole notion of tradition and identity of persons with their work has been radically changed.

Scientific and technological innovation is, for the most part, no longer episodic. Technological change has been routinized. Not only has abstract knowledge come to the center of the world's political economy, but there is also a tendency to produce and trade in symbolic significations rather than concrete products. Today, knowledge rather than traditional skill is the main productive force. The revolution has widened the gap between intellectual, technical, and manual labor, between a relatively small number of jobs that, owing to technological complexity, require more knowledge and a much larger number that require less; as the mass of jobs are "deskilled", there is a resultant redefinition of occupational categories that reflects the changes in the nature of jobs. As these transformations sweep the world, older conceptions of class, gender, and ethnicity are called into question. For example, on the New York waterfront, until 1970 the nation's largest, Italians and blacks dominated the Brooklyn docks and the Irish and Eastern Europeans worked the Manhattan piers. Today, not only are the docks as sites of shipping vanishing, but the workers are gone as well. For those who remain, the traditional occupation of longshoreman – dangerous, but highly skilled – has given way, as a result of containerization of the entire process, to a shrunken workforce that possesses knowledge but not the old skills.[4] (. . . T)his is just an example of a generalized shift in the nature and significance of work.

As jobs have changed, so have the significance and duration of joblessness. Partial and permanent unemployment, except during the two great world depressions (1893–1898 and 1929–1939) was largely episodic and subject to short-term economic contingencies, has increasingly become a mode of life for larger segments of the populations not only of less industrially developed countries, but for those in "advanced" industrial societies as well. Many who are classified in official statistics as "employed" actually work at casual and part-time jobs, the number of which has grown dramatically over the past fifteen years. This phenomenon, once confined to freelance writers and artists, laborers and clerical workers, today cuts across all occupations, including the professions. Even the once buoyant "new" profession of computer programmer is already showing signs of age after barely a quarter of a century. We argue that the shape of things to come as well as those already in existence signals the emerging proletarianization of work at every level below top management and a relatively few scientific and technical occupations.

At the same time, because of the permanent character of job cuts starting in the 1970s and glaringly visible after 1989, the latest recession has finally and irrevocably vitiated the traditional idea that the unemployed are an "industrial reserve army" awaiting the next phase of economic expansion. Of course, some laid-off workers, especially in union workplaces, will be recalled when the expansion, however sluggish, resumes. Even if one stubbornly clings to the notion of a reserve army, one cannot help but note that its soldiers in the main now occupy the part-time and temporary positions that appear to have replaced the well-paid full-time jobs.

Because of these changes, the "meaning" (in the survival, psychological, and cultural senses) of work – occupations and professions – as forms of life is in crisis. If the tendencies of the economy and the culture point to the conclusion that work is no longer significant in the formation of the self, one of the crucial questions of our time is what, if anything, can replace it. When layers of qualified – to say nothing of mass – labor are made redundant, obsolete, *irrelevant,* what, after five centuries during which work remained a, perhaps *the,* Western cultural ideal, can we mean by the "self"? Have we reached a large historical watershed, a climacteric that will be as devastating as natural climacterics of the past that destroyed whole species?

Some of these new epochal issues have been spurred by a massive shift in the character of corporate organization. Beginning in the 1970s much of the vertical structure of the largest corporations began to be dismantled. New kinds of robber barons appeared; among them, Bernard Cornfeld and James Ling were perhaps the most prominent pioneers in the creation of the new horizontal corporate organizational forms we now call conglomerates. Ling's empire, for example, spanned aircraft, steel, and banking. Textron, once a prominent textile producer, completely divested itself of this product as its business expanded to many different sectors. U.S. Steel became so diversified that it replaced *steel* with X in its name shortly after it bought Marathon Oil in 1980. And Jones and Laughlin, a venerable steel firm, became only one entry in Ling's once vast portfolio of unconnected businesses. Every television watcher knows that Pepsi-Cola has gone far beyond producing soft drinks to operating a wide array of retail food services; by the 1980s it owned Pizza Hut and several other major fast-food chains.

New forms of organization such as mergers and acquisitions, which have intensified centralized ownership but also decentralized production and brought on the shedding of whole sections of the largest corporations, have spelled the end of the paternalistic bureaucracy that emerged in many corporations in the wake of industrialization and, especially, the rise of the labor movement in the twentieth century.

Large corporations such as IBM and Kodak, for example, have reversed historic no-layoffs policies that were forged during the wave of 1930s labor organization as a means of keeping the unions out. Equally important, layoffs as a mode of cost cutting have been expanded to include clerical, technical, and managerial employees, categories traditionally considered part of the cadre of the corporate bureaucracies and therefore exempt from employment-threatening market fluctuations. The turnover of ownership and control of even the largest corporations combined with technological changes undermines the very concept of job security. The idea of a lifetime job is in question, even in the once secure bastions of universities and government bureaucracies. Thus, the historic bargain between service workers and their employers, in which employees accepted relatively low wages and salaries in return for security, has, under pressure of dropping profit margins and a new ideology of corporate "downsizing", been abrogated.

For the corporate conglomerate, the particular nature and quality of the product no longer matter since the ultimate commodity, the one that subsumes and levels all others, is the designating language, the representing language in the terms of forms of credit. That is to say, along with the technical changes, which are knowledge changes, the changes in representation are not only parallel, but in conflict. Knowledge itself, once firmly tied to specific labor processes such as steelmaking, now becomes a relatively free-floating commodity to the extent that it is transformed into information that requires no productive object. This is the real significance of the passage from industry-specific labor processes to computer-mediated work as a new universal technology.

Science and technology (of which organization is an instance) alter the nature of the labor process, not only the rationalized manual labor but also intellectual labor, especially the professions. Knowledge becomes ineluctably intertwined with, even dependent on, technology, and even so-called labor-intensive work becomes increasingly mechanized and begins to be replaced by capital- and technology-intensive – *capitech-intensive* – work. Today, the regime of world economic life consists in scratching every itch of everyday life with sci-tech: eye glasses, underarm deodorant, preservatives in food, braces on pets. Technology has become the universal problem solver, the postmodern equivalent of deus ex machina, the ineluctable component of education and play as much as of work. No level of schooling is spared: students interact with computers to learn reading, writing, social studies, math, and science in elementary school through graduate school. Play, once and still the corner of the social world least subject to regimentation, is increasingly incorporated into computer software, especially the products of the Apple corporation. More and more, we, the service and professional classes, are chained to our personal computers; with the help of the modem and the fax we can communicate, in seconds, to the farthest reaches of the globe. We no longer need to press the flesh: by E-mail, we can attend conferences, gain access to library collections, and write electronic letters to perfect strangers. And, of course, with the assistance of virtual reality, we can engage in electronic sex. The only thing the computer cannot deliver is touch, but who needs it, anyway?[5]

Each intrusion of capitech-intensiveness increases the price of the product, not makes it cheaper, because the investment in machines has to be paid off. For example, getting on E-mail is not free; in 1993 dollars it costs about ten dollars a month for the basic service. Joining a conference or forum network might cost an additional ten or fifteen dollars, and each minute on the E-mail line carries an additional charge, although it is not as high as the charge for traditional voice-based telecommunications. Like the 900 number used to get vicarious sexual experience or esoteric information, computer-driven information is not free. Of course, as scientific, technical, academic, and other professionals feel that they "need" access to information that, increasingly, is available only through electronic venues, the cost of being a professional rises, but the privileges are also more pronounced.

The new electronic communication technologies have become the stock-in-trade of a relatively few people because newspapers, magazines, and television have simply refused to acknowledge that we live in a complex world. Instead, they have tended to *simplify* news, even for the middle class. Thus, an "unintended" consequence of the dissemination of informatics to personal use is a growing information gap already implied by the personal computer. A relatively small number of people – no more than ten million in the United States – will, before the turn of the century, be fully wired to world sources of information and new knowledge: libraries, electronic newspapers and journals, conferences and forums on specialized topics, and colleagues, irrespective of country or region around the globe. Despite the much-heralded electronic highway, which will be largely devoted to entertainment products, the great mass of the world's population, already restricted in its knowledge and power by the hierarchical division of the print media into tabloids and newspapers of record, will henceforth be doubly disadvantaged.

Of course, the information gap makes a difference only if one considers the conditions for a democratic, that is, a participatory, society. If popular governance even in the most liberal-democratic societies has been reduced in the last several decades to *plebiscitary* participation, the potential effect of computer-mediated knowledge is to exacerbate exclusion of vast portions of the underlying populations of all countries.

The problem is not, as many have claimed, that the U.S. economy has gone global. Not only has *every* economy become global, but in fact economies have been "global" for centuries.[6] International trade and investment were part of the impetus that brought Columbus to these shores more than five hundred years ago. The movement of both capital and labor across geographic expanses has been, since 1492, a hallmark of U.S., Caribbean, and Canadian economic development. From its days as a series of English, French, and Spanish colonies, the geographic expanse that, eventually, became the United States and later Canada was, because of fertile agricultural and horticultural production, a valuable source of food, raw materials, and tobacco for Europe. Only after 1850, more than three centuries after Columbus, did the U.S. economy enter the industrial era, the major products of which – textiles, iron, steel, and later machine tools, for example – were closely intertwined with the European economy.

In fact, the era of U.S. international economic dominance began, at the beginning of the twentieth century, with its leadership in the development of industrial uses for electricity, oil, and chemicals. The application of electricity to machinery and chemical manufacturing eliminated vast quantities of industrial labor and accelerated the process whereby science, rather than craft, drove the production process. The primacy of knowledge is reflected as well in the rationalization, by assembly-line methods, of automobile production even though, at least until the late 1970s, this type of mass production required vast quantities of semi-skilled labor. Needless to say, under pressure from growing international competition, the introduction of computer-mediated robotics and numerical controls has, since the late 1970s, enabled auto corporations to substantially reduce their labor forces and impose other efficiencies in production.

In retrospect we can see how temporary U.S. domination of world industrial markets really was. Despite truly remarkable industrial development, agricultural products are still the most important U.S. export commodities today. In the wake of the rise of Middle Eastern, Soviet, and Latin American oil production in the interwar period, the rapid recovery of European industrial capacity by the 1960s, especially in conventional mechanized industries such as autos and steel, and the truly dramatic development of Japanese export industries in consumer durable goods such as cars, electronics, and computer hardware as well as basic commodities, the U.S. economy had little else besides agriculture and its substantial lead in the development of informatics to commend it to foreign markets. Only France and Canada were able to offer significant farm competition, and Japan was the only significant competitor in computer hardware, though the explosion of the personal-computer market was initiated by IBM. The major industrial commodities in which the United States still enjoys a comfortable lead are computer chips and software. Japanese-made IBM clones have outdistanced the parent in the production and sales of personal computers. And it has taken the alliance of Intel, the world's premier chip producer, and Microsoft, whose lead in software is quite wide, to fend off Japanese and European competition.

What is new is that after a century of expansion and then world economic, political, and military dominance after World War II, the U.S. lead remains only in these sectors – and in military production. The United States is now the only military superpower. Still a formidable economic and political force, the United States nevertheless no longer commands, in terms of either production or, increasingly, consumption, anything like its former authority. Moreover, the United States has lost its great historical leadership and ability to mobilize science in the service of technological change. Today, not only Japan, Korea, and Germany but also China and India are producing engineers and scientists who compare favorably with those employed in the West.[7] Consequently, U.S. companies engaged in the production of high technologies such as robotics, lasers, and other computer-mediated industries are either relocating in these regions – not for their cheap manual labor, but for their cheap technically and scientifically trained labor – or are in fact communicating with this labor.

New uses of knowledge widen the gap between the present and the future; new knowledges challenge not only our collectively held beliefs but also the common ethical ground of our "civilization". The tendency of science to dominate the labor process, which emerged in the last half of the nineteenth century but attained full flower only in the last two decades, now heralds an entirely new regime of work in which almost no production *skills* are required. Older forms of technical or professional knowledge are transformed, incorporated, superseded, or otherwise eliminated by computer-mediated technologies – by applications of physical sciences intertwined with the production of knowledge: expert systems – leaving new forms of knowledge that are *inherently* labor-saving. But, unlike the mechanizing era of pulleys and electrically powered machinery, which retained the "hands-on" character of labor, computers have transferred most knowledge associated with the crafts and manual labor and, increasingly, intellectual knowledge, to the machine. As a result, while each generation of technological change makes some work more complex and interesting and raises the level of training or qualification required by a (diminishing) fraction of intellectual and manual labor, for the overwhelming majority of workers, this process simplifies tasks or eliminates them, and thus eliminates the worker.

The specific character of computer-aided technologies is that they no longer discriminate between most categories of intellectual and manual labor. With the introduction of computer-aided software programming (CASP), the work of perhaps the most glamorous of the technical professions associated with computer technology – programming – is irreversibly threatened. Although the "real" job of creating new and basic approaches will go on, the ordinary occupation of computer programmer may disappear just like that of the drafter, whose tasks were incorporated by computer-aided design and drafting by the late 1980s. CASP is an example of a highly complex program whose development requires considerable knowledge, but when development costs have been paid and the price substantially reduced, much low-level, routine programming will be relegated to historical memory.

The universal use of computers has increased exponentially the "multiplied productive powers" of labor.[8] In this regime of production, the principal effect of technological change – labor displacement – is largely unmitigated by economic growth. That is, it is possible for key economic indicators to show, but only for a short time, a net increase in domestic product without significant growth of full-time employment. On the other hand, growth itself is blocked by two effects of the new look to working in America. Labor redundancy, which is the main object of technological change, is, indirectly, an obstacle to growth. In the wake of the shrinking social wage, joblessness, the growth of part-time employment, and the displacement of good full-time jobs by mediocre, badly paid part-time jobs tend to thwart the ability of the economic system to avoid chronic overproduction and underconsumption.

The global metastate

Thus, for many employers, the precondition of weathering the new international economic environment of sharpened competition is to ruthlessly cut labor costs in order to reverse the free fall of profits. The drop of profits over the past five years may be ascribed to a number of factors including declining sales; increased costs of nearly all sorts, but especially of borrowing; and the high price of expensive technologies used to displace even more expensive labor. But many corporations experience profit loss in terms of falling prices, a telltale sign of *overproduction* in relation to consumption. Along with labor-displacing technological change aimed at reducing the size of the labor force, wages must be reduced and benefits cut or eliminated, especially those that accrue on the basis of length of employment. And, wherever possible, employers are impelled to export production to areas that offer cheap labor and, like Mexico, free plants, water, and virtually no taxes. These measures produce chronic overproduction of many commodities that formed the foundation of postwar domestic growth: cars, houses, and appliances. Consistent cost cutting leads to a domestic labor force that suffers short-term – that is, security-free – jobs. This situation is exacerbated by the accelerated globalization of production and the current international recession, so that raising the level of exports as a means to overcome the structural crisis within the national economy is much more difficult to achieve even as it plays a greater role in foreign policy. In fact, the very notion of "exports", just like the notion of a purely national working class in a global economy, is problematic if not already anomalous.

Here, from the economic perspective, we can observe the effective breakdown of the purely "national" state and the formation of what might be called the "metastate", in which the intersection of the largest transnational corporations and the international political directorates of many nations constitute a new governing class. Institutional forms of rule – multilateral trade organizations such as the General Agreement on Tariffs and Trade (GATT) and the North American Free Trade Agreement; proliferating international conferences on terrorism, technological change, and new forms of international economic arrangements in which business leaders, diplomats, academics, and other "experts" regularly consult; and increasingly frequent summits among government leaders of the key national states, usually flanked by trade representatives recruited from the international business establishment – are taking over.

Until recently, from the perspective of these metastates, to the extent that currency regulation remained a national affair, national states were important as the major means for valorization of capital. Labor was regulated within the framework of national law, and police forces and armies were raised in this way. Of course, the nation, with or without the state, remained the context within which culture and ideology are produced, itself an aspect of control, at least from the perspective of international business. Although these functions are still partially served by national states, we may discern, in the various forms of spurious capital formation made possible by informatics, a definite decline in the valorization functions of national treasuries; the emergence of a de facto international currency undermines the power of the dollar, the yen, and the mark as universal media of exchange. Further, international capital has forced many states to relax enforcement of protective labor codes if not the law itself, leaving employers freer to pay lower wages, export jobs, and import (undocumented) labor. The very idea of national "border" in all except its most blatant geographic connotation is becoming more dubious as labor flow becomes heavier between formally sovereign states. Finally, while elements of national culture remain, the past quarter century is definitively the era of media and cultural internationalization, precisely because of available technologies as well as the proliferation of transnational production and distribution companies for (primarily) U.S. cultural products. The international culture industry has destroyed all but a few national film industries (in Europe, in France and Germany but not in Britain and Italy; in Asia, in India; and in Latin America, Argentina's is dead, Mexico's weak, and Brazil's almost non-existent). American television syndication has reached deeply into the world market, and only Great Britain and, to a lesser degree, France have achieved transnational dissemination in Western countries.

The pressure on profits and the imperative to subsume labor under the new global arrangements is the "rational" basis for the decimation of the industrial heartlands – of the United States as well as European countries such as France and Great Britain – manifested in plant closings, drastic workforce reductions, and the definitive end of the social compact that marked the relationship between a significant portion of industrial labor and corporations since the New Deal and the postwar European compromise between capital and labor. Ronald Reagan's dramatic and highly symbolic firing of 11,000 air traffic controllers in 1981 may be remembered as the definitive act that closed the book on the historic compromise between a relatively powerful, if conservative, labor movement and capital. As the American unions whimpered but offered little concrete resistance, employers' groups quickly perceived that it was possible to undertake a major frontal assault on labor's crucial practice, collective bargaining. The ensuing decade witnessed rapid deterioration in union power and *therefore* a decline in real wages (what income can actually buy) for a majority of workers. Millions of women entered the wage–labor force in part to mitigate the effects of a fairly concerted employer/conservative campaign to weaken unions and to reduce wages and salaries beginning in the 1970s.[9]

In the 1980s, the two-paycheck family became a commonplace. Of course, the entrance of large numbers of women into the wage-labor force was also a sign of their growing refusal to accept subordination within the male-dominated family. At the same time, as the computerization of the labor process accelerated, millions of well-paid industrial jobs were eliminated by technological change and others migrated to the global South, both within the United States and in other parts of the world.

Recall that one of the major terms of the compromise between labor and management forged in the 1930s and 1940s was the exchange of the job control inherent in traditional crafts for high wage levels, which, in the era of U.S. domination of world markets for autos and steel, for example, spread from the crafts to many categories of unqualified labor. When the U.S. labor force was about 60 million, most of the 20 million industrial workers belonged to unions that negotiated steadily increased wages and benefits. At the end of World War II, union strength had grown to nearly a third of the labor force. By 1990, however, when the non-farm labor force had reached about 105 million and factory and transportation employment was about 22 million, unions represented only 16 percent of the labor force, 12 percent in the private sector. Although in key industries such as autos, communications, chemicals, oil, electrical, and steel unionization as a percentage of the non-supervisory workforce had not significantly diminished, collective bargaining no longer determined general wage levels. In fact, union wages were being driven by the low-wage non-union sector abroad as well as at home. Having surrendered job control, workers were unable, and often unwilling, to control the pace and effects of technological change lest the employer close up shop, and their diminished political power made unions virtually incapable of stemming capital flight. Needless to say, union concessions in the form of wage and benefits reductions in the 1980s failed to halt industrial migration. This resulted in lower living standards for many Americans.

As we have argued elsewhere, the surprisingly feeble union response to the concerted employer offensive on the social compact that drove labor relations for almost forty years may be attributed to one of the tacit provisions of that compact: that labor accept its role as merely another variable "factor" of the costs of doing business.[10] Fulfilling labor's historical social justice agenda became dependent on the health of American business and subordinate to the exigencies of U.S. foreign policy.

Organized labor's ideological subordination in the first decades after World War II seemed to serve American workers' interests well. Real wages rose nearly every year until 1967 and, with short disruptions, continued to improve until the late 1970s. During this period, the AFL-CIO was perhaps the most reliable and powerful non-governmental organization that provided a social base for U.S. foreign policy, especially its periodic war aims, but also its program of intervention in Europe, Africa, and Latin America, where American unions supplied training and financial assistance to "free" (read anticommunist) trade unions.[11]

As important as this full-throated patriotic fervor was for disciplining American workers, at least politically, perhaps the most important result

of labor regulation since the New Deal was the emergence of a highly autocratic – in some cases semi-feudal – labor bureaucracy to administer the
terms of regulation, especially the crucial task of keeping workers in line.
The labor baronate is among the most stable of U.S. institutions. In fact,
many large unions resemble, in their culture as much as their structure,
the large corporations with which they bargain. Far from the social movement in which they had their roots, many unions became, in effect, the
mirror image of the corporations with which they bargain collectively.
Although, since the 1930s, unions have modified the old doctrine of business unionism by adopting a distinct political agenda, their daily operation
resembles that of an insurance company, and union leaders take on the aura
of corporate executives.

Even before the debacle of the 1980s, unions in private production and
service sectors had ceased to grow, even as they experienced enormous expansion at all levels of public employment after President Kennedy's 1961
executive order sanctioning union recognition and bargaining for federal
employees. Yet in banking and financial services, in the crucial industrial
South, and among the rapidly expanding scientific and technical categories,
organized labor made almost no inroads, even during the booming 1960s
when ostensibly prolabor Democratic administrations were in power. The
1947 Taft–Hartley amendments, especially the anticommunist provisions
and restrictions on the use of the strike weapon, halted labor's forward
march during the 1950s, and labor's vaunted legislative clout was unable
to rescind this blight even under the most favorable political circumstances;
the cold war continued to drive labor relations, but, perhaps significantly,
except for teachers and other public employees, hospital workers, and agricultural workers, unions had ceased to be a dynamic force in U.S. society.

Computers and economic growth

In sectors run by computer-mediated work, productivity outstrips growth.
Now, *productivity* is a hotly disputed term. The conventional economists'
definition focuses on the formula of measuring the ratio of the price of
goods and services, adjusted for inflation, to labor costs. In these terms
labor productivity, which has stagnated since the recession, grew in 1992
by nearly 3.5 percent, while the gross domestic product (GDP) increased
by less than half that percentage.[12] But in specific sectors, such as industrial
production, productivity is much higher, perhaps 5 percent, which, in view
of the relative stagnation of manufacturing, accounts for the substantial
reduction of the labor force in these sectors. Computer-mediated work has
spread from offices and the industrial sectors where a high level of corporate
concentration prevails (such as autos, machine tools, and steel) to light
manufacturing and, more recently, to the professions. Economic growth,
which has proceeded in the last decade at a very modest rate (1 to 3 percent

a year), is structurally unable, in the long run, to overcome the job-reducing effects of technological and organizational changes. This relatively new development contrasts sharply with the two great periods of U.S. growth in this century: 1900 to 1925 and the years between 1938 and 1970. Although the average annual growth rate was about 3 percent during the period after 1938, the level of technological displacement was relatively low and offshore capital flight virtually absent, except in shoes and the needle trades. However, the internal capital flight began at the turn of the twentieth century, principally in textiles, garments, shoes, lumber, oil refining, and steel. While the distribution of industry changed within the United States from the Northeast to the Middle West and the Southeast, the national workforce grew substantially and so did income.

Of course, much of the prolonged era of general expansion of the economy and the proliferation of jobs corresponded to spurious growth associated with the permanent war economy. That is, much of U.S. economic activity in the last great expansion period is attributable to enormous state investments in military goods that do not circulate but remain within a self-contained defense sector. "Real" growth, that is, the accretions of capital stock for the civilian sectors of the economy, was severely limited by what might be termed "disaccumulation", defined here as investments in sectors such as public employment, military expenditures, and financial services that exist to get rid of surplus capital.[13] As we have noted, from the perspective of the individual or institutional investor, putting money in these activities may yield higher returns and are evaluated by neoclassical criteria as a "rational" choice. But spurious capital formation, favored since the 1950s over industrial production and transportation, conspired to accumulate debt rather than capital and contributed to the relatively slow growth rate.

From the craft era to Fordism

Once craftspersons controlled production. From the point of view of the labor process, the skilled worker of the early, manufacturing phase of capitalism was really no different from the artisan who owned as well as operated the shop. The artisan designed the product and made and chose the tools needed to shape the raw material and the tools needed to convert the raw materials into a finished product. In manufacturing, the main change was the shift in property relations. The craftsperson now worked for an employer who may or may not once have worked at the bench. More typically the employer was a merchant who supplied the building, some of the tools, the raw materials, and the means to bring the product to the market. The procedures of the traditional craft(s) still dominated the labor process, which, in that period, remained virtually unchanged.

The industrializing era of the late nineteenth century was marked by the growing rationalization of the labor process. The introduction of rationalized methods of production and scientifically designed machinery simultaneously reduced, but did not obliterate, the crafts. The machine was designed to "transfer" craft knowledge to those who organized production, and to machines that were designed by engineers, who became technical adjuncts of management. Artisans began to lose their design function, except for the modifications required to adapt machines to specific production requirements. The crafts were progressively reduced to making tools and maintaining or fixing machinery designed by an engineer.[14]

Marxist theorists of the labor process have attempted to account for this rationalization process by citing the pressure of capitalist competition on profits and have tended to reduce explanation to its economic dimension. But concrete studies of the labor process reveal, time and again, the degree to which reducing the worker to an interchangeable part by means of "rational" organization and machine technology rationalization (which was, at that stage of development, a kind of analog to actual work and worker) is also paralleled and dominated by the struggle among the workers, management, and the owners for *power*. The chief weapons of craft resistance are the traditional skills shared by the community of craftspersons and their *culture*, which prescribes *how* things are to be done consistent with the moral economy implicit in their culture. As E.P. Thompson and Harry Braverman have suggested, the struggle of capital to dominate the labor process has for centuries been linked to breaking craft culture, not only by bitter tactics such as provoking strikes and lockouts to smash craft unions, but also by making mechanization and rationalization a "natural" process that is regarded as socially progressive. What could not be accomplished by Taylorism was finally achieved by computerization.[15]

A case in point is the transformation of the relatively "crude" division of labor in carriage production to the extreme rationalization of the Ford assembly line in the second decade of the twentieth century. Henry Ford was able to portray the introduction of the conveyor belt and the breakdown of assembly tasks to fine details as a function of "efficiency". By the 1920s, together with Frederick Winslow Taylor's reports of his own industrial engineering innovations at Midland Steel, Frank Gilbreth's work in "scientific rationalization", and Lillian Gilbreth's application of the Taylorist system to the household, the assembly line as an emblem of industrial efficiency became a new "common sense".[16] People debated whether goods made by such methods were equal or superior in quality to those made by the older craft methods, but there was virtually no debate about whether these commodities could be made at prices most working people could afford. Selling the idea of a car in every garage was one of the major rationales, and also the promise that, with the introduction of mass production, one could purchase almost any product, even a house, from a Sears catalog. Fordism – including mass production, relatively high wages, and mass consumption through a liberal credit system – quickly became the

American *cultural ideal*.[17] Thanks to mass production and easy credit, the prevailing ideology was that nearly every hard-working American could own a house, a car, and appliances without saving for a lifetime. Of course, this new common sense was frequently violated by the persistent evidence that many who had successfully internalized the common sense of hard, steady work as the path to success often had trouble paying the rent, let alone affording a late-model car.

Yet there is little doubt that the economic and social history of the past century may be identified, to a considerable degree, with the conjunction of a new regime of capital accumulation based on the expansion of consumer credit (debt) with the new cultural ideal in which the categories of want and need were melded so that absolute need became confused with want.[18] Or, to put it another way, the distance between want and need were so confused that large segments of the population were taught to experience a sense of deprivation as their inability to achieve what has been established as the distinctly "American" living standard grew. In this regime of regulated accumulation, there is little point to comparing U.S. living standards in terms of the conventional measures of the earlier industrializing era when the issue was whether or not workers had adequate food, clothing, and shelter (could meet their needs). Although there is growing evidence that for an important and growing minority of the populations of advanced industrial societies these "necessities" have been denied, the economic/cultural situation of perhaps a majority of citizens of these countries is still framed by expectations created during the "Fordist" age. Despite determined efforts by ideologists as well as political leaders to complete a post-Fordist counter-revolution, selling, as it were, lowered expectations (new ideology, which began to be sold during the great oil "crisis" of the mid-1970s), large segments of the U.S. population have internalized a contrary, if materially antiquated, cultural ideal.

In the rise of the Taylorist–Fordist regime, the "mass", semi-skilled worker or artificer is organized into a highly cooperative division of labor and assigned specific tasks that are closely integrated by managers and engineers who monopolize, and thus keep secret, as much knowledge as they can.[19] In the early mechanical era, the conflict between employers and their agents with the artisans, who still possessed considerable know-how, led to hard-fought strikes, machine breaking, and other forms of protest. The battle extended into the twentieth century, for even though artisans were being driven from their central place in the production process, they remained indispensable as long as tool and die making could not be performed by unaided machines, machines that could not yet fully build other machines and were unable to repair themselves. After the crafts were broken up into detailed and repetitive tasks, these detail workers (mass workers, in our usage) became interchangeable like standardized machine parts. This situation, felicitous for management, diminished but did not eliminate the capacity of the mass worker for self-organization. When the mass production workers organized after the turn of the twentieth century into strong industrial unions and were able to form alliances with the somewhat more privileged "skilled" workers (themselves performing only some of the segments that once constituted a traditional craft) and with workers in other plants within the same company and industry, they were able to exercise a substantial degree of power that mediated, if not reversed, management's monopoly over the labor process. Employers counterattacked, beginning in the 1920s, first by moving plants, especially in light industry, to non-union regions of the country and then by globalizing industrial production so that the mass worker, who benefited from the concentration of production in a few large factories, was considerably weakened. And, lacking a truly inter-national movement to coordinate labor's resistance, unions in industries such as textiles and shoes were decimated even as unions in other industries were still expanding.

The heart of management's power was its ability to control the labor process, especially to develop technologies of production and administration that progressively eliminated large quantities of labor and further trans-ferred worker know-how to machines. By the middle of the twentieth century, most key industries, while still ensconced in the mechanical mode of production, were already highly rationalized. The conveyor-driven assembly line was only one of the methods of control. The fabrication of almost all major appliances, clothing, processed food, and machinery itself was organized according to the rules of detailed rationalization even when no conveyor belt was used. For example, a power press operator spent the entire shift stamping out a single sheet metal part of a television set, a section of an auto body or of a washing machine. Machine tool operators worked on lathes that had already been set up and whose cutting tools were presharpened, producing thousands of screws, nuts, and other small parts. In another part of the shop a drill press operator spent the entire day performing a single operation on a machine tool designed for the special-ized function of cutting holes.

Specialization also arose within engineering: quality control, industrial, and design engineering became subspecialties, and managers and engineers at first recruited from the ranks of craftworkers were increasingly consid-ered professionals, even when they did not have academic credentials. The professionalization of engineering signaled a regime in which large segments of industrial production became based on applications of natural science after about 1850; this process accelerated after the Civil War. By the begin-ning of the twentieth century, formal credentials increasingly became a condition for advancement beyond the level of foreman within large enter-prises. Gradually, management was recruited from the growing ranks of those trained in business and professional schools, but the front lines still remained a shrinking site where a sliver of manual labor could enter the ranks of low-level management. Plant superintendents intimately familiar with most of the jobs because they had performed most of them during their years as manual workers began to be replaced by administrators with academic credentials who relied on a staff of production specialists. The plant manager became a kind of cost accountant and personnel manager and, above all, a corporate politician without shop floor background. As is evident from this description, the emergence of management and engineering is closely linked to the process of rationalization, that is, to the expanded requirements for control of labor.

This, of course, is a highly schematic account; the "pure" type never corresponded to the actual labor process in which the craftworker, the "mass worker", and the engineer modified each other's core functions through conflict as well as cooperation. This non-correspondence between model and performance attests to the persistence of tacit as opposed to formal, abstract knowledge. To the extent that craft and other categories of manual labor had a primary relationship with "nature" throughout the industrializing era, they remained indispensable for transforming materials into products. The craftsperson's intimate knowledge of the "feel" of materials such as wood and metal is an integral feature of the labor process: the blacksmith "knows", tacitly and by "touch", how much heat to apply to metal in order to soften it for fabrication, just as the shoemaker can discern the texture of leather without referring to a manual. It may be argued that the power of scientific knowledge to transform the labor process in the image of capitalist rationality relies, historically, upon two developments: the invention of artificial materials based on the chemistries of hydrocarbons and petrochemicals, from which synthetic fibers and especially plastics may be produced; and the rationalization of the labor process via innovations such as those introduced by Frederick Winslow Taylor and Henry Ford, the aim and result of which is the subordination of craft. Chemistry as the basis of synthetics technologies replaces natural products such as textiles, leather, and metals whose quality depends, crucially, on traditional craft-wrought knowledge. And crafts are broken up by techniques of organization.

These technological innovations occurred in the context of the dramatic improvement of communication and transportation technologies – the telegraph, the telephone, the airplane, the motor vehicle – that helped extend the market for goods and information beyond conventional borders. We do not claim a direct relationship between scientific knowledge, invention, and economic relations. Indeed, many scientifically based technologies were invented before the conditions for their wide dissemination were present. Yet we do not doubt that futuristic dreams, in both fiction and popular philosophy and science – the aspiration to fly, to reach the moon and the planets, to achieve the laborless factory – are conditioned by the *dialectic* between scientific discovery, economic development, and political struggle. Jules Verne's celebrated nineteenth-century journeys to the bottom of the

sea, to the center of the earth, and to outer space presupposed the emergence of rudiments of scientific and technological possibility and the
collective perception that the economic means were, at least hypothetically,
available. Similarly, in 1914, H.G. Wells's novel *The World Set Free* fore-
told the discovery of nuclear chain reaction and the consequent development
of an atomic bomb that changes the face of world politics and culture.

Of course, from Mary Shelley's *Frankenstein* to Fritz Lang's *Metropolis* to
Phillip K. Dick's novels of simulacra *Do Androids Dream of Electric Sheep?*
(made into the movie *Blade Runner*), *We Can Build You*, and *The Three
Stigmata of Palmer Eldritch* (among many others), writers and film-makers
have envisioned the dystopian consequences of fulfilling what is, perhaps,
the most vivid capitalist fantasy, the automatic factory and human-free
work. Most recently, Alvin Toffler and Jacques Attali have offered futur-
ologies that confirm prognostications of the workerless factory and office.[20]
With computer applications in virtually every aspect of work and play,
none of these once unimaginable dreams is beyond practical possibility.

The second consequence of the replacement of mechanical tools of both
production and administration by computers is the transformation of the
occupation structure of the old mechanizing era. In this transformation,
every new technological generation transfers more skill to the computer,
and the life of each generation of computer technology is, in terms of
acquired knowledge, radically foreshortened. In fact, the point of the technological change is to elide a work regime fatally subject to human error
in which tolerances are extremely narrow; in the mechanical era, hand tools
such as micrometers and calipers were important verification devices.

Culture as habit formation includes language and discourse as well as
algorithms and other practices. These practices often involve the habituation
of the body as well as the "mind" in ways that render a practice largely
second nature. For example, the skilled worker in a cold rolling mill adjusts
the rollers by "feel" to attain the desired width of the sheet or wire. Similarly,
"feel" is the major instrument of micromeasurement by the machinist on
work in which tolerances are extremely narrow; micrometers and calipers
are important verification devices. But as any experienced machinist or tool
and die maker will attest, intuition plays the major role in meeting "close
tolerances".

In the period of automatic production, the motions, practices, skills, and
intuition of the mechanic are copied and programmatically simulated and
mimicked by an instrument. As exemplified by computers, the digitaliza-
tion of machinery signifies the final triumph of science and technology over
craft, abstract over concrete labor, the "mind" over the "body", or, to be
more exact, the ideology of the dominance of the intellect over the body-
subject. Number is the language of science; the body is the language of
craft. Or, put more precisely, although number is latent in older forms
of analog machines, its full impact as a governor of labor is still mediated

by traditional skill. In contrast, while it is true that the engineer, for example, working with a computer-aided drafting and design program still relies to some degree, on hunch and intuition and must understand mathematics in order to make choices among several options, the program allows only a finite menu of options. Although designing a switch or transformer, routine electrical engineering work, is never an entirely spontaneous activity, the three-dimensional graphics on the computer screen partially displace the imagination, at least for routine designs, while at the same time stimulating the imaginative dimension of more complex design work.

Writing programs and designing systems that displace or otherwise alter the character of intellectual labor is, at first, heady stuff for high-level computer engineers. One must reproduce, rationalize, and transform, in the logical language of computers, aspects of professional knowledge, rather than the classical manual task. But, after barely two decades of experiment with and perfection of these programs, impelled by the cost-cutting imperative, programmers found ways to displace their own work. Today computer-aided software programming eliminates much of the routine work of the programmer, just as, in the 1970s, numerical controls and robotics eliminated vast quantities of craft and unqualified labor. Knowledge, once the vehicle of the unprecedented expansion of our collective dominion over nature, including traditional skill, has turned on itself. Its *tendency,* if not a completed task, is toward the self-regulated workplace in which no category of labor is spared, even some categories of management.

Of course, not all paid work is obsolete, especially work that entails the perfection of control, but this is the tendency that results from the displacements currently in process. The new computer-mediated technologies bifurcate paid work in a new way. Much of this work, in both its "manual" and its "intellectual" incarnations, is now engaged in the labor of *control* of living labor or its machine form. In other words, where in the previous regime of mechanical production the skilled worker was partially disempowered by the rationalization of the traditional crafts and transformed into a mass worker, the technologies of many knowledge-based industries require a more qualified worker.

For example, production workers in oil refineries are required to understand and to monitor fairly complex computer-mediated production systems and be able to operate similarly intricate environmental and safety equipment. The environmental equipment conforms to state and federal anti-pollution requirements, but the safety equipment is installed to protect expensive machinery as much as the workers. And, to operate these systems properly requires the production worker to have some scientific and technical knowledge as distinct from mere familiarity with operational procedures and rules. Hence, production workers in this industry, perhaps the most sophisticated and costly of advanced technologically based industries, must undergo some degree of scientific education as opposed to manual or clerical training. But in 1991 there were fewer than 50,000 production and maintenance workers in U.S. oil refining as compared to nearly 200,000 in 1960. Technological change has produced similar reductions in steel, electrical equipment, auto, and even traditionally low-technology industries such as garments and textiles, where computers are now typically attached to sewing machines and to looms. This trend is, of course, much better known in offices, where computer-mediated electronic devices dominate the labor of both clerical workers and professionals.

(. . .) Our broad conclusion is that the highly publicized benefits of these technologies for work and its culture are vastly overblown. For an ever smaller number of people in virtually all occupations, the qualifications required by computers have created new opportunities for satisfying and economically remunerative work. But for the immense majority, computerization of the workplace has resulted in further subordination, displacement, or irrelevance. (. . . T)he transformation of production from mechanically based technologies to what some have termed the "mode of information" not only changes the notion of the "subject", as Mark Poster has observed, but also changes the prospects that paid work can remain the defining activity of human existence.[21] It is not a question of posing labor against "leisure", for in this dichotomy work remains dominant. Rather, we pose questions that, although they have been on the agenda of philosophers and cultural theorists for much of this century, have not (yet) intruded into the precincts of social policy – except welfare. To raise the question of the partial eclipse and decentering of paid work is to ask crucial questions concerning the purpose of education, the character of economic and social distribution, and, perhaps more profoundly, what it means to be human.

Notes

1   Steve Lohn, "Top IBM Issue: How, Not Who", *New York Times*, March 25, 1993.
2   The concept of human capital in its classic enunciation is in Gary Becker, *Human Capital: A Theoretical and Empirical Analysis with Special Reference to Education* (New York: Columbia University Press, 1964). Building on the work of T.W. Schultz, Becker argues that the growth of physical capital (machinery, buildings, and so forth) accounts for "a relatively small part of the growth of income" when compared to "education and skills". Hence his argument that education, which, presumably, upgrades skills and knowledge, is crucial for growth policies.
3   The words used by the secretary of labor after the Bureau of Labor Statistics reported an increase of 365,000 jobs in February 1993 (*New York Times*, March 24, 1993).
4   William DiFazio, *Longshoremen: Community and Resistance on the Brooklyn Waterfront* (South Hadley, Mass.: Bergin and Garvey, 1985).
5   Phillip K. Dick, *The Three Stigmata of Palmer Eldritch* (London: Jonathan Cape and Granada Books, 1978). First published in 1964, Dick's novel foreshadows the development of virtual reality technology, linking it to a future when most

people can no longer live on Earth but are afforded the means to simulate a life on this planet from a position somewhere in the galaxy.

6 Immanuel Wallerstein, *The Modern World System* (New York: Academic Press, 1974). Building on the work of "dependency" theorists such as Giovanni Arrighi, Cardozo and Faetto, Andre Gunder Frank, and, especially, the Annales school of French historiography (Braudel, Lucien Febvre), Wallerstein demonstrates that, since the sixteenth century, capitalism has been a global system, albeit one of unequal exchange.

7 In 1992, Indian engineers and computer scientists emerged as world-class players in high-tech design. American and European corporations began letting contracts to Bombay- and Delhi-based software firms.

8 Karl Marx, *Grundrisse* (New York, Vintage, 1973), 701–5.

9 In the United States, nearly 70 percent of women had entered the labor force by 1990. In recent years, many have been able to obtain only part-time jobs.

10 Stanley Aronowitz, *False Promises: The Shaping of American Working Class Consciousness*, with a new introduction and epilogue (Durham, N.C.: Duke University Press, 1992 [1973]); *Working Class Hero* (New York: Pilgrim, 1983).

11 Beth Sims, *Workers of the World Undermined American Labor's Role in U.S. Foreign Policy* (Boston: South End Press, 1992). For an earlier study of this question, see also Ronald Radosh, *U.S. Labor and American Foreign Policy* (New York: Random House, 1971).

12 *Wall Street Journal*, March 9, 1992.

13 Martin Sklar, "On the Proletarian Revolution and the End of Political-Economic Society", *Radical America*, June 1969. This remarkable article provides a theory, from the perspective of political economy, of the end of real capital accumulation. According to Sklar, the major tendency of contemporary advanced capitalist societies was towards an overaccumulation of capital; thus, the task of investment is to get rid of this surfeit, to disaccumulate capital. Hence advertising, the production of waste in the form of planned obsolescence, the proliferation of 'services', and, of course, in the United States, massive military expenditures.

14 Harry Braverman, *Labor and Monopoly Capital* (New York: Monthly Review Press, 1974).

15 E.P. Thompson, *The Making of the English Working Class* (New York: Knopf, 1963).

16. Frederick Winslow Taylor, *Principles of Scientific Management* (New York: Norton, 1967 [1911]); Lillian Gilbreth, *The Homemaker and Her Job* (New York: Appleton, 1927). Gilbreth's book is an application to "women's work", more specifically the work of the "mother" who must provide a "place of rest" by making invisible the myriad household tasks, of the principles of scientific management developed with her husband, Frank, and Taylor.

17 Christian Palloix, 'From Fordism to Neo-Fordism', in *The Labour Process and Class Strategies* (London: Conference of Socialist Economists, 1976); Bernard Doray, *From Taylorism to Fordism*, trans. David Macey (London: Free Association Books, 1988).

18 Michel Aglietta, *A Theory of Capitalist Regulation*, trans. David Fernbach (London: New Left Books, 1976).

19 Sidney Pollard, *The Genesis of Modern Management* (Cambridge, Mass.: Harvard University Press, 1965); Daniel Nelson, *Managers and Workers* (Madison: University of Wisconsin Press, 1975).

20 Alvin Toffler, *The Third Wave* (London: William Collins, 1980): Jacques Attali, *Millenium: Winners and Losers in the Coming World Order* (New York: Random House, 1991).

21 Mark Poster, *The Mode of Information* (Chicago, University of Chicago Press, 1990).

Chapter 5

Jobs and people

John Grieve Smith

The predominance of monetarist thinking in recent years has been associated with a revival of the prewar view that the cure for unemployment lies in 'the labour market', rather than in strengthening the demand for goods and services. The phrase 'the labour market' often seems one of the economic profession's more unhappy pieces of jargon. It conjures up visions of people being auctioned like cattle, or of agricultural workers in the nineteenth century coming to the County Town for the Michaelmas hiring, and in doing so suggests that, if the price for their labour was right, everyone would get a job. But (. . .) the supply and demand for labour is different from that for anything else, in that the receipts from selling labour (i.e. wages and salaries) are a major component of the demand for it (or the goods that labour is needed to produce).

Labour market fallacies

The misleading thesis that unemployment reflects an imbalance between the supply and demand for labour that can be remedied by adjusting the price still, however, underlies a variety of current proposals for tackling unemployment, most of which have in common the fact that they would worsen the lot of the unemployed and the ordinary wage earner. The simple version is that cutting wages will reduce unemployment. The more sophisticated variant is that while lower real wages will not in themselves lead to higher employment, they are a necessary consequence of it. (Keynes originally made this assumption in the *General Theory* but later modified his views.)[1] In each case the proposition rests on the fallacious assumption that the average productivity of labour falls as output and employment increase. This assumption, so basic to nineteenth-century economic theory, may have some validity in agriculture, assuming that successively less productive land is brought into production as demand increases (as in Ricardo's theory of rent); but it bears little relation to the facts of modern industrial life.

The classical economists were wedded to the idea that average costs would rise, rather than fall, as output expanded, because it was a necessary concomitant of their theory of 'perfect competition' which assumed that a firm could sell as much as it wished of its product at the existing market price: for if a firm's average costs did not rise with increasing output, there would be no limit to how much it could produce or sell. But in reality the market for any one firm's products is finite and depends on their quality, brand image, service, local connections and so on: although a firm's costs may decline when it produces and sells more, its ability to do so is (as we all know) limited by market factors, and at some point cutting prices to expand sales will bring prices below costs.[2] In the real world competition is not perfect and costs do not increase as output expands.

Productivity, costs and output

In industry today the two key issues are: (a) how is productivity related to output within a plant; and (b) how does average productivity compare in different plants which only come into (or out of) use as output rises (or falls)? In general, average productivity rises with output in an under-used plant: not because the marginal productivity of successive new workers increases, but because additional operatives (each with more or less the same productivity) dilute the overhead costs of managers, and so on. This is, of course, why it is worthwhile for firms to pay premium rates for overtime or night and weekend working. This effect usually more than compensates for any question as to whether the new recruits are less able or well-trained than those already on the job. The one situation where increasing output may lead to a fall in productivity is where the plant is already working virtually at full capacity and inefficient methods of working have to be adopted to squeeze out the extra output.

As far as successive plants are concerned, the position is not symmetrical between closing a succession of plants in a recession and opening new plants in a recovery – assuming that the closed plants are closed for good, which is generally the case. When plants are closed, the least efficient are closed first; so that cutting output reduces costs. But when successive new plants are brought in over a period of recovery, they should each be more efficient and lower in cost than their predecessors; so that expanding output by expanding capacity results in lower costs.

In considering therefore the implications for real wages of expanding demand and output, the most realistic general assumption is that average productivity will improve rather than decline. These facts are widely known to those who work in industry, and were recognised by many economists 60 or 70 years ago.[3] Roy Harrod wrote in 1967:

> During the 'twenties many of us were deeply interested in Keynes's advocacy of measures to promote fuller employment. According to the traditional theory, success in this would entail higher marginal costs

and lower real wages. And yet there was a great paradox. If an academic economist left his ivory tower and mingled a little with industrialists in the field, he could not help being impressed with the fact that the great majority of these industrialists affirmed that they could produce at lower cost, both in the long *and* in the short period, if only they had a bigger demand to satisfy. There seemed to be a stark contradiction between the views of the industrialists and the theory of perfect competition. And, of course, if the industrialists were right, this would be helpful for Keynesian policy.[4]

Most of the current discussion of unemployment, together with much modern economic theory, still implicitly assumes, however, that lower real wages or labour costs are needed to increase employment; for example, proposals to deregulate the labour market, reduce taxes on employment or subsidise the employment of certain types of worker. Common observation suggests the reverse: that where current output is economic, additional output at today's prices and wages will almost always be equally, or more, profitable.[5] It is lack of demand, not the need to cut the price of labour, that holds back output and employment

It is well nigh incredible that one of the most important basic assumptions of neo-classical economics has no empirical foundation and receives so little critical comment. But then, as Galbraith has said:

> reputable or, as it is often called, mainstream economics has for some centuries given grace and acceptability to convenient belief – to what the socially and economically favoured most wish or need to have believed . . . To serve these ends, it must be emphasised, the required doctrine need not be subject to serious empirical proof.[6]

Thus the doctrine of diminishing returns led to the convenient conclusion that those who were out of work were there through their own fault in demanding too high a price for their labour; and hence reducing wages would benefit both employers of labour and the unemployed.

One of the consequences of the common but erroneous assumption that lower real wages are necessary to reduce unemployment is to build up a quite misleading picture of the 'cost' of achieving full employment. The first point is that in any event reducing unemployment means that more goods and services are produced and the community is that much better off. Second, if the additional workers do not reduce the average level of productivity, their pay packets can be as high as those of people already in work without presenting problems either of profitability to the employer or of excessive demand on the additional resources. There is not therefore a problem of 'insiders' and 'outsiders' with the marginal workers needing to be worse paid if they are to be employed at all; as, for example, James

Meade suggested in his final work, *Full Employment Regained?*, which was much concerned with the redistribution effects of the 'relatively low real wage rates needed to maintain Full Employment'.

Reducing wages is neither a necessary nor an effective solution to unemployment. It is true that keeping down real wages and other costs relative to our competitors can improve one country's competitive position and thus increase its employment at the expense of others. But in a situation where virtually all industrial countries are suffering from heavy unemployment (partly hidden rather than apparent in the case of Japan), such beggar-my-neighbour policies merely shift unemployment from one country to another and do not represent an acceptable solution. Adjustments in relative costs between countries are better handled by exchange rate policy than by trying to cut wages to this end (. . .); and exchange rate adjustments should be limited to the needs of the balance of payments and not regarded as a means of exporting unemployment.

Intensifying the search for jobs

There is, however, another set of labour market proposals which do not depend on assuming that productivity falls as employment increases. The theoretical justification for these is that by intensifying the search for jobs, wages will rise more slowly and unemployment can be kept lower without inflation, i.e. the NAIRU (Non-accelerating Inflation Rate of Unemployment) will be reduced. Such proposals concentrate on getting particular sections of the unemployed back into work. Three groups attract particular attention: those who are alleged to prefer to remain unemployed, the long-term unemployed and school leavers. In all three cases, however, there seems no reason why such action should in itself increase the total number of jobs available.

As far as the first category is concerned, while there may be a small minority of people who are not actively seeking employment because they feel they are better off unemployed either because they are in a benefit trap, or have given up hope of a job, there is no reason why making life on the dole more unpleasant for them (or lessening the reduction in benefits if they get work) should increase the total number of jobs; and it seems doubtful whether such measures would have any significant effect on wage demands. But in their popular text book on unemployment, Layard, Nickell and Jackman go so far as to maintain that 'The unconditional payment of benefits for an indefinite period is clearly a major cause of high European unemployment.'[7] We should be worrying more about the effects of the continual erosion of benefits on the plight of the vast majority of those who are desperate for work rather than the small minority who are out to beat the system. Experience shows that if demand is strong enough and jobs become available, there is no problem of people preferring to live on benefit.

The idea that over-generous benefits are keeping up the number of unemployed at a time when there is a widespread shortage of jobs is both cruel and mischievous.

This type of thinking, combined with the desire to keep down the cost of social security benefits, has provided a pretext for a series of measures to restrict the value of the benefits available to the unemployed and aggravate their financial plight. Whereas in 1978/9, on average the unemployed received from benefits 55 per cent of their former income from work, by 1987 this ratio had fallen to 39 per cent.[8] In 1987, for about 70 per cent of those unemployed, unemployment-related benefits replaced less than half their previous earnings.[9] Another and more recent measure of increasing financial hardship among the unemployed is available from the Department of Social Security (DSS) report on *Households below Average Income*.[10] In 1992/3, 75 per cent of families suffering from unemployment had an income less than half average income, as compared with 58 per cent in 1979 (in both cases after allowing for housing costs). The number of children in families with incomes less than half the national average had risen from 1.4 million to 4.3 million. The policy followed since 1984 of linking benefits to prices rather than earnings has meant that the erosion of the value of benefits is still continuing. Such harsh restrictions not only cause severe financial hardship, but also serious stress and worry.

Ethnic minorities

Ethnic minorities have been particularly badly hit by unemployment. The Labour Force Survey for Spring 1995 showed that while the (ILO) unemployment rate (. . .) was 8 per cent for white workers, it was 19 per cent for non-whites. Pakistani/Bangladeshi workers had the highest rate of 27 per cent, with Afro-Caribbeans at 24 per cent. In Greater London 11 per cent of whites were unemployed but 24 per cent of non-whites. Black workers were also likely to be unemployed for longer than whites: 60 per cent of Afro-Caribbean workers unemployed in the Spring of 1994 had been without work for over one year compared to 44 per cent of unemployed white workers.[11]

Racial discrimination in one form or another must be a factor in this situation. The percentage of highly qualified non-whites unemployed (6.9 per cent) was more than double the rate (3.1 per cent) for highly qualified white people. The situation tends to be prolonged by the fact that the jobs that non-white workers do get are often those most vulnerable to redundancy.

Long-term unemployment

Long-term unemployment has become an increasing problem as unemployment has risen and jobs have been harder to get. In the summer of 1995,

1.0 million people claiming unemployment benefit had been out of work for over a year. It is obviously important to help those concerned get back into employment. The main problem facing the long-term unemployed is probably not, as is generally suggested, that their skills have become rusty or their work experience out of date, but that many employers are reluctant to recruit them; this reflects a more general tendency for employers to favour those already in work over those who are unemployed. The reason for this is simple. When making people redundant, managers try so far as possible to keep those workers that they consider the best and get rid of those that they consider less competent. Thus when they come to recruit again, they assume that other employers have been behaving in the same way. (Even university appointment boards work on this assumption.) Similarly, the longer people have been out of work, the more likely managers are to assume that the fact that they have failed to impress other recruiters must mean that they are not strong candidates. This factor obviously has less force in depressed areas where unemployment has been consistently high for some time. But the higher unemployment has become and the greater the number of people who apply for any particular job, the more likely are recruiters to fall back on general criteria such as age, or whether the applicants have been out of work for long, when they have to sift through numerous candidates.

The long-term unemployed therefore need particular help to overcome their perceived lack of ability, whether or not this perception is justified. The fallacy, however, is to assume that reducing the numbers of long-term unemployed will in itself have any significant effect in reducing total unemployment. Subsidising employers who take on the long-term unemployed (or unemployed young people) will generally mean that they will employ such people instead of someone else, not that they will increase their labour force. This is borne out by a study of the effects of the Government's Pilot Workstart Schemes made by the Institute of Employment Studies.[12] This scheme offered employers a subsidy of £60 a week for 26 weeks and then £30 a week for 26 weeks for each full-time recruit who had been continuously unemployed for two years (four years in London). Whereas the study found that the subsidy had been effective in getting employers to take on the very long-term unemployed, the scheme did not appear to have had much effect on total employment. In only 17 per cent of cases were jobs created as a result of the subsidy where there would otherwise have been no vacancy; and there is no evidence that these represented any increase in total employment. If a garage or dry cleaner in the scheme took on an extra person and got more work, its competitor elsewhere may have had to make someone redundant.

Youth unemployment

The age group worst hit by unemployment (with some of the most serious consequences) is the under-twenties. In the summer of 1995 over 20 per cent of

16- to 19-year-olds who had left school were unemployed. There are powerful reasons for providing special assistance to young people who are unemployed, particularly in areas of persistently high unemployment; but the most effective way to help young people is to strengthen the general demand for labour. Special measures to help them or any other particular groups of unemployed people are of only limited benefit when there is a general shortage of jobs, and should not be regarded as a means of reducing total unemployment.

Similar considerations apply to regional measures, of which little has been heard in recent years, partly because the experience of different areas of the country has been less varied than in the past. While in October 1995 unemployment in Northern Ireland and the Northern Region was over 10 per cent, Greater London was almost as bad with 9.6 per cent. If, however, the general level of unemployment were to fall appreciably, there would once again be more conspicuous differences between areas. There would then be considerable scope for assisting such areas by special incentives for industrial development or additional investment in infrastructure.

The changing labour market

One source of confusion in discussing the causes of, and remedies for, mass unemployment is the effect of certain structural changes in the labour market, many of them predating the abandonment of full employment. Perhaps the most dramatic of these is the increase in the number of women in, or seeking, employment. In 1971, only 57 per cent of women of working age were in the labour force; 20 years later the proportion had risen to 71 per cent. The increase was most marked in the 25–34 year-old group where the participation rate rose from 45 per cent to 70 per cent as more women with school-aged children remained at work.[13] Approaching half of women's jobs were part-time, which can take a variety of forms.

> 'Part-time' employment includes the clerical worker on a regular, 24-hour-a-week contract; the DIY sales operator working a 3-day 'weekend' for full-time wages; the local authority job-sharer on 17 hours per week with membership of a pension scheme; the shop assistant whose hours vary each week; the cleaner who works for 3 hours per week, and the production-line operator on a zero hours contract.[14]

Over the same period, 1971–91, the participation rate for men of working age fell slightly from 91 per cent to 88 per cent as the demand for labour weakened. The change was noticeable among older men: in 1991 less than half men aged between 60 and 64 were in work. There seems little doubt that if the demand for labour were stronger, both more men and more women would enter or remain in the labour force who today form part of the one million 'hidden' unemployed.

The increase in the number of women working has led to a consequential increase in the number of households with two earners, while at the same time higher unemployment has increased the number of households with no earners. Between 1975 and 1990 the proportion of households with two adults of working age where both worked rose from 51 to 60 per cent, but the proportion with no earner rose from 3 to 11 per cent.[15]

A return to full employment in the 1990s would mean a higher proportion of part-time jobs for women than it did in the 1960s. But there is no reason to suppose that if the demand for labour were stronger there would be any mismatch between the demand and supply of full-time versus part-time jobs. Most employers have considerable scope for flexibility in deciding whether to employ full-timers or part-timers according to the wishes of their potential employees. The key point about the relation of full employment to the revolution in women's working patterns and family life is that it would shift the balance of choice from the employer to their employees. 'Flexibility' in conditions of work is desirable if it means that women (and men) can adjust their working pattern to the needs of family life (and other personal circumstances, such as studying for additional qualifications). 'Flexibility' is much less desirable, where as now, it is synonymous with insecurity and means that people can be laid off at short notice or expected to work unreasonable hours. In most EU countries, minimum wages, working conditions and social security contributions apply regardless of hours; in the UK, no such principle of 'equal treatment' applies, and both employment legislation and the structure of national insurance contributions create important incentives towards part-time employment.[16] In times of buoyant demand the good employer will reach an appropriate *modus vivendi* with his or her staff that can be beneficial to them both.

The number of men and women remaining at work over the age of 60 would seem likely to increase substantially if the demand for labour were stronger. Many of those dropping out of the labour force at the present time do so not from choice. Indeed with improved health and longer life expectation, more people than in the past will want to continue working after the age of 65, in some cases part-time rather than full-time. With a stronger demand for labour there will be more scope for them to do so. Compulsory retiring ages will at the same point become an anachronism. The only potential factor working the other way is that, among higher income groups, people may find it easier to accumulate the financial resources needed for earlier retirement, but only by accepting a greater drop in their standard of living than if they had retired later. Full employment could revolutionise the whole problem of the so-called 'demographic time bomb' by raising the proportion of older people at work. This is just one facet of the fact that any return to full employment would be that many people not now seeking jobs – the so-called 'economically inactive' – would return to the labour market.

Hidden unemployment

The official unemployment figures show the number of people claiming unemployment (or unemployment-related) benefits on a particular day in the month. Continual changes in the rules governing eligibility for such benefits have tended to reduce the figures and cast doubt on their validity as an indicator of the 'true' unemployment (. . .). Both the Royal Statistical Society[17] and the House of Commons Employment Committee[18] have suggested that the present situation is unsatisfactory and that more use should be made of the information obtained in the regular Labour Force Surveys based on questioning households.

The Surveys show that there are around a further one million people not claiming unemployment benefit, but actively seeking work: the 'hidden unemployed'. This applies particularly to the large numbers of women who want a job but who are not eligible for unemployment pay or actively seeking work, and to older men. The Unemployment Unit publish a regular series of estimates of 'broad' unemployment based on the Labour Force Surveys. These include people who want work, and are available to start in two weeks but have not been looking for work. In the summer of 1995 when the claimant count averaged 2.3 million, their figure for 'broad unemployment' was 3.5 million.[19]

The extent of 'hidden' unemployment varies according to how strict a definition of seeking work is adopted. John Wells has produced a similar estimate (on a slightly different basis), raising the official total of 2.81 million unemployed in the summer of 1993 to an alternative figure of 4.07 million.[20] The importance of these estimates lies not so much in the exact figures as the evidence that there are many people not counted in the official unemployment statistics who would take jobs if the demand for labour were stronger. Hence to reduce the number of those officially unemployed by, say, one million, would require considerably more than one million new jobs as some of the hidden unemployed or economically 'inactive' came back into the labour market.

Work-sharing

The idea of 'work-sharing' (i.e. spreading the available work more widely) has obvious attractions at a time of heavy unemployment. But it is a dangerous fallacy to think that there is a pre-determined demand for labour or fixed amount of work to go round. (Indeed on present policies if unemployment were appreciably decreased in this way, the Treasury and the Bank might well be seeking to restrict demand for fear of inflation.) It is, however, absurd and anti-social when work is scarce, that many men (in particular) are forced by their employers to work excessively long hours for fear of losing their jobs. Britain's failure to ratify the Social Chapter aggravates this situation. In many other EU countries standard weekly working hours are set by law. Thus one positive response to the 'work-sharing' approach is that it provides an additional argument for limiting hours worked where they could otherwise be excessive on social grounds.

Where the concept of work-sharing does seem appropriate is in employers' response to temporary recessions in demand. (. . . O)ne of the problems of returning to full employment is to rebuild our capacity in the widest sense, not just of plant – and maintain it at a level compatible with full employment during any temporary recessions. Part of such a process must be to keep a firm's labour force as far as possible intact during recession by reducing hours rather than numbers. This accords with Japanese and German practice, but is increasingly difficult where industrial decisions are dominated by the myopic reaction of city financial analysts. Whereas in the past, managers who could not sustain or expand their business enough to employ their existing workforce were regarded as having failed, today, 'down-sizing' the workforce is applauded as a sign of management virility.

Is there a shortage of unskilled jobs?

Another fashionable labour market theory is the so-called 'shortage of unskilled jobs'. But most of what has been written about the problem of unemployment among the unskilled is based on the inaccurate assumption that the 'demand for unskilled labour', in the sense of the number of jobs that the unskilled succeed in getting, is a direct reflection of the type of jobs available. It clearly is not. If an unemployed university graduate replaces someone with no qualifications in a job stocking the shelves in the local supermarket, there has in this sense been a decline in 'the demand for unskilled labour' but not a loss in unskilled jobs. Any statistical analysis of job losses based on the educational qualifications of those in or out of work must be regarded in this light. Most of the statistics purporting to prove that the industrial countries are suffering 'from a loss of unskilled jobs' can equally well be interpreted as demonstrating that the unskilled are the least effective competitors in the competition for the available jobs.

While the detailed statistical analyses show that the unskilled have the highest incidence of unemployment, relative changes in recent years do not fall in any simple pattern or support any general thesis about unskilled jobs. Nickell and Bell have analysed the disparate movements of unemployment among the skilled and unskilled in a number of OECD countries.[21] They treat as 'skilled' those with a high educational qualification; e.g. in the UK, A levels, or a professional qualification or a degree. The 'unskilled' are defined as those who leave school with no qualifications. This leaves, of course, a middle group accounting for about one-third of the male working population. (The figures refer only to men on the grounds that factors other than education are more important in determining the cause of female unemployment.) Nickell and Bell distinguish two phases over the last 20 years or so. In the period from the early or mid-1970s to the late 1980s the countries where data are available fall into two groups. The first group, consisting of the US, Japan, Norway and Sweden, experienced small increases in unemployment and the increase was concentrated on the unskilled. The second group, consisting of Germany, the Netherlands, Spain, the UK and Canada, experienced larger rises in unemployment with a significant rise in unemployment among those who had been through higher education. In the subsequent sharp recession in the early 1990s, the further rise in unemployment involved substantial increases in unemployment among both skilled and unskilled.

The emphasis on skilled as against unskilled jobs in this and other studies rests on the unrealistic assumption that there are two (or more) groups of jobs with a corresponding number of classes of potential workers, and that Group 1 jobs can only be filled by Group 1 people. In real life there are relatively few jobs, particularly in industry, which can only be filled by people with specific qualifications. Where the restriction is most highly specified it is generally a question of public safety (e.g. doctors or electricians) or semi-restrictive practices (e.g. lawyers and accountants); and many of these jobs are in non-industrial sectors. In industry, most former demarcations covering skilled jobs for time-served apprentices have gone by the board. It is strange that the concept of a sharp division between skilled and unskilled should suddenly come to the fore at a time when the old distinctions between skilled craftsmen and unskilled labourers is no longer so important, and the workforce has a much more closely graduated spectrum of skills, training and ability.

In practice there is a range of people of varying degrees of ability, experience and qualifications that can fill a vacant post, and employers try to get the best person they can. When demand for labour is strong, employers have to be content with people at the bottom of the range of available skills, education or ability. But when demand is weak, employers can be more selective and posts tend to be filled by people at the top of the ability range. The knock-on effect is that the less skilled or less able fall off the bottom of the jobs ladder. In other words, the fact that a higher proportion of the less skilled and less educated may be unemployed reflects the fact that they lose out in the battle for jobs, rather than the nature of the jobs available. This is particularly true in the service trades where the 'better educated' tend to get the available jobs, and may in many cases be heavily over-qualified for the work in hand; for example, university graduates are taking lower-grade jobs. Hence as unemployment rises it tends to be concentrated on those at the bottom of the hierarchy of skills and ability. This also helps to explain why higher unemployment is associated with growing inequality of earnings, as the less well-placed have to compete most fiercely for jobs.

Is this then a justification for arguing that those out of work can only command lower wages than those at work? The answer is 'No' because, for the reasons discussed earlier, costs tend to decline as output increases irrespective of any minor difference in the ability or productivity of the people employed. Take a hotel, for example: if its room occupancy increases and an extra chambermaid has to be employed at the same rate of pay as the others, its profitability will rise whether or not she is just as efficient. Postwar experience suggests that it is only when unemployment is very low, and then only to a limited extent, that those unemployed may differ markedly in efficiency from those in work.

None of this is to deny the merits of more and better education and training. But it does suggest that we should not try to create more unskilled jobs by further cheapening the cost of unskilled labour or other means. If there are enough jobs in total to go round, all the evidence of wartime and postwar history is that few people will be excluded from work because the jobs are too skilled or the workforce too unskilled.

North–south

The emphasis on unemployment among the unskilled has encouraged the popular thesis that unemployment in the more highly industrialised countries reflects increased competition from developing countries with a very low cost of unskilled labour. This thesis has been developed in most detail by Adrian Wood in his study on North–South Trade.[22] But the fact that competition may be most acute in such industries does not mean that the remedy is to reduce wages for the unskilled workers in Europe, or that we have to beat such competition to ensure full employment. (. . .). Europe's competitive strength lies in developing the more advanced industries and in effect creating more 'skilled' jobs.

Wood argues that even if the trade effects balance out, the industrial countries require less labour to make an equivalent value of relatively high technology machinery to export to the developing countries than the jobs we lose by importing an equivalent value of labour-intensive products, such as textiles. It may (to take imaginary figures) only need 70 British workers to produce the machinery needed to buy the textiles from China that previously needed 100 British workers to produce, so 30 jobs have been 'lost'; but this merely means that we can have a satisfactory balance of payments and employ more labour to meet our own needs. Whether or not we have full employment in such a situation is a matter of the level of demand in the UK. Competition from the developing world is not an argument against following more expansionary policies in the industrialised countries. It is the developing world that has a balance of payments problem, rather than the industrial countries taken as a whole. The correct policy is to expand demand in the industrial countries to reduce unemployment, and broadly speaking leave market forces to determine the long-term pattern of the industrial structure.

The real problem for the industrial countries is not the threat of cheap imports of labour-intensive products, but the difficulties of adjusting to a changing industrial structure: as, for example, in the case of localities strongly dependent on steel or shipbuilding where production has been shifting away from the older industrial countries. The problem of such adjustments is most acute when unemployment is generally high. Where there is a strong demand for labour, the creation of new industries and jobs in declining areas is very much easier; as was apparent in the massive restructuring of the British steel industry in the 1970s with extensive plant closures in towns highly dependent on the industry.

Skills and training

Peter Robinson has examined the relationship between unemployment and skills or qualifications using some of the same data as Nickell and Bell. He, however, draws a distinction between 'skills', covering literacy, numeracy, personal and job-specific skills, and formal 'qualifications' such as A levels.[23] Where employers reported recruitment difficulties they attributed them to lack of 'skills' rather than 'qualifications'. But there is little or no statistical evidence about skills in this broad sense, as there is about educational qualifications. Robinson points out that the proportion of the unemployed who are unqualified has been declining significantly. Although the less qualified are most easily pushed off the jobs ladder, a large number of the unemployed are well qualified. By 1994, 40 per cent of unemployed men had A level or equivalent qualifications or some form of higher education, and only 30 per cent had no formal qualifications; whereas in 1979, 70 per cent of unemployed men had no formal qualifications. This reflects both the tendency for more qualified people to become unemployed as total unemployment rises and the fact that the proportion of the workforce with educational qualifications has risen sharply in recent years: between 1984 and 1994 the proportion with higher educational qualifications rose from 12 per cent to 19 per cent. Robinson concludes that it is 'misleading to paint a portrait of the unemployed in the mid 1990s as being primarily unqualified'.

The two questions that need to be asked about training programmes for the unemployed are (a) whether they will reduce unemployment in total and (b) whether they will help those concerned to get jobs. There is no reason to think that such programmes by themselves will lead to any increase in jobs. As to the effects on individuals, Robinson finds no evidence in the US or Europe that large-scale training programmes positively help the individuals concerned. While some forms of education and training, or special schemes for young people and the long-term unemployed, may help particular individuals or groups to compete in the jobs market, they will not in themselves create more jobs. Such schemes may form a useful part of an overall strategy for full employment (as in Sweden), and better education and training can be valuable in improving industrial efficiency, but it is misleading to regard them as a significant instrument for reducing unemployment on their own. Any political platform to reduce unemployment based solely on such measures is guilty of offering a false prospectus.

The growth of inequality

The weakening in the demand for labour since the end of the 1970s has been a major factor in the striking growth of inequality in the UK in this period: it has both widened the disparity of earnings and added large numbers of unemployed to the pool of low-income families. The Rowntree Report on Income and Wealth[24] concluded that:

> Internationally the UK was exceptional in the pace and extent of the increase in inequality in the 1980s . . . The speed with which inequality increased in the UK between 1977 and 1990 was faster than in any of the other countries listed with the exception of New Zealand over the four years to 1989.

The Report found that 'Since 1979 the lowest income groups have not benefited from economic growth.' DSS figures for 1992/3[25] show that, after allowing for housing costs, the real income of the poorest 10 per cent had fallen by 17 per cent since 1979, and the real income of the next lowest 10 per cent has remained virtually unchanged. The number of families with less than half the average income had risen from 4.4 million to 11.5 million within the same period. Apart from the growth in the number of unemployed, the situation has been aggravated by the policy of freezing unemployment and other benefits in real terms whilst wages and salaries have continued to show real increases.

A further source of growing inequality has been the fact that the pay of the higher paid has risen more rapidly than that of the lower paid. The Rowntree Report found that after 1978, the real wages of the lowest paid third of male workers showed little change and were actually lower in 1992 than 1975; but real wages in the middle third rose by 35 per cent, and in the top third by 50 per cent. Women's wages showed a similar trend. We should be suspicious of any measures which could make this trend worse under the pretext of cutting unemployment.

It is noteworthy that the 'labour market' approaches to curing unemployment would tend to worsen still further the position of the less well-paid wage earner. Just as readiness to sacrifice jobs to control inflation reflects a particular set of political and social values, so too does the idea of reducing wages still further for those who are already worst paid. As we have already shown, any intellectual justification for them rests on the erroneous assumption of 'decreasing returns', i.e. that higher production is uneconomic without lower wages. Moreover, there is clearly no historical justification for thinking that greater inequality and a weakening in the protection of labour are a precondition for a return to full employment. On the contrary, low pay and insecurity are not a recipe for full employment, but a consequence of a weak demand for labour. The period of full employment was one where labour was stronger and society more egalitarian. For this reason many of those who press strongly for labour market measures to weaken the position of employees have no real desire to return to a state of full employment. Those who do should not follow their lead. The re-emergence of mass unemployment has already taken sufficient toll in terms of increased poverty and growing inequality without deliberately aggravating it by further measures to deregulate the labour market or depress the wages of the unskilled.

Notes

1 Keynes, J. M., 'Relative Movements of Real Wages and Output', *Economic Journal*, March 1939.
2 There is a classic statement of this in Hicks, J. R. (1939), *Value and Capital*, Oxford, Oxford University Press.
3 Jonathan Michie reviews the literature on this in Michie (1987), *Wages in the Business Cycle*, London, Pinter.
4 Harrod, R. (1972) 'Increasing Returns' in *Economic Essays*, London, Macmillan.
5 The accounting treatment of the cost of existing, as opposed to new, capital equipment may, however, distort the lower real cost of new equipment.
6 Galbraith, J. K. (1992) *The Culture of Contentment*, London, Sinclair-Stevens.
7 Layard, R., Nickell, S. and Jackman, R. (1992) *Unemployment, Macroeconomic Performance and the Labour Market*, Oxford, Oxford University Press.
8 Wells, J., 'The Costs of Unemployment', mimeo (1993). Calculated from the DSS Reports on *Incomes In and Out of Work*.
9 Garman, A., Redmond, G. and Lonsdale, S., *Incomes In and Out of Work*, DSS Research Report No. 7.
10 DSS, *Households below Average Income, A Statistical Analysis 1979–1992/3* (1995).
11 TUC, *Black and Betrayed* (October 1995).
12 Atkinson, J. and Meager, N. 'Evaluation of Work Start Pilots', *Institute of Employment Studies*, Report 279.
13 Rosewell, B. 'Employment, Households and Earnings', in Meadows, P. (ed.) (1996) *Work Out – or Work In?*, York, Joseph Rowntree Foundation.
14 Hewitt, P., 'The Place of Part-Time Work', in Meadows, *Work Out – or Work In?*, op. cit.
15 Rowntree Foundation (1995) *Inquiry into Income and Wealth*, York, Joseph Rowntree Foundation.
16 Hewitt, 'The Place of Part-Time Work'.
17 Royal Statistical Society, *Report of Working Party on the Measurement of Unemployment in the UK* (April 1995).

18 House of Commons Employment Committee, *Unemployment and Employment Statistics* (February 1996).
19 Unemployment Unit, *Working Brief* (February 1996).
20 Wells, J. (1995) 'Unemployment, Job Creation and Job Destruction in the UK since 1979', in Arestis, P. and Marshall, M. (eds), *The Political Economy of Full Employment*, London, Edward Elgar.
21 Nickell, S. and Bell, L.A., 'The Collapse of Demand for the Unskilled and Unemployment Across the OECD', *Oxford Review of Economic Policy* (Spring, 1995).
22 Wood, A. (1994) *North–South Trade, Employment and Inequality*, Oxford, Oxford University Press.
23 Robinson, P., 'Skills, Qualifications and Unemployment', *Economic Affairs*, Vol. 16, No. 2 (Spring, 1996).
24 Rowntree Foundation, *Inquiry into Income and Wealth.*
25 DSS, *Households below Average Income, A Statistical Analysis 1979–1992/3.*

Chapter 6

Evaluating the assumptions that underlie training policy

Ewart Keep and Ken Mayhew

The aim of this chapter is to examine the assumptions underlying British training policy in recent years. It argues that many of these assumptions are questionable, and explores the policy implications of this clash between official perceptions and reality. In particular, Britain's skill problem is at least as much one of low demand for skills as one of inadequate supply. Policy concentrates on enhancing supply in a system which is employer-led and which to a large extent ignores deep-seated reasons for lack of employer demand. Thus its effectiveness is likely to be limited.

1 The assumptions that lie behind policy

Analysis of official policy statements reveals a series of interlinked beliefs underpinning initiatives in the 1980s and early 1990s. The main ones have been:

- that training and development act as key determinants of economic success, at the levels of both national economy and individual firm;
- that the UK increasingly will require a labour force consisting of highly educated, skilled, flexible and autonomous workers;
- following on from this, a belief that UK employers will require a highly educated and trained workforce at all levels;
- that a market-based approach, with little place for direct legislative backing for training, is best;
- that this approach will work because the payoff from training, whether for the employer or the employee, will generally be positive;
- that employment and promotion opportunities ought to be strongly influenced by formal skills and qualifications;
- that control of the new training system should be vested with employers, upon whom falls primary responsibility for deciding the nature and volume of training that is required.

We consider each of these assumptions.

2 The link between VET and economic success

What evidence is there to support the notion that levels of training affect economic performance? Beyond a commonsense belief of long standing that this must be so, the evidence is patchy. At the level of the national economy, there is no lack of comparative studies which indicate that other developed countries have more highly qualified workforces (NEDO/MSC/IMS, 1984; Worswick, 1985; Daly, 1986). It is also true that most of these countries have achieved higher rates of long-term growth than Britain, and there is a general presumption that there is a direct link between national economic efficiency and high levels of vocational education and training. Though not everyone accepts this linkage (see, for example, Pratten (1990) and Shackleton (1992)), comparative studies of VET mapping the scale of the UK's relative deficiencies have been used to define the terms on which debate about the need for improvements in national training effort has been conducted (Keep, 1991, pp. 25–6).

However, problems occur when we come to look for proof at the level of the individual firm of links between training and good performance. The evidence here indicates that the linkages are complex and indirect. The difficulty stems in part from the fact that it is not always certain to which aspects of company performance training is being linked. If high levels of productivity, or the production of high-quality goods and services is the measure of success, then the evidence available from the studies conducted by NIESR in, for example, clothing (Steedman and Wagner, 1989), furniture manufacturing (Steedman and Wagner, 1987), and retailing (Jarvis and Prais, 1989) suggests a link. However, if profitability, share value or return on investment are the measures of success, the story is much less clear. For example, a large-scale study of management training in the UK found that 'there is no clear evidence on which to conclude that an association exists between return on capital and the proportion of managers trained' (Mangham and Silvers, 1986, p. 20).

Moreover, as the NIESR matched plant comparison studies and other evidence suggests, significant sectors of the UK economy have survived and probably in their own terms viewed themselves as successful, at least to date, despite low levels of productivity, high scrap and wastage rates, and the adoption of product market strategies that require only very low levels of skill. There are also examples of large companies that have been highly profitable without laying much overt stress on having a highly qualified workforce. Equally, investment in training has not guaranteed corporate success.

Disentangling the beneficial results that derive exclusively from training, as opposed to other variables, is a complicated task and there is a danger of confusing cause and effect, not least because of the complex 'virtuous circle' relationships that often exist between skill levels and choice of product market strategies. Many companies recognise this. As *A Challenge to*

Complacency noted, 'we found few firms which were prepared to state that they believed in a direct causal relationship from training to profits' (Coopers and Lybrand, 1985, p. 10), though many companies were willing to acknowledge a linkage between training and quality.

The fact that many firms are often apparently less than convinced of a link between training and profits has important consequences for the success of an employer-led training strategy and for reliance on a market-based approach to investment in human capital. This is an issue to which we will be returning later in the chapter.

3 The nature of the UK's future work and occupational structure

The next two assumptions are interlinked: firstly, that the future of work in the UK will increasingly require highly educated and skilled, flexible, autonomous workers; and, following on from this, a belief that UK employers will require a highly educated and trained workforce at all levels. These assumptions are reflected in the work of popularisers of a vision of 'post-industrial' society, such as Toffler, Handy, and Drucker, and in macro-economic models of labour market developments, such as those undertaken by the Institute of Manpower Studies (IMS) and the Institute of Employment Research (IER).

It has been a commonplace assertion during the last decade that Britain is faced with a fundamental choice about the basis on which the economy faces international competition. One major strand of the official prescription for economic development in the UK has tended to embrace a particular conception of a competitive strategy based upon high-quality, technologically advanced, flexible production. Coupled with this have been frequent references to the changing structure of employment. The decline of manual occupations, craft apprenticeships and craft-based occupations, the reduction of manufacturing jobs, the rise in demand for technicians, and the growth in white-collar and professional employment are constant themes in official policy statements (see, for example, MSC (1981, 1983a, 1983b), ED (1988) and CBI (1989)). Increasing competition and demand for quality, coupled with these shifts in occupational structure, are seen as pointing to a future where an independent, self-reliant, flexible and highly skilled workforce will be a necessity (IoD, 1991).

It is undoubtedly true that there have been very significant changes in the composition of the workforce, with a considerable growth in 'higher level' occupations, particularly the professions. This has coincided with an increase in the number of people within the workforce holding qualifications. Projections of future skill demand appear to show a continued rise in employment in white-collar, higher-level occupations and a continued decline in manual, semi-skilled and craft occupations (see for example, ED (1992)).

However, there have also been developments that may point to a rather different view of skill requirements within the national economy.

3.1 The growth of small firms

Government policy since 1979 has placed great importance on an 'enterprise culture', a standard bearer of which was to be a revitalised small business sector. Small businesses accounted for a disproportionately large share of total job creation. In the services sector, between 1987 and 1989, firms with fewer than ten employees accounted for half of net job creation. In the production sector over the same period, firms with fewer than ten employees accounted for 40% of net job generation (Daly et al., 1992). By 1989 firms employing between one and five people accounted for 87.7% of all the businesses in the UK, and 22.4% of all employment; and firms with fewer than fifty workers accounted for 98.8% of the total number of businesses, and 42.3% of employment (Daly and McCann, 1992, p. 48).

Significant sections of the revitalised small firms sector do not chime well with the vision of those who embrace hopes of a high-skill, high-tech UK economy competing successfully in world markets. For instance, Storey's studies of small firm formation in Cleveland in the 1970s and 1980s showed that in the 1980s small firms were often being established in non-tradeable areas, with only 1% of sales being made outside the UK (Storey, 1982; Storey and Strange, 1992). Moreover, no less than 26% of all new firms in Cleveland in the 1980s were engaged in hairdressing, car breaking and garage activities – not sectors whose growth suggests a massive increase in demands for higher-level skills and formal qualifications.

Moreover, a variety of econometric studies (Booth, 1991; Green, 1991) have indicated that small firms are significantly less likely to train their employees than are larger ones, even allowing for the nature of the goods and services they produce. As Finegold (1992) notes, *Training in Britain* (TA, 1989) suggested that the majority of all training days were accounted for by enterprises with more than 1,000 employees. Yet the number of enterprises of this size was only about a thousand and they employed no more than 27.5% of the workforce (Daly and McCann, 1992).

Data from a 1992 ED survey of small firms' training needs conducted by IFF (IFF, 1992) and from the survey of individuals' perspectives on training, undertaken as part of the *Training in Britain* study (Rigg, 1989) tend to confirm that training provision is relatively weak in very small firms. The IFF survey showed that less than 20% of establishments with between one and four employees were providing off-the-job training, as compared with more than 40% of establishments with between ten and twenty-four employees. The *Training in Britain* survey of adults suggested that workers in establishments with fewer than five people were half as likely to have been trained in the last three years as other employees (Rigg, 1989).

3.2 The growth in self-employment

Between 1981 and 1991 self-employment increased by 1.1 million (a rise of 52%) to a total of 3.3 million (Campbell and Daly, 1992). The incidence of training among the self-employed is far lower than for the employed workforce. The 1992 Labour Force Survey indicated that whereas 14.9% of the sample as a whole had received job-related training in the preceding four weeks, the figure for the self-employed was only 6% (ED, 1992, p. 57).

3.3 The growth in part-time work

There has been a significant increase in part-time employment in the UK, with the result that by 1988 there were more than five million part-time workers, representing almost a quarter of all employees. The vast bulk of part-time jobs are concentrated in relatively low-level occupations such as clerical work, selling, catering, cleaning, hairdressing and other personal services. Such is the clustering in lower-status, lower-skill occupations that Dex remarks, 'part-time work appears to be being defined as inherently low skilled' (1988, p. 290). An Employment Department analysis of the 1992 LFS data commented that, 'a large proportion (14 per cent) of women full timers received training, more than men or women working part time . . . Nearly as many women work part time as full time and very few of the former received training' (Labour Market Quarterly Report, February 1992, p. 6). If the proportion of part-time jobs is growing, then it is at least possible that the proportion of jobs regarded by employers as unskilled is also growing. As in the case of small firms, econometric evidence suggests that, even controlling for other variables, part-time employment involves relatively little training.

Finally, forecasts of future employment growth suggest that, while the largest expansion of job opportunities will be concentrated in the managerial, professional and technical levels (ED, 1992, p. 19), 'personal and protective services represent the main growth area for employment outside the managerial and professional occupations with an additional 300,000 (16 per cent) by the end of the century' (ED, 1992, p. 20). The only other area showing above average rates of growth will be sales-based occupations. Thus the skill requirements of managerial, technical and professional occupations may justify the forecast decline in skilled craft employment in manufacturing, and the continued growth of employment in the relatively low-skilled parts of the service sector, such as personal and protective services, where part-time employment is also prevalent.

The foregoing comments about small firms, self-employment, part-time work and shifts in occupational structure are not meant to suggest that the trends towards a higher global requirement for skill within the British economy reported by bodies such as the IER and IMS are wrong. They simply point to countervailing developments in the structure of employment that mean that there are large areas of employment where skill requirements and training effort are and will remain limited and where there may be active de-skilling of segments of the workforce.

4 The need for a highly trained workforce

This brings us to the belief that UK employers will require a highly educated and trained workforce at all levels. In general the high-skills route is probably the only one that advanced, high-wage economies can sustain in the long term (Streeck, 1989); and indeed it is this realisation which, at least in part, motivates the training debate. Nevertheless, in the shorter term it is perfectly possible for high-skill, high-wage sectors to coexist with low-wage, low-skill sectors (Ashton *et al.*, 1987; King, 1990, pp. 150-1; McNabb and Ryan, 1990). At the same time, while the changes in organisational structure and workforce utilisation that are being advocated by the evangelists of a high-skill, high-tech future may be the best strategic direction in which to proceed, they are not the only options available to many UK enterprises, at least in the short- to medium-term. These alternatives include increasing use of crude work-intensification practices, low pay, insecure and casualised employment, and the subcontracting of more complex parts of production.

There is some ambiguity in the government's stance towards the choice of competitive strategy. On the one hand, ministers and civil servants have painted the vision of a high-wage, high-tech, high-skill future outlined above. On the other, the utilisation by companies of strategies centred on price-based competition would not be inconsistent with those strands of government policy which have sought to emphasise low wage costs as a source of competitive advantage, and which have laid considerable stress on the benefits to be reaped from possessing the most deregulated labour markets in Europe (Emerson, 1988).

Utilisation of competitive strategies based on price rather than quality plays an important role in determining managements' perceptions of the levels of skill they require. The case for up-skilling and high-value-added strategies may also be undermined by the structure of demand in the UK economy. Producing high-tech, high-quality goods and services that require high levels of skill is not, in itself, intrinsically important to a company. The issue of overriding concern is whether or not its product market strategy allows it to survive and to make adequate (however defined) levels of profit. If companies can achieve these ends through the production of low-cost, low-quality, high-volume goods and services that require minimal skill levels, then there is little reason for them to alter their strategies.

For example, much has been made in recent years of the improvement in profit that retailers can realise by abandoning a pile-it-high-and-sell-it-cheap approach, and moving upmarket, thereby achieving higher value added per unit of goods or service sold. The examples of retailers like Marks and Spencer and J. Sainsbury are held out as proof of the value of adopting such a strategy, and others, for example Tesco, have followed in their footsteps. However, the pursuit of a price-based competition strategy may be highly rational if the goods and services which companies are producing are aimed largely at certain segments of the UK home market. Put simply, Britain contains a large number of people of modest disposable income, who are not in a position to purchase expensive, high-quality goods and services. There is likely to be a significant market for goods and services that have low cost as their main selling point.

Given the influences outlined above, it is hardly surprising that the product market strategies of sections and skill requirements of the British economy exhibit considerable diversity. There is little doubt that there are companies, such as British Steel (Morris *et al.*, 1991), Rover Group (Muller, 1991), and ICI, where competitive strategies based on high-quality production and high value added mean that a more flexible, autonomous and highly skilled workforce is regarded as an essential prerequisite for success. There are a great many other employers (Keep, 1990) pursuing product market strategies based on the production of low-quality, low-cost goods and services using Taylorist methods of work organisation, who are more likely to want a cheap, relatively low-skilled workforce of people who do what they are told.

4.1 Low-skill jobs

Of the existence of a significant number of these types of jobs there can be little doubt. As Sir Bryan Nicholson, chair of the National Council for Vocational Qualifications (NCVQ) has commented, 'there are jobs in the British economy that can be achieved with only modules of NVQ Level 1' (Nicholson, 1991). A report on skills in the plastics industry, commissioned by the Training Agency, the EITB, and the Plastics Processing Industry Training Board (Rigg *et al.*, 1989), demonstrated that not only was training provision in the sector weak, but that many employers viewed training for process operators as a waste of time because the skill requirements of the job were so limited. One employer commented that the requirements for being a process operator were 'two arms and two legs' (1989, p. 52).

Perhaps some of the clearest indications that many employers believe in the necessity of only a very limited span of training for many employees came when the move from one-year to two-year YTS was announced (Chapman and Tooze, 1987, p. 60). Jim Foulds, the personnel director of DRG Group, commented:

> Given the nature of many of the jobs available, it is already hard to provide sufficient content for the one-year scheme and still be credible

in the eyes of those concerned. Youngsters are quick to see the difference between the training being given and the tasks which they will be required to do . . . The crux of the issue on the move from one-year to two-year YTS is that we are moving from building a bridge between education and business, something most businesses can cope with, to real vocational education and training, something many of the schemes may have difficulty in coping with.

(Milton, 1986, p. 29)

The presence of a substantial residual of jobs where low skills are likely to remain the norm for the foreseeable future, casts serious doubt on the ability of the new market-based training system to function as intended. The existence of a large number of such employment opportunities will help to undermine the training strategy being advocated by government and bodies such as the CBI. For example, the planned reform of the youth labour market, via the introduction of Training Credits, is crucially dependent upon the removal of the significant number of dead-end jobs without training which are currently on offer to young people. In the absence of any statutory obligation to provide training for young employees, there are good reasons for doubting that employers in low-skill sectors will cooperate (Cassels, 1990, pp. 32–7; Lee *et al.*, 1990).

4.2 Discrimination and equality of access to training

Official training policy in the 1980s had relatively little to say about issues of equality of access to training for disadvantaged groups. Failure to address these issues is an important omission given the volume of econometric and survey evidence suggesting that, holding other variables constant, gender, race and age can play a crucial role in determining access to training opportunities.

Even worse, these other variables are not in fact constant. For example, the distribution of women across occupational groupings is heavily skewed. They are under-represented in skilled manufacturing employment. Indeed women's share of skilled work in manufacturing in Britain has shrunk throughout this century (Purcell, 1988, p. 168). This skewed distribution, as Cockburn (1987) demonstrates, tends to exhibit a capacity to be self-sustaining. The young are channelled by the existing structure of employment and gender segregation into making 'realistic' choices about training and career opportunities, i.e. choices that reflect existing patterns of segregation. The result is the danger of a vicious circle that ensures that the employment pattern of the past remains more or less unchanged in the future.

What is the impact of this on training? The most obvious is that many people may be being misdirected into occupations where their talents cannot be made best use of. Attempts by individuals to challenge these divisions indicate that the ability of a trainee to exercise choice of future occupation is currently heavily circumscribed by gender barriers, as, for example, Cockburn's (1987) work on YTS underlines.

Gender also plays a major part in defining what is skilled work. As Dex comments, 'there is a sense in which "unskilled" comes to be defined as anything which women do' (1988, p. 289). In some sectors access to skilled status, and the pay that goes with it, is largely a factor of gender. Thus, 'for a woman to become skilled in the clothing industry, she would have to change her sex' (Dex, 1988, p. 290). One consequence of gender-based definitions of skill, and of poorer pay and promotion opportunities, is to make investment by women in their own training highly problematic. Given the record of employers in investing more heavily in training men than women, current public policy of leaving training decision making in the hands of employers does not augur well for women (Payne, 1990).

In the mid-1980s, the major force that had been expected to provide the impetus for a market-based challenge to discrimination was enlightened self-interest on the part of companies, in the light of demographic change (specifically falling numbers of young people entering the labour market) and associated shifts in the structure of the UK labour market. The subsequent sharp and prolonged recession has created very different labour market conditions, including a significant increase in youth unemployment. The tight labour market that was supposed to drive employers towards enlightened self-interest has vanished, and it is uncertain when, and indeed if, it will return.

There is a more deep-seated reason to doubt that a market-based approach reliant on voluntarism, exhortation and a willingness on the part of employers to change themselves, would be able to deliver significant shifts in the divisions that structure occupational choice and opportunity. Discrimination and segregation of career and training opportunities start early on in life, well before people reach the labour market. Attempts at fundamental change therefore have to address broader questions than simply the training opportunities that are being offered. Certainly the evidence of YTS and YT suggests that the largest attempt to provide structured vocational preparation for young people in the UK has had little more than marginal effects upon traditional gender divisions within training provision and occupational choice (Cockburn, 1987; TA *Youth Training News*, No. 55, June/July 1989, p. 24; Lee *et al.*, 1990).

Gender is but one example of discrimination within the training and labour markets. Much the same sorts of difficulties arise with regard to race and age. Current policies have tended to passively reflect rather than actively challenge the status quo. Efforts to promote change have been largely limited to exhortation.

5 Market-based approaches to training

As there is insufficient space here to probe every aspect of reliance on market mechanisms, what follows concentrates on the key question of the payoffs that result from investment in training. An individual worker or an employer will make an investment in training only if the net payoff is perceived to be positive. First the payoffs to the individual are examined, and then the company's perspective.

5.1 The growing emphasis on the individual

Of late, perhaps because of some of the difficulties with achieving greater employer investment, the individual 'has taken centre stage in government policy on training in Britain' (Payne, 1992, p. 1). Government policy asserts that, 'for individuals, investment in training is the best way to ensure both greater job security and enhanced earnings over the course of their working lives' (ED, 1988, p. 59). Investment by an individual is likely to take the form of time, effort, and income forgone while under training. Unless the subsequent payoffs are positive, in terms of higher subsequent lifetime earnings, a training market is unlikely to produce significant increases in the supply of skills. Thus reliance on a training market supported by individual investment carries with it a conviction that a strong link exists between qualifications and skill, and employment and promotion opportunities.

5.2 Skill and reward structures

The evidence to support such assumptions is in many instances weak. Indeed, with the possible exception of degree-level education, there is very scant evidence that British pay and reward structures are able to provide substantial incentives to the individual to acquire skills. To begin with, the financial returns available to young people who invest in obtaining post-16 vocational and academic qualifications are often extremely poor. Research by Bennett et al. (1992) showed that the returns to post-compulsory education and training are mixed, with degrees and higher-level vocational qualifications generally enhancing lifetime earnings, but with low-level vocational qualifications, and for many males even A-levels, producing only very modest and in some cases negative returns. They conclude that low demand for skills from employers produces inadequate returns to young people who invest in skills and qualifications, and that this situation in turn reduces the demand of young people for post-compulsory education and training. Thus, 'many young people are quite rational in not pursuing training – it does not give them great enough reward' (1992, p. 2).

These findings reflect broader problems with the links between skill and reward in the workplace. As the survey of employers' training activities reported in *Training in Britain* (TA, 1989) demonstrated, more than a quarter of those establishments that train regarded it 'as a serious drawback that newly trained employees might want more money' (Mayhew, 1991). Training poses this problem because, in many UK enterprises, 'pay and status are rarely linked to the attainment of qualifications or to attendance at training courses, so they provide little incentive to British employees to seek further training' (Coopers and Lybrand Associates, 1985, p. 13). Differentials in the UK between the skilled and unskilled are often low by international standards (Layard *et al.*, 1992).

While the overall picture on differentials is gloomy, there are signs that some British employers are beginning to shift payments systems and reward structures towards a greater recognition of skills *(Employee Development Bulletin,* 31, July 1992, pp. 2–7). The development of skills-based pay is so far limited, but the fact that some major employers are making moves in this direction may be an indication that UK employers are at last beginning to realise the significance of links between investment in skill and pay.

5.3 The influence of past deficiencies on perceived payoffs

Another problem with relying on individual investment in a training market is the fact that the likelihood of obtaining training is heavily correlated with the individual's position within occupational and management hierarchies. Research suggests that an individual's capacity to perceive the benefits of training is structured by levels of prior educational qualification and the degree to which the receipt of training has already figured in their working lives. Hence those most in need of training, because they have to date received very little, are often the least likely to perceive it as being of value (Rigg, 1989; Fuller and Saunders, 1990). In the absence of access to well-developed internal labour markets (ILMs) for many manual and semi-skilled employees (Millward and Stevens, 1986), such beliefs may be well-founded.

5.4 Job structures, ILMs and internal progression

The idea that the individual can be expected to foot the bill for his or her own training presupposes certain features of the labour market in which the individual is working, or seeking work. A recent White Paper on training proposes that:

> Skills and qualifications will be crucial factors shaping the prospects of individual people at work. For many they may make the difference between success and failure. They have the potential to enable individuals to take control of their working lives and shape them – far more than was possible in the past – into careers that reflect their personal ambitions and preferences. The aim must be to enable them to obtain the skills and qualifications they need and want . . . It is central to the White Paper as whole.
>
> *(People, Jobs and Opportunity*, 1992, p. 23)

The authors of this statement appear to assume the job structures that pertain in professional jobs are also found in other forms of employment. Yet to talk about careers, in any meaningful sense, for many employees is simply to ignore reality. For the majority of process and non-craft skilled workers in many sections of manufacturing industry well-formed ILMs and job security are often lacking, whilst opportunities for progression are minimal with the current employer and limited within the sector as a whole. In the clothing industry, for example, the current situation is that, 'a typical female machinist enters the industry in her early twenties and retires from the industry maybe forty years later – as a machinist' (Bosworth *et al.*, 1990, p. 45).

Retailing, cleaning, distribution, hotels, food and tobacco, clothing and textiles, catering, and leisure and tourism would be examples of sectors where well-developed ILMs and career structures frequently do not exist. These sectors employ a significant proportion of the national workforce. In order to progress, workers employed in such sectors must take the risk of changing jobs and employer.

5.5 The role of skills and qualifications in recruitment

Even where job ladders and ILMs do exist, research suggests that initial access to employment, and promotion thereafter, may not be closely linked to the possession of formal skills and qualifications (Jenkins and Troyna, 1983).

Research such as that undertaken by Collinson for the EOC (1988) suggests that problems of informality in recruitment and promotion procedures means that, even in large, sophisticated organisations, 'formal' skills and qualifications may count for relatively little in securing employment or a better job within the organisation, since other criteria dominate the selection process. These criteria include the possession of 'informal' or tacit skills, as well as social and behavioural characteristics – personality, attitude, motivation, health and fitness, appearance, age, marital status, stable work record. In recruiting young workers, research certainly suggests that qualifications may come a long way down the list of desired characteristics. An Employment Department study undertaken in 1990 (ED, 1991) showed that vocational qualifications figured eighth out of nine in the ranking of things employers desired of school-leaver candidates. There are strong indications that social criteria often play a dominant role in the selection of adult workers, in particular the acceptability of candidates in terms of their potential ability to 'fit in' in the workplace (Oliver and Turton, 1982).

As Wood points out (1988), social characteristics and skills may be valid criteria to take into account when seeking to recruit, as the productive process, particularly in the case of the delivery of services, is about social processes and skills as well as technical ones. Nevertheless, insofar as recruitment is dependent upon a range of characteristics and attributes, of which formal skills and qualifications are but one part, and not always the most important, then the case for the individual worker to invest in the acquisition of skill may be weakened.

5.6 Training and qualification as positional goods

Training aims to raise the capacity of individuals, or groups of individuals, to deal with problems, undertake new tasks, and assume greater responsibilities. As such, sooner or later, it is likely to disturb existing hierarchies and power relationships within the workplace.

Much of the research on British attitudes towards training has tended to explore the proposition that its benefits have not been fully appreciated. Perhaps one element of the problem is quite the reverse. Perhaps the lack of greater investment in training stems, at least in part, from a very real appreciation by some managers, and other sections of the workforce, of the disadvantages that can accrue from having better educated and trained employees and co-workers. Training may be seen as a threat of erosion of managerial power relationships, traditional pay relativities and status divides.

5.7 The company's perspective on investment in training

Many companies see training not as an investment, but as a cost (Coopers and Lybrand Associates, 1985; Hyman, 1992). However, to the extent that training is treated as an investment, research within companies indicates that it is but one of a range of possible solutions to skill shortages – others include recruitment, changes in payment systems, or investing in technology to downgrade skill requirements (Pettigrew et al., 1989, pp. 18–20). It would seem logical to assume that attempts are made, however informally, to weigh the relative costs and advantages of each option.

One of the factors that is likely to complicate this process is the difficulty posed by the 'poaching' of skilled labour. The essence of the problem is easily stated. If a shot of training is transferable rather than specific, then the skills acquired are capable of being used by other employers in addition to the one who pays for the training. In other words there is an externality problem (. . .). In order to recoup his costs, at some point the employer will have to pay the worker less than what other employers who have not borne the initial cost can afford to pay. Companies may rationally choose not to train and to rely on poaching skilled labour from those firms that do. The problem comes in the fact that the more companies that adopt this stance, the fewer remain to undertake training, and the greater the risk they bear of losing those they have trained. Thus, the aggregated result of individually rational self-interested actions may be a self-defeating collective under-supply of training (Streeck, 1989).

Both practitioner and academic opinion is sharply divided as to the importance of the problem that poaching poses. Many employers believe it is a major obstacle. The CBI's Vocational Education and Training Task Force cited poaching of skilled labour as one of the 'four basic weaknesses that will need to be tackled if the skills gap is to be bridged successfully' (1989, p. 33), and a case study from the steel industry (Morris *et al.*, 1991) reveals the degree to which British Steel regarded investment in multi-skilled craft workers as a risk because of the danger of poaching. By contrast, the authors of *A Challenge to Complacency* were 'not convinced that poaching is a major deterrent to the total volume of training undertaken – even if it is for some individual (usually small) firms' (Coopers and Lybrand Associates, 1985, p. 11).

Even if the potential difficulties posed by externalities are left to one side, the process of evaluating the return on a company's investment in training remains problematic. The fundamental difficulty is the weakness of the information on both the costs and benefits of training (Pettigrew *et al.*, 1989; Coopers and Lybrand Associates, 1985). As *Training in Britain* (TA, 1989) indicated, only 19% of training establishments attempted to assess the benefits arising from training, and just 3% tried to measure cost against benefit. If the return on training is relatively uncertain or difficult to forecast, the case for spending on training may be harder to sustain. Indeed, the inability to calculate returns on investment in training might help breed a culture which reinforces the tendency to think of training not as an investment, but rather as a cost (Mayhew, 1991).

Firms may be further encouraged in this view by financial institutions. What is known about the basis upon which many UK takeover bids are made contrasts sharply with the rhetoric about the importance to competitive advantage of investment in training and development. A study by London Business School and Egon Zehnder International (LBS/EZI, 1987) suggested that in only 37% of takeovers had any attempt been made by bidders to evaluate or audit the human resources of the bid target. Even in those cases where efforts were made, they appeared chiefly to be limited to obtaining very basic information about the pensions and salaries of the target's senior managerial employees. Nor has training figured to any great extent in the factors that City analysts choose to use in assessing the future prospects of companies (Coopers and Lybrand Associates, 1985, pp. 13–14).

5.8 The volatility of the UK economy

A further factor which affects the ability of both individuals and their employers to be assured of a reasonable payback on investment in human capital is the volatility of the UK economy. CBI analysis of OECD figures (CBI, 1991, pp. 26–9) shows that the UK has 'experienced a more volatile economic cycle than Germany and Japan, particularly in the 1970s and 1980s' (CBI, 1991, p. 26). The volatility of the UK economy renders problematic investment in anything that has long lead-times and a relatively slow pay back, like training. *A Challenge to Complacency* tends to confirm this problem. It noted that 'overall, uncertainty was the reason most commonly cited by the companies we interviewed for not doing more training' (Coopers and Lybrand Associates, 1985, p. 10). This uncertainty, and the misgivings it promotes about sustained investment in training, may be well placed. The recessions of the early 1980s and 1990s have witnessed the scrapping of significant investments, in terms of both physical capital (plant and equipment) and human capital through the redundancy of skilled workers.

To summarise, major difficulties confront a market-based approach to training in the UK. The failure of reward systems to link skill adequately with pay, the lack of ILMs and job structures that offer opportunity for advancement, the insecurity of employment in many sectors, the weak connection between qualifications and recruitment, the difficulties posed by the role of skills as positional goods and the threat effect of a more meritocratic approach to hiring and promotion, the uncertainty of the payoff from training *vis-à-vis* other forms of investment, the volatility of the UK economy, and the product market strategies being pursued by firms in many sectors, all pose questions for the viability of a system geared solely to responding to market forces.

6 The primacy of the employer in the new system

The final assumption underpinning the new training system is that the views of employers should be afforded primacy within it. The institutional structure that the government has erected to facilitate and oversee the new training market thus hinges upon the actions and abilities of employers. The creation of TECs, Industry Lead Bodies, NCVQ, and the National Training Task Force all reflect beliefs that managers, particularly private sector managers, have access to a set of techniques, knowledge and skills that are not available to other sections of the population, and that possession of these attributes make them uniquely qualified to 'solve' a series of deep-seated structural problems in the country's education and training system.

6.1 The prospects for an employer-led system

After a period in the 1980s when employers did increase their spending and give training to more of their employees, it might seem churlish to doubt this strategy, but there are reasons for concern. There is some suggestion that much of the increased activity involved the relatively narrow fields of developing personal skills and IT competencies (Gallie and White, 1993). More generally the evidence that is available tends to cast doubt on the idea that British management, taken as a whole, constitutes an elite capable on its own of fundamental transformation of VET provision. The general training record of UK private sector companies is, by European standards, relatively poor. Indeed, British managers' perceptions of the value of training are part of the problem which they are now being expected to single-handedly solve.

We do not suggest that all British employers are incompetent or are poor trainers. There are within the UK economy companies, such as ICI and British Steel, which are world leaders in their field, and whose training matches best practice abroad. The problem comes in the fact that the variation in performance between the best and the worst UK manufacturing employers is extremely wide and too few UK companies are world-class players (CBI, 1991).

We would also argue that this situation is caused by a series of deeply rooted and interrelated forces within the UK's industrial structure – forces which constrain the choices open to management.

6.2 The weakness of personnel management

One set of structural factors comes in the shape of the distinctive historical legacy of the UK's industrial relations system and the attitudes it has spawned towards the management of the employment relationship. Many companies lack the types of sophisticated personnel management systems necessary to make effective training and utilisation of workers' abilities a reality. Moreover, a significant proportion of firms offer their employees extremely limited opportunity for progression. This situation reflects a continuing belief on the part of many managements that their staff are 'incapable of thought' (James, 1991, p. 4; see also Plowman 1990).

The reasons for this belief are various. An important one is the legacy of low-trust industrial relations, where passive consent rather than active commitment was the norm, and where knowledge and skill were the contested terrain over which managers and workers (particularly craft workers) fought for control of the work process. The overall effect has been to encourage a reliance by many UK firms on a narrow managerial elite leading a mass of ill-trained workers. It is noticeable that those companies that have invested heavily in training (BS, Rover Group, Norsk Hydro) have normally done so as simply one part of a broader shift to very different models of industrial relations and personnel management, which stress commitment, trust, good communication between management and employees, and the breakdown of status divides (Fox, 1988; Muller, 1991; Williams et al., 1990).

Unfortunately, as Whipp (1992) indicates, the creation and implementation of human resource management (HRM) policies even within large, relatively sophisticated British companies has often proved halting. Furthermore, there is some evidence which suggests that sophisticated personnel management policies of the type espoused by HRM textbooks may only be appropriate to those product market strategies and production technologies and processes that demand workers with skills that are difficult to replace, and 'to workers who have jobs that are or could be redesigned to engender commitment, individual initiative' (Lloyd and Rawlinson, 1992, p. 189). As the NIESR studies suggested, there are sectors of the British economy where such conditions may not pertain. Lloyd and Rawlinson (1992), for example, demonstrate the irrelevance of HRM techniques to firms in the clothing industry, who see low-cost labour, piecework wage systems, and de-skilling as more accessible routes to competitive advantage. Furthermore, insofar as some government policies, such as the abolition of wages councils, encourage reliance on low wages as a source of competitive advantage, they arguably reduce the pressure on companies to contemplate more radical redesign of jobs and production systems that might enhance opportunities for skill acquisition and utilisation.

It might be argued that this situation is being improved by the 'demonstration effect' of inward investors. However, the evidence for a positive effect on training and skill usage is not encouraging. For example, Peck and Stone's (1991) study of 105 inward investors in north-east England indicated that they employed a higher proportion of unskilled and semi-skilled operatives than native companies, and that over half of the foreign-owned companies relied upon poaching to meet their skill needs. Furthermore Knell's (1992) examination of two large inward investors in West Yorkshire concluded that 'the existing stock of skills in a locality exerts a powerful influence on the ongoing nature of indigenous and inward investment, which as a consequence adapts to, rather than attempts to transform, inherited weaknesses in the local labour force' (1992, p. 18).

Overall, the evidence for a widespread and thoroughgoing transformation of British personnel management and IR along the lines of the sophisticated HRM model is limited (Edwards et al., 1992; Sisson, 1992). Some organisations have attempted to introduce isolated aspects of human resource management (HRM), with greater or lesser degrees of effectiveness, but a coherent, consistent approach has often been lacking (Edwards et al., 1992; Storey, 1992). This incoherence may in turn reflect the low priority that has been afforded to IR and human resource issues in strategic decision making within many British businesses. Sir John Cassels' comment, made apropos of the 'demographic timebomb' is apposite, 'the unfortunate truth is that . . . in personnel matters (because labour is so cheap?), most employers live hand-to-mouth and the idea of taking a strategic view and of doing so at board level is quite alien' (Cassels, 1989, p. 6).

6.3 Short-termism in the British economy

Many commentators have suggested that the failure of senior British managers to deal with personnel issues strategically, and their weak performance in making long-term investments in research and development and training, has stemmed in part from the short-term pressures generated by the structure of UK finance capital and the City's preoccupation with the maximisation of short-term profit. Others, such as Marsh (1990) and the CBI Task Force on relations between the City and industry (CBI, 1987) have sought to refute these allegations.

Perhaps the point to be emphasised is that even those who dismiss arguments about structural short-termism within capital markets in the UK are often inclined to criticise the tendency for the management systems of large UK organisations to produce an internal dynamic that encourages a short-term perspective on decision-making (Marsh, 1990). Whatever the reality of external pressures on companies to take a short-term view, many corporate headquarters have developed internal financial control mechanisms that 'peer at the business through numbers' (Goold and Campbell, 1986). These mechanisms create internal markets within companies, whereby subsidiaries focus on short-term performance as a means of winning investment from the corporate HQ, which acts as a banker. Companies managed on this basis are unlikely to be committed to developing sophisticated human resource strategies, or to make substantial long-term investments in training and developing their workforce.

In more general terms, the distinctive dominance of the finance and accounting function within British management (Armstrong, 1987) has encouraged a situation where management accountancy provides the 'core organisational technology of modern management'. The result has been to concentrate a disproportionate degree of managerial attention on labour cost containment, rather than on increasing the 'performance capacity of labour' (Hyman, 1992, p. 17). In some instances, concentration on labour costs has led to the curtailment of training expenditure, which by accounting convention figures as a cost that is incurred, not as an investment that will produce productivity benefits (CBI, 1985).

The pressures created by financial control systems can be reinforced by their linkage to the reward structure. To the extent that reward systems such as performance-related pay are geared to the achievement of short-term goals, particularly short-term profit maximisation, they may discourage long-term thinking and encourage managers to avoid or defer investment that will only pay back in the long-term, such as training and R&D (Murlis, 1990; Marsh, 1990). By contrast with British and American practice, Japanese companies reward their executives very differently, using systems that place considerable emphasis upon long-term performance within the organisation (Marsh, 1990).

One reason underlying the rise in financial control systems and portfolio planning techniques has been the growth of conglomerates and diversified companies within the UK economy since the Second World War. By 1980, no less than 67% of the top 200 manufacturing and services businesses in the UK could be regarded as being diversified, while only 9% remained in the single business category. The results have been the use of internal control structures that make predominant use of financial criteria of performance, and which place heavy reliance on portfolio management techniques. Portfolio management means that the centre has little long-term commitment to any particular business. If it starts to fail, the preferred option may be to sell it and use the money raised to buy something more profitable. This situation has obvious implications for long-term planning and investment in human resources (Purcell, 1989).

It is probably no accident that those firms normally held up as examples of good training practice in Britain in the 1980s, e.g. British Steel, ICI, ICL and motor vehicle builders such as Ford, have tended to be single business or related business firms, rather than diversified conglomerates.

6.4 British employers' commitment to the UK economy

Some of the problems of limited demand for skills may be rooted in other developments within the industrial structure of the UK. Large companies dominate output (in 1983 those employing 500 plus represented about 75% of manufacturing value added), and have generally dominated formalised training provision. However, there is a problem in assuming that large UK companies are quite what they seem to be any more. The growth of global competition and the removal of exchange control regulations meant that the 1980s witnessed a very significant shift overseas. Many companies that we tend to think of as 'British' no longer employ the majority of their workforce in this country.

To take just one example, Pilkingtons is usually seen as a major British glass manufacturer, but by 1990 only about 21.6% of the company's workforce was actually employed in the UK, and the company has recently announced the decision to transfer the corporate HQ for its flat glass making businesses to Brussels. Policy makers tend to continue to refer to many of the household names of the British economy as 'big British companies', when in fact they have become multinational enterprises within which the British component of the company's operations, whether measured in terms of employment, or sales, or turnover, has become a dwindling proportion of the whole. For instance, evidence suggests that no more than 40% of the turnover of the top 20 UK-owned engineering companies is now generated within the UK (Williams et al., 1990).

Since the end of exchange control regulations many British-owned companies have been directing an increasing proportion of their investments overseas. In 1987, for example, UK firms spent $31.7 billion on acquisitions in the USA alone (Rodgers and Tran, 1988). Between 1980 and 1988 outward investment by UK companies was in total $133.2 billion. Of course an obvious response is that it is all a matter of swings and roundabouts

– the arrival of foreign-owned firms in the UK balances the picture. Against this it is important to note that, over the same period, inward investment into the UK by foreign-owned firms did not balance this outflow, running at slightly less than half ($64.7 billion) the outward figure (CBI, 1991, p. 34). In 1990 inward investment did exceed outward investment, but this year is the exception rather than the rule.

A survey of the annual report of *The Times* Top 100 Companies for the year 1989/90 indicates the extent of these developments. Annual reports were trawled for data on the distribution of employment between UK and overseas operations. In some cases the details were not available. In others, figures for the UK were aggregated with those for Europe. Moreover, of the 100, several are foreign-owned subsidiaries of overseas multinationals, such as IBM and Esso. Nevertheless, from the data available it was apparent that of the British-owned firms, at least seventeen now employ the majority of their workforce outside the UK. These were, BP (73.9% of employees overseas), Shell Transport and Trading, ICI, BAT (93% overseas), Unilever, Glaxo (65.5% overseas), GKN (56.8% overseas), Redland (69% overseas), Cable and Wireless (75.1% outside Europe), BTR, RTZ (71.2% overseas), Lonrho (89.6% overseas), Beecham Group (68.5% overseas), Cadbury Schweppes (55.1% overseas), Pilkingtons, BOC, and Tate & Lyle.

Other large companies show signs of moving in this direction. These include GEC (with more than a quarter of its workforce overseas), Trust Houses Forte (with 20% overseas), Reed International (41% overseas), Coats Viyella (46.3% overseas), Dixon Group (26.4% overseas), Racal (44.7% outside Europe), Allied Lyons (30% of full-time employees outside the UK), P & O (42.6% outside the UK), and Courtaulds (44% overseas).

While growing internationalisation is a common phenomenon among the developed countries, the British economy is distinctive. Whereas 40% of the total employment of British-owned companies was located abroad, the proportion for American and German-owned companies was 25%, and only 20% for French and Japanese-owned companies (Marginson, 1992). These structural features of ownership, investment and employment have implications for UK training policy. At least some major firms now find themselves with domestic operations that are a dwindling and increasingly marginal proportion of the company's overall activities, and investment in them and the people they employ may no longer be regarded as crucial to the long-term well-being of the firm.

At the very least, the increasing globalisation of economic activity and the UK's tendency to be in the vanguard of overseas investment, raise questions for policies that implicitly link the success of individual major companies to the overall health of the UK economy and its skills supply system, and which explicitly see major UK firms as the engine that drives changes in that skill system. Companies have a choice about where they locate production and where they find skills. If skill supply and a well-educated and trained workforce is a problem in the UK, why not shift that section of production that demands those skills overseas?

6.5 Employer leadership and the low skills equilibrium

Outlined above has been a series of structural factors that, it can be argued, weaken the ability and willingness of many British employers to make major adjustments to their current skill requirements. Perhaps most importantly of all, as Finegold and Soskice (1988) have argued, much of the British economy is arguably trapped in a 'low-skills equilibrium'. Many UK employers find themselves caught in a vicious circle of self-reinforcing factors that perpetuate limited demand for training and skills. Amongst these factors is the possibility that, in the past, firms were forced into a low-skill, low-quality strategy because of their inability to acquire skilled workers. The resort by some sectors of the British economy to product market strategies based on a concentration on simple, standardised products and services and upon low-cost, low-skill competition (see Saunders, 1978; Carter, 1981; Reich, 1983; New and Myers, 1986; Sharp *et al.*, 1987; Steedman and Wagner, 1987; Greenhalgh, 1988; Fonda, 1989; Steedman and Wagner, 1989; Jarvis and Prais, 1989; Mason *et al.*, 1996), creates a weak demand for skill. This weak demand for skill within the economy reduces the incentives to training, which in turn produces a poorly skilled workforce. Lack of skill then inhibits moves towards competitive strategies that stress quality as opposed to cost. As evidenced above, the job structures found in many sectors of the economy reflect the broad effects of this problem.

The possible existence of a low skills equilibrium, within at least some parts of the UK economy, in the context of a national training system where employers are the sole determinants of what constitutes an adequate level of training, could be a system that meets the short-term perceived private demands of companies, while failing to supply sufficient training to satisfy the social and strategic needs of the national economy.

7 Conclusions

7.1 The concentration on supply at the expense of demand

Many of the assumptions that have formed the basis of policy have been founded on the underlying prior belief that it is weakness in the supply of skills, rather than weakness in demand, that is the root of Britain's difficulties. During the 1980s vocational education and training (VET) policy was dominated by attempts to adjust the institutional mechanisms of VET supply, in the belief that if only supply could be boosted, demand would take care of itself. History suggests that the opposite may be true.

The example of YTS is a useful one. Moves from a one-year to a two-year scheme revealed that simply offering employers a new supply mechanism through which to upgrade skills failed to produce any fundamental change, because the underlying attitudes towards skill and the demand for it did not change (Chapman and Tooze, 1987). Indeed, British employers may often be providing their workforce with levels of VET which are more or less appropriate to the product market strategies which they are following, and which reflect the levels of service which they currently aim to provide. Case studies conducted in twenty companies as part of the *Training in Britain* exercise, reached the conclusion that 'training decisions are not strongly influenced by the VET infrastructure' (Pettigrew *et al.*, 1989, p. 107).

It follows that attempts to boost the supply of VET without simultaneously tackling those structural characteristics within firms that limit demand for higher levels of education and skill run the risk of creating a situation where the returns from investment in VET will be inadequate – to the individual, to their employer, and to society as a whole. Does this mean that current VET policies are doomed to failure? The answer to this question depends on how one chooses to define the overall thrust of Britain's current education and training strategy. If the aim is to provide a training system that meets, more or less adequately, the current needs of British employers, then success may be possible. If, on the other hand, the policy objectives are more ambitious, and encompass goals such as much greater equality of access to training opportunities, and the provision of levels of training equal to those in other developed economies, levels which could support the general transformation of the British economy towards a high-skill, high-productivity, high-wage equilibrium, then the prospects for success are much less rosy.

7.2 Policy and the internal workings of the firm

Although in the early 1980s the MSC and the Central Policy Review Staff (CPRS) pointed to the problems for training policy created by various rigidities in the deployment of skilled labour within firms, such as demarcation issues, there has been relatively limited interest from policy makers in addressing the internal workings of the firm, in particular the crucial questions of job design and work organisation. This despite the fact that a growing volume of research indicates that the demand for skill and its effective utilisation within the productive process are inextricably bound up with the ways in which work is organised and the employment relationship is managed (see, for example, Lam and Marsden (1992) and Campbell and Warner (1991)). In view of the importance of the ways in which companies deal with skill in the workplace, and the relationship of this with business strategy, Hendry (1990) concludes that, 'it makes more sense to try to influence a company's business and technology strategy than its training activity alone' (1990, p. 6).

The difficulty for policy makers has been that while a convincing case can be made to suggest that questions of training and skill supply are inextricably linked with other issues such as work organisation, job design, product market strategies, employee participation and involvement, and reward systems, these issues have been defined, by the parameters within which training policy has normally been discussed, as falling within the confines of managerial prerogative. For the state, or other outside parties, to intervene in these crucial areas has generally been regarded as fruitless or as anathema. Where interventions have occurred, they have done so either as part of government's attempts to promote, in the face of threatened EC legislation, a distinctive, British voluntarist approach to employee participation, or, in the case of reward structures, as elements within policies designed to weaken trade unions and collectivism.

These examples aside, intervention has been deemed to represent an industrial policy of the sort that the government has refused to countenance. While many other developed countries, such as Germany and Japan, have favoured the use of broad industrial policies that establish a contextual framework within which companies can direct their efforts, the UK in the 1980s firmly rejected such notions. In the place of such corporatist devices, market forces and the 'enterprise' of individual entrepreneurs and company managements have been regarded as sufficient to maximise economic efficiency. The result has been that many of the key variables that determine the demand for skill and its efficient utilisation have remained firmly 'off limits' to any form of outside influence. One of the few admissions that the internal workings of the firm have to be addressed if training policy is to succeed, comes in the Investors in People (IIP) initiative.

The current inability of policy to confront head-on the question of skill utilisation in the workplace, and its relationship with other aspects of the management of work organisation and of the employment relationship, raises questions about the ability of those policies, and the institutions they have spawned, to tackle the underlying problems. For so long as the employing organisation, and the use to which it puts skills, remains more or less a 'black box', it seems improbable that lasting progress towards a fundamental transformation of Britain's skill supply and utilisation can be made.

For a long time economists have stressed the importance of externalities in causing the amount of training and consequently the supply of skills to be less than is socially optimal. This chapter argues that leaving aside such externality problems, employers as a whole exhibit a low demand for skilled labour. This may well represent a rational short-term strategy, but for many firms carries substantial longer-term dangers. Meanwhile for the economy as a whole this strategy imposes a rather different type of externality. We have described a 'systems flaw', to which there is no easy policy response; but recognition that it exists would be an important first step.

References

Armstrong, P. (1987), 'The Rise of Accounting Controls in British Capitalist Enterprises', *Accounting Organizations and Society* 12(5), 415–36.

Ashton, D., M. Maguire and M. Spilsbury (1987), 'Labour Market Segmentation and the Structure of the Youth Labour Market', in P. Brown and D. Ashton (eds), *Education, Unemployment and Labour Markets*, Lewes: Falmer.

Bennett, R., H. Glennerster and D. Nevison (1992), *Learning Should Pay*, Poole: British Petroleum.

Booth, A. L. (1991), 'Job-Related Formal Training: Who Receives it and What is it Worth?', *Oxford Bulletin of Economics and Statistics* 53(3), 281–94.

Bosworth, D., C. Jacobs and J. Lewis (1990), *New Technologies, Shared Facilities and the Innovatory Firm*, Aldershot: Avebury/Gower.

Campbell, A. and M. Warner (1991), 'Training Strategies and Microelectronics in the Engineering Industries in the UK and Germany', in P. Ryan (ed.), *International Comparisons of Vocational Education and Training for Intermediate Skills*, London: Falmer.

Campbell, M. and M. Daly (1992), 'Self-employment into the 1990s', *Employment Gazette*, June.

Carter, C. (ed.) (1981), *Industrial Policy and Innovation*, London: Heinemann.

Cassels, J. (1989), 'Facing the Demographic Challenge', *Personnel Management* November, 6.

—— (1990), *Britain's Real Skill Shortage and What to Do about it*, London: Policy Studies Institute.

CBI (1985), *Change to Succeed – The Nationwide Findings*, London: Confederation of British Industry.

—— (1987), *Investing for Britain's Future: Report of the City/Industry Task Force*, London: Confederation of British Industry.

—— (1989), *Towards a Skills Revolution*, London: Confederation of British Industry.

—— (1991), *Competing with the World's Best – The Report of the CBI Manufacturing Advisory Group*, London: Confederation of British Industry.

Centre for Economic Performance (1991), 'Corporate Governance Meeting, June 1991', Working Paper No. 151, London School of Economics, CEP, mimeo.

Chapman, P. G. and M. J. Tooze (1987), *The Youth Training Scheme in the United Kingdom*, Aldershot: Avebury.

Cockburn, C. (1987), *Two-Track Training*, Basingstoke: Macmillan.

Collinson, D. (1988), *Barriers to Fair Selection: A Multi-sector Study of Recruitment Practices*, London: HMSO.

Coopers and Lybrand Associates (1985), *A Challenge to Complacency: Changing Attitudes to Training*, Sheffield: Manpower Services Commission/National Economic Development Office.

Daly, A. (1986), 'Education and Productivity: A Comparison of Great Britain and the United States', *British Journal of Industrial Relations* 24(2), 251-67.

Daly, M. and A. McCann (1992), 'How Many Small Firms?', *Employment Gazette* February, 47–51.

Daly, M., M. Campbell, G. Robson and C. Gallagher (1992), 'Job Creation 1987–89: Preliminary Analysis by Sector', *Employment Gazette* August, 387–92.

Dex, S. (1988), 'Gender and the Labour Market', in D. Gallie (ed.), *Employment in Britain*, Oxford: Blackwell, pp. 281–309.

ED (Employment Department) (1988), 'Employment for the 1990s', Cmnd 540, London: HMSO.

—— (1991), 'Into Work', *Skills and Enterprise Briefing*, Issue 15/91 October, Sheffield: ED.

—— (1992), *Labour Market and Skills Trends 1993/94*, Sheffield: ED.

Edwards, P., M. Hall, R. Hyman, P. Marginson, K. Sisson, J. Waddington and D. Winchester (1992), 'Great Britain: Still Muddling Through?', in A. Ferner and R. Hyman (eds), *Industrial Relations in the New Europe*, Oxford: Blackwell.

Emerson, M. (1988), 'Regulation or de-regulation of the labour market?', *European Economic Review* 32, 775–817.

Finegold, D. (1992), 'The Implications of "Training in Britain" for the Analysis of Britain's Skill Problem: A Comment on Paul Ryan's "How Much Do Employers Spend on Training"', *Human Resource Management Journal* 2(1), 110–15.

Finegold, D. and D. Soskice (1988), 'The Failure of Training in Britain: Analysis and Prescription', *Oxford Review of Economic Policy* 4(3), 21–53.

Fonda, N. (1989), 'In Search of a Training Strategy', *Personnel Management* April, 6–7.

Fox, J. (1988), 'Norsk Hydro's New Approach Takes Root', *Personnel Management* January.

Fuller, A. and M. Saunders (1990), 'The Paradox in Open Learning at Work', University of Lancaster, Institute for Post-Compulsory Education, mimeo.

Gallie, D. and M. White (1993), *Employee Commitment and the Skills Revolution*, London: Policy Studies Institute.

Goold, M. and A. Campbell (1986), *Strategies and Styles: The Role of the Centre in managing Diversified Corporations*, Oxford: Blackwell.

Green, F. (1991), 'Sex Discrimination in Job-related Training', *British Journal of Industrial Relations* 29(2), 295–304.

Greenhalgh, C. (1988), *Employment and Structural Change: Trends and Policy Options*, Oxford University, mimeo.

Hendry, C. (1990), 'Corporate Strategy and Training', paper presented to the National Economic Development Office 'Training Policy Seminar', Coventry, University of Warwick, Centre for Corporate Strategy and Change.

Hirsch, F. (1977), *The Social Limits to Growth*, London: Routledge & Kegan Paul.

Hyman, J. (1992), *Training at Work: a Critical Analysis of Policy and Practice*, London: Routledge.

IFF (Industrial Facts and Forecasting) (1992), *Small Firms' Skill Needs and Training Survey*, London, IFF.

IoD (Institute of Directors) (1991), *Performance and Potential – Education and Training for a Market Economy*, London: IoD.

James, G. (1991), *Quality of Working Life and Total Quality Management*, Work Research Unit Occasional Paper No. 50, London: ACAS, WRU.

Jarvis, V. and S. Prais (1989), 'Two Nations of Shopkeepers: Training for Retailing in Britain and France', *National Institute Economic Review* 128, 58–74.

Jenkins, R. and B. Troyna (1983). 'Educational Myths, Labour Market Realities', in B. Troyna and D. I. Smith (eds), *Racism, School and the Youth Labour Market*, Leicester: National Youth Bureau.

Keep, E. (1990), 'Training for the Low-paid', in A. Bowen and K. Mayhew (eds), *Improving Incentives for the Low-Paid*, London: Macmillan/NEDO.

—— (1991), 'The Grass Looked Greener – Some Thoughts on the Influence of Comparative Vocational Training Research on the UK Policy Debate', in P. Ryan (ed.), *International Comparisons of Vocational Education and Training for Intermediate Skills*, London: Falmer, pp. 23–46.

King, J. (1990), *Labour Economics*, London: Macmillan.

Knell, J. (1992), 'TNCs and the Dynamics of Human Capital Formation: Evidence from West Yorkshire', Leeds University, School of Business and Economic Studies, mimeo.

Lam, A. and D. Marsden (1992), 'Shortages of Qualified Labour in Britain: A Problem of Training or of Skill Utilisation?', paper presented to CEDEFOP conference on vocational training, Berlin.

Layard, R., K. Mayhew and G. Owen (1992), *The Training Reform Act of 1994*, Swindon: ESRC and the Centre for Economic Performance.

LBS/EZI (1987), *Acquisitions, The Human Factor*, London: London Business School.

Lee, D., D. Marsden, P. Rickman and J. Duncombe (1990), *Scheming For Youth. A Study of YTS in the Enterprise Culture*, Buckingham: Open University Press.

Lillard, L. A. and H. W. Tan (1992), 'Private Sector Training: Who Gets it and What Are its Effects?', in R. G. Ehrenberg (ed.), *Research in Labor Economics*, Greenwich, CT: JAI Press, pp. 1–62.

Lloyd, C. and M. Rawlinson (1992), 'New Technology and Human Resource Management', in P. Blyton and P. Turnbull (eds), *Reassessing Human Resource Management*, London: Sage, pp. 185–99.

Mangham, I. L. and M. S. Silvers (1986), *Management Training: Context and Practice*, University of Bath, School of Management, ESRC/DTI report.

Marginson, P. (1992), 'Multinational Britain: Employment and Work in an Internationalised Economy', paper for the Warwick VET Forum Conference 'Multinational Companies and Human Resources: a Moveable Feast?', Warwick University, 22–24 June 1992.

Marsh, P. (1990), *Short-termism on Trial*, London: Institutional Fund Managers Association.

Mason, G., B. van Ark and K. Wagner (1996) 'Workforce Skills, Product Quality and Economic Performance', in A. L. Booth and D. J. Snower (eds) *Acquiring Skills: Market Failures, their Symptoms and Policy Responses*, Cambridge: Cambridge University Press.

Mayhew, K. (1991), 'Training – The Problem for Employers', *Employment Institute Economic Report* 5(10), March/April.

McNabb, R. and P. Ryan (1990), 'Segmented Labour Markets', in D. Sapsford and Z. Tzannatos (eds), *Current Issues in Labour Economics*, Basingstoke: Macmillan.

Millward, N. and M. Stevens (1986), *British Workplace Industrial Relations, 1980–84*, Aldershot: Gower.

Milton, R. (1986), 'Double, Double, Toil and Trouble: YTS in the Melting Pot', *Personnel Management* April. 26–31.

Morris, J., N. Bacon, P. Blyton and H. W. Franz (1991), 'Beyond Survival: The Influence of New Forms of Work Organisation in the UK and German Steel Industries', paper prepared for Employment Research Unit conference on 'The Future of Employment Relations: International Comparisons in an Age of Uncertainty', Cardiff.

MSC (1981), *A New Training Initiative: An Agenda for Action*, London: Manpower Services Commission.

—— (1983a), *Towards an Adult Training Strategy – A Discussion Paper*, Sheffield: Manpower Services Commission.

—— (1983b), *Adult Training Strategy: Proposals for Action*, London: Manpower Services Commission, mimeo.

Muller, F. (1991), 'A New Engine of Change in Employee Relations', *Personnel Management* July, 30–3.

Murlis, H. (1990), 'A Long-term View of Reward Systems', *Personnel Management* August, 10.

NEDO/MSC/IMS (National Economic Development Office/Manpower Services Commission/Institute of Manpower Studies) (1984), *Competence and Competition*, London: National Economic Development Office.

New, C. C. and A. Myers (1986), *Managing Manufacturing Operations in the UK 1975–1985*, London: British Institute of Management.

Nicholson, B. (1991), Response given at LSE Centre for Economic Performance/Anglo-German Foundation Seminar on the UK and German training systems, 8 October 1991.

Oliver, J. and J. Turton (1982), 'Is There a Shortage of Skilled Labour?', *British Journal of Industrial Relations* 20(2), 195–217.

Payne, J. (1990), *Women, Training and the Skills Shortage. The Case for Public Investment*, London: Policy Studies Institute.

—— (1992), 'Motivating Training', paper presented to the CEP project on VET, January, mimeo.

Peck, F. and J. Stone (1991), *New Inward Investment in the Northern Region Labour Market*, Newcastle Economic Research Unit, Newcastle upon Tyne Polytechnic.

People, Jobs and Opportunity (1992), Cm 1810, London: HMSO.

Pettigrew, A., C. Hendry and P. Sparrow (1989), *Training in Britain: Employers' Perspectives on Human Resources*, London: HMSO.

Plowman, B. (1990), 'Management Behaviour', *TQM Magazine* 2(4), 217–19.

Pratten, C. (1990), 'The Limits to Training', *Financial Times*, 3 April.

Purcell, J. (1989), 'The impact of corporate strategy on human resource management', in J. Storey (ed.), *New Perspectives on Human Resource Management*, London: Routledge, pp. 67–91.

Purcell, K. (1988), 'Gender and the Experience of Employment', in D. Gallie (ed.), *Employment in Britain*, Oxford: Blackwell, pp. 157–86.

Reich, R. (1983), *The Next American Frontier*, Harmondsworth: Penguin.

Rigg, M. (1989), *The Impact of Vocational Education and Training on Individual Adults*, London: HMSO.

Rigg, M., I. Christie and M. White (1989), *Advanced Polymers and Composites: Creating the Key Skills*, Sheffield: Training Agency.

Rodgers, P. and M. Tran (1988), 'US Feathers Ruffled at British Invasion', *Guardian*, 26 April.

Saunders, C. T. (1978), 'Engineering in Britain, West Germany and France: Some Statistical Comparisons of Structure and Competitiveness', Sussex European Papers, No. 3, Falmer: University of Sussex.

Shackleton, J. R. (1992), *Training Too Much?*, London: Institute of Economic Affairs.

Sharp, M., M. Shepherd and D. Marsden (1987), *Managing Change in British Industry*, Geneva: International Labour Office.

Sisson, K. (1992), 'Change and Continuity in UK Industrial Relations: "Strategic Choice" or "Muddling Through"?', paper for the meeting of the International IR/HR Project, Warwick University, Industrial Relations Research Unit, mimeo.

Steedman, H. and K. Wagner (1987), 'A Second Look at Productivity, Machinery and Skills in Britain and Germany', *National Institute Economic Review* November, 84–95.

—— (1989), 'Productivity, Machinery and Skills: Clothing Manufacture in Britain and Germany', *National Institute Economic Review* 128, 40–57.

Storey, D.J. (1982), *Entrepreneurship and the New Firm*, London: Croom Helm.

Storey, D.J. and A. Strange (1992), *Entrepreneurship in Cleveland 1979–1989: A Study of the Effects of the Enterprise Culture*, Employment Department Research Series No. 3, Sheffield: Employment Department.

Storey, J. (1992), *Developments in the Management of Human Resources: An Analytical Review*, Oxford: Blackwell.

Streeck, W. (1989), 'Skills and the Limits of Neo-Liberalism: The Enterprise of the Future as a Place of Learning', *Work, Employment and Society* 3(1), 89–104.

TA (1989), *Training in Britain: Employers' Activities*, Sheffield: Training Agency.

Whipp. R. (1992), 'Human Resource Management, Competition and Strategy: Some Productive Tensions', in P. Blyton and P. Turnbull (eds), *Reassessing Human Resource Management*, London: Sage, pp. 33–55.

Williams, K., J. Williams and C. Haslam (1990), 'The Hollowing Out of British Manufacturing and its Implications for Policy', *Economy and Society* 19(4), November, 456–90.

Wood, S. (1988), 'Personnel Management and Recruitment', in P. Windolf and S. Wood (eds), *Recruitment and Selection in the Labour Market*, Cambridge: Gower.

Worswick, G. D. N. (ed.) (1985), *Education and Economic Performance*, London: Gower.

Chapter 7

Expanding employment

Council of Churches for Britain and Ireland

The challenge to society, as the nature of work changes, is to find good work for everyone to do in the economy of the future. In responding to that challenge the first, and most obvious, need is to expand employment (or self-employment), so that we are not constrained by a scarcity of jobs. (. . . W)e shall be arguing that this can be achieved, provided that it is given a high enough priority in the choices of individuals, and also most importantly in the conduct of public policy. (. . . W)e would [also] argue that the issues involved are not just technical ones. The questions of fact about how the economy functions and the questions of value about how its functioning should be improved are very closely related to one another and cannot be discussed satisfactorily if they are kept totally separate.

It is important to understand why people are unemployed, their objectives and the constraints they face; equally it is important to understand the aims which motivate employers and how they see their own social obligations. Labour market behaviour expresses social values, which economic policy must either counteract or reinforce. Economic policy is not just a kind of engineering, it must be based on a sympathetic interaction between different groups of human beings, including the policy makers themselves. But it also requires its own variety of expertise. There is no merit in well-meaning people suggesting impractical solutions. But equally, if there is no real commitment to the objectives of expanding employment, practical obstacles will all too easily be seen as insuperable.

We begin by asking what kinds of employment could most readily be expanded. Then we shall ask what kinds of action governments can take to increase employment in the context of a market economy with a large public sector. We need to be clear, or as clear as we can be in the present state of knowledge, about how creating a higher level of employment risks increasing the rate of inflation, and what that implies for the longer-term effectiveness of different kinds of policy action. (. . .)

What kind of employment could expand?

In 1994 the Organisation for Economic Co-operation and Development (OECD) concluded its extensive review of unemployment in advanced industrial countries, called simply *The Jobs Study*. We do not find ourselves in agreement with all its policy recommendations, but it provides an authoritative summary of what might be called the 'conventional wisdom' amongst economists and policy makers, not just in our own countries, but also worldwide in the early 1990s. We begin with two quotations from the summary report called *Facts, Analysis, Strategies* (p. 33).

> The basic answer to unemployment problems lies in creating more jobs. Although it is impossible to predict what these jobs will be, they are likely to share some basic characteristics. New jobs are likely to appear in the service sector, which already accounts for more than half of total employment in most OECD countries. The service sector is producing a higher proportion of new jobs as the demand for new services increases. Some of these are new types of jobs. Others are activities that formerly were performed within manufacturing enterprises, but are sub-contracted.

The 'service' sector of the economy includes all activities which consist of 'doing' rather than 'making', for example private sector activities like catering and banking or mainly public sector activities like health and education. Employment in activities which produce 'goods' rather than 'services', for example manufacturing or agriculture, has declined and is unlikely to increase in the future. This much is uncontroversial. The next quotation is not quite such plain sailing.

> Many new jobs are likely to be low-productivity, low-wage jobs. From one point of view, this is intrinsically undesirable. Yet at the same time there are also calls explicitly to foster the creation of low-productivity jobs, especially in the non-tradeable sector, in order to absorb significant numbers of low-skilled unemployed workers. Policy has to find a balance between these two considerations.

On this question, we would comment first that some (but not all) service jobs which are called 'low productivity' as measured by market valuation may be very worthwhile in terms of human relationships. We would also question whether such jobs need to be as low-waged as they commonly are. (The privatising and contracting out of public services may have reduced costs, but often by reducing the bargaining power of employees who in any case include many who are low paid.) However, the reference to the 'non-tradeable sector', that is to activities which do not compete with imports or try to sell on a world market, must surely be correct.

We would wish to see employment expanded in all sorts of directions if that were possible, but given the growth of competition with developing countries and the introduction of new technologies, we are more likely to see net job reductions in manufacturing, transport or 'high-tech' services. Our particular concern, given the threat of unemployment, is to see a very substantial increase of employment which does not require an initial level of education and training beyond the reach of most of the existing labour force. Many such jobs will fall within the definition of the service sector, but others will be elsewhere in the economy for example in construction and the maintenance of existing buildings and works.

The record of job creation in Britain in recent decades is not good compared with other advanced industrial economies. In Britain the decline in employment in manufacturing has been particularly sharp: from 1970 to 1990 the number of manufacturing jobs halved (see Figure 7.1). It has been a feature of relatively successful industries like chemicals, as well as others like motor vehicles, where, until quite recently, output was also falling sharply. By contrast employment in services has been rising. Between 1970 and 1990 there was a substantial increase in employment of women in that sector, while employment of men also held up well. However,

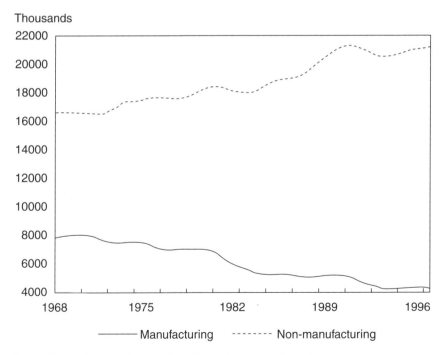

Figure 7.1 Employment in manufacturing and non-manufacturing

comparing the growth of service sector employment in Britain with other countries over the same period, suggests that growth could well have been more rapid. In America, employment growth in services through the 1970s was twice as fast as in Britain. In banking, for example, new technology may actually have increased rather than decreased employment in America, as the range of services on offer has been widened. In health services the rise in employment in America has been truly spectacular, whilst in Britain it has been held back severely by the lack of funds for the NHS.

It is unlikely that the new jobs which can be created will be in the same sectors as continuing job losses occur. There is a natural and understandable reluctance to move from one industry, which has been traditional in a family or a community, to work of a quite different kind. We have already mentioned the view expressed to us in South Yorkshire, that the only 'real' jobs are jobs in coal or steel. This is not an attitude that we can encourage or condone. There has to be mobility and the acceptance of change. Old forms of employment need to be run down, but at a pace which takes account of the human as well as the economic costs. New forms of employment need to be created, jobs of which in due course we can be at least as proud.

At one time those who could not find work in their native place were expected to migrate, either within their native country or abroad. In the nineteenth century there was massive emigration from both Britain and Ireland to America, Australia and elsewhere. Within Britain there was also massive internal migration, typically from rural to urban areas. Migration is still of major significance to the economy of Ireland and to several regions of England, Scotland and Wales. We do not see it, however, as playing an important role in solving the problems of unemployment identified in this enquiry.

Migration is an expensive solution to a regional unemployment problem because it requires the old infrastructures of housing, roads and amenities to be written off and a new infrastructure built. It is usually cheaper, in purely economic terms, to bring the work to the people rather than vice versa (as communication becomes cheaper this argument is becoming stronger). Private firms will not take account of infrastructure costs in making their decisions where to locate production. It is worthwhile therefore preserving, and perhaps increasing, the tax and other incentives to create jobs in areas where they are most needed.

Economics apart, it is also a strong argument against migration that it destroys local communities, separates families and weakens the link between generations. In the process people are pulled up from their social roots, and perhaps their moral and religious roots as well. For some this may be stimulating or even liberating, but for many it is a confusing and isolating experience.

What can governments do to expand employment?

Twenty years ago the OECD published a report called *Towards Full Employment and Price Stability*. This was at a time when unemployment in the OECD area was about 20 million, compared with about 35 million today. It said 'The fundamental aim of policy is to return to reasonable rates of growth and high levels of employment'. It was assumed that governments could reduce unemployment to tolerable levels, if they went to the task with sufficient determination and skill. Now people are not so sure. *The Jobs Study* of 1994 included many policy recommendations to improve employment prospects. It said 'there is no single recipe for full employment, but a menu of measures that can help move OECD economies towards higher employment with good jobs'. This nicely dodges the question of whether full employment can be achieved at all. The OECD as an organisation is not as certain about that as it was twenty years ago. It also says that its recommendations 'do not apply to governments alone. In many cases responsibility for action to improve employment performance lies most directly with employers, trade unionists and individual workers.' That is certainly true, but we need to press the point that governments do have the power to act decisively if they choose.

One limitation to the powers of governments results from the growth of international markets, which has accelerated since the 1970s. The global market for capital is especially active and can frustrate national economic policies if exchange rates or interest rates become unstable. This was true even in the 1970s, as the sterling crisis of 1976 demonstrated, and it has become even more true since the abolition of exchange controls throughout Europe. This certainly restricts the ability of national governments to conduct independent monetary policies or to borrow on a scale that 'the markets' believe to be imprudent.

The international mobility of production itself also has implications for the taxation of profits and investment income. The Republic of Ireland for example has been very successful in attracting firms to locate in that country by offering them a relatively generous taxation regime. To a lesser extent Britain is doing the same. Within Europe as a whole there is pressure to harmonise as many rates of tax as possible so as to avoid a competition to attract investment which would ultimately undermine the tax-raising powers of all the governments concerned. These are real limitations to the powers of national governments, meaning that some economic policies now have to be conducted by governments jointly in agreement with one another. That much is true about internationalisation and globalisation, but it does not mean that governments in Britain or Ireland have no powers to create jobs or encourage job creation.

Most labour is not internationally mobile at all. Labour markets, except for some special highly skilled occupations, are national or even local in extent. Regulation and the structure of taxation falling on labour does not have to be the same in different countries. The systems are in fact very different in Britain and Ireland. If the Irish government decides, for example, to pay a higher rate of social security benefit than the British government, the British unemployed cannot migrate en masse to take advantage of it. There is a real choice here to be made by each government separately, for which each government must take the responsibility. A similar point could be made in relation to the taxation of domestic property, earned income and household expenditure, as well as most forms of public expenditure.

According to the ILO (1997) report already quoted:

> It is not true that globalization is an overwhelming supra-national force that has largely usurped national policy autonomy. There is still considerable policy autonomy and national macroeconomic structural and labour-market policies are still the dominant influence on economic and labour-market outcomes in any country.

It is to national governments therefore that we would look mainly for policy action to expand employment. There is, however, an important role for local government as well as national. On our visits we have learnt much about the concern at local or regional level to devise economic programmes which will stimulate local employment as well as economic activity. It is sad to see their efforts often frustrated by their lack of real authority, or by their inability to generate enough revenue to have a large impact on their own labour markets. On the other hand we appreciate the need for an equitable sharing of resources between regions and local authorities at a national level, which must be the responsibility of national government. We have been led to believe that competition between local authorities for shares in both private investment and public funding can be wasteful and unfair in its results, however good it may be at stimulating local initiatives. We certainly see a vital role for local government in the process of employment expansion, but it must be within the framework of a national strategy to achieve that end at a national level as well.

Cyclical and structural unemployment

A quite different limitation on the powers of government arises from the nature of the market economy itself. If the pressure of demand rises too high then inflation will accelerate. This happens whatever the reasons for the increase in demand – it does not have to be an increase deliberately engineered by an act of policy by a government which wants to see unemployment fall. The nature of this constraint is the subject of continuing debate amongst economists. It depends on how much unemployment is interpreted as cyclical and how much as structural in its origins.

Unemployment rises and falls with the pressure of demand in the economy. This accounts for most of the movement in unemployment from year to year. In Britain, for example, the unemployment rate reached 12½ per cent in the aftermath of the recession at the beginning of the 1980s, but fell to 7 per cent after the boom at the end of the decade and then rose to over 10 per cent again in the next recession. These are very large swings, creating and destroying millions of jobs. Clearly it would be very attractive to keep the pressure of demand high all the time, so that jobs were always at least as easy to find as they were at the peak of the last boom. It is also clear, however, that this cannot be achieved simply by expanding demand. When the economy 'overheats' the result is accelerating inflation, which must sooner or later halt economic growth and push unemployment back up again.

We recognise that this relationship between unemployment and inflation does limit what governments or central banks can do to expand employment by stimulating demand. This does not mean, however, that the management of demand and the conduct of monetary policy are purely technical matters on which the experts should be given a free hand. The variations from year to year in the demand for labour or the swings in unemployment and vacancies which result are themselves a cause of social as well as economic upheaval. Greater stability in the pressure of demand for labour is itself a very worthwhile policy aim.

It has become almost uncontroversial to say that the objective of monetary policy should be low inflation or price stability. This will be the declared aim for the European central bank if monetary union goes ahead as agreed in the Maastricht Treaty. It is, of course, a necessary aim for any central bank to adopt. But, consistent with that aim, policy can and should also seek to limit the variation from year to year in the pressure of demand, especially as that affects the labour market. It seems to us that this very important function of monetary policy has not, in recent years, been given as much emphasis as it deserves.

The main challenge to economic policy, however, is to reduce the level of unemployment which is sustainable and consistent with low inflation or price stability in the longer term. This level is variously described as the 'natural' rate, the 'equilibrium' rate or the NAIRU (non-accelerating-inflation rate of unemployment). Alternatively it can be called structural unemployment, as opposed to the component of unemployment which is merely cyclical. The distinction is very helpful in theory, although the figures corresponding to it are always uncertain and controversial. It may be helpful again to quote the OECD *Jobs Study* report (p. 32): 'an often discussed aspect of the unemployment problem is how much is cyclical and how much is structural . . . In practice, however, there are many definitions of structural unemployment, and there is no unambiguous way of providing a decomposition, especially as there seems to be strong interaction between the two. Factors that increase structural unemployment will often exacerbate cyclical unemployment; while cyclical unemployment, if it persists, may well lead to an increase in structural unemployment.' In other words, no one knows for certain how much unemployment is due to the ups and downs of the economy from year to year, and how much is due to more lasting causes; and anyway the ups and downs themselves may have lasting effects. This last point certainly reinforces the need to avoid sharp cyclical contractions of demand as a means of repressing inflation. The effect of a recession on unemployment may be long-lasting or even permanent.

The level of structural unemployment is not constant over time and it seems to be very different in different countries. There is no simple, well-defined cause and no simple, obvious cure, but there are many different factors influencing structural unemployment, and many of them could be altered by government policy.

Obviously the existence of social security benefits must have an influence on the level of unemployment, and especially the numbers of claimants unemployed. In poor countries which cannot afford social security systems recorded unemployment percentages are often very low. In America, where there is no equivalent to Income Support, unemployment has usually been lower than in Europe. In America more poor people have work than they do in Europe, but that does not mean that they are necessarily better off as a result.

For a significant group in Britain, mainly parents with several dependent children, the relationship between benefit levels and wages is such that it is difficult to find work which does not involve an actual loss of weekly income. This situation could certainly be improved by government policy, as indeed it has been in recent years through the provision of benefits to people in work. (. . .)

It is very likely that the structure of taxation also affects unemployment, although the magnitude of its influence is debatable. It is generally recognised in Continental Europe that the high level of taxes and social security contributions which have to be paid by employers is a disincentive to job creation. When these charges are lowered the result will be either more employment or higher wages, or some combination of the two. Again this is something which is directly under the control of national governments.

A less tangible, but very important, influence comes from what is called 'mismatch'. The pattern of demand for labour does not match the pattern of supply, and relative wages and salaries do not move to clear the market. There can be mismatch between regions, industries, possibly genders and certainly between skills. In a time of rapid technical change these mismatches get worse. There can be an excess of demand over supply for some kinds of labour alongside an excess of supply over demand for others. Retraining and relocating the labour force takes a long time and is expensive. There may be a good social reason why it cannot happen at all. It may seem, at first sight, that there is not a great deal that governments can do to correct mismatch, but we hope to show that it would not be impossible to shift the pattern of demand significantly whilst acting on the supply side as well.

Finally many economists, notably Richard Layard (. . .) believe that the level of unemployment which is sustainable depends on the average duration of unemployment itself. The higher the proportion of people who have been unemployed for long periods, the more difficult it will be to reduce unemployment in total. It is as if the long-term unemployed have been cut off altogether from access to jobs, and for that reason play no part in the labour market at all. The market settles down, according to this view, at a level of short-term unemployment which is the equilibrium or point of balance between supply and demand. Then the long-term unemployed have to be added on to that equilibrium of short-term unemployment to arrive at the level of unemployment in total.

Looking at it this way suggests an important conclusion. If special measures can be devised to overcome the problems of the long-term unemployed then this will be a means of reducing total unemployment and not just of reducing its average duration. (. . .) We continue (. . .) looking at measures to increase the demand for labour, first in the private and then in the public sector.

Expanding employment in the private sector

Employment growth in the private sector depends directly on the decisions made by employers (or the self-employed) to maintain and to increase the size of the business that they run. Public policy can influence that decision, but it is the entrepreneur who takes it, and who takes the risk that goes with it. The success of any economic strategy in a market economy like our own depends on the courage and the hope in the future shown in the actions of large numbers of individual owners and managers. The economy will flourish and employment expand only if these qualities are nurtured and supported by public opinion and by public policy. This point has been made to us frequently in our enquiry – and not only by representatives of the business community itself. What is needed in the future is not so much growth in private sector output, profits and dividends, as growth in private sector jobs. The risk which entrepreneurs seem most reluctant to take is the risk of creating employment – yet it is on this most of all that public support for entrepreneurship rests.

(. . .)

In several of the regions we have visited the economic regeneration and employment growth we have seen have been the result of inward investment, that is the decision of foreign firms to locate new production in our country. It seems crucially important to the expansion of employment in the private sector that this inflow should continue. (Moreover, it is inevitable, and not always a matter of regret, that domestically owned firms choose to locate some of their production overseas.) One key decision is where a multi-national allocates its centres of research, development and innovation. It has been suggested to us that this matters more even than the location of its head office. Our countries have a good reputation for the quality of their higher education and, in many fields, for the quality of their scientific research as well. In the long run the quality of the academic research base is critical to the wealth of the whole community and hence its ability to create employment either in the public or in the private sector.

One means of increasing the demand for labour in the private sector would be to change the structure of taxation to encourage more labour-intensive methods of production. Firms, when they decide to hire or to fire, look at the effects of that decision on their own profitability, not at the wider social costs or benefits of what they do. At present the structure of taxes encourages labour saving which is not cost effective in social terms. When an employer takes on an additional full-time employee the cost includes not only the gross wage but also some social security contributions. The employee receives a net wage which excludes some more social security contributions as well as income tax. The cost to society is much less than that, because society as a whole has use of the contributions and taxes paid both by the employer and the employee. Moreover society as a whole pays for the benefit income which some at least of the workers would receive if they were unemployed. It would make more sense to subsidise employment than to tax it, because then employers would be encouraged to do what it is in the social interest for them to do – that is to use more labour, when they have that option, and less capital and other scarce resources.

Reducing the burden of taxation and insurance contributions that fall on employment would, as we have suggested above, increase either jobs or pay, or both. We believe that there is a strong case for reducing the costs of employing labour and also the taxes and insurance contributions paid by workers themselves on employment income. But the case is most compelling in relation to relatively low-skilled jobs. These are the jobs held by people most at risk of unemployment, and the jobs which most unemployed people have the best hope of securing. The effects of reducing taxes and charges on low skilled jobs in particular would be either to create more jobs of the right kind to cut unemployment or else to raise the take-home pay of relatively poor people in work. Either way it helps to achieve social aims.

The European Commission (1994) favours such a change in the structure of taxation in the White Paper mentioned above. It refers to 'statutory charges' on labour, including taxes as well as social security contributions. These amount on average in Europe to 40 per cent of Gross Domestic Product (GDP) to 37 per cent in the Irish Republic, 34 per cent in the UK and 30 per cent in the USA (1991 figures quoted in the White Paper). 'In order to help maintain employment and create new jobs without reducing wage levels,' the White Paper states, steps must be taken to reduce non-wage costs, particularly for less skilled labour . . . The reduction of statutory charges on labour should apply as a priority to the lowest earnings. This would make it possible to limit the budgetary cost of the measure per job saved or created while responding to the scale of unemployment among the least skilled workers.

Inevitably the question then arises as to what taxes should be raised to compensate for the loss of revenue. The European Commission very properly does not duck this issue. The White Paper considers options to raise the taxation of energy use, or consumer spending (VAT) or income from financial capital. It quotes estimates of the effects of a tax switch throughout Europe. Suppose that employers' social security contributions are reduced by just 1 per cent of GDP 'targeted on categories of workers with a low level of skills' and the revenue is recouped by an energy tax. The econometric model used shows a reduction in the unemployment rate of 2½ percentage points over four years (White Paper, p 150).

We do not attach any great significance to these precise numbers. If the policy is as effective as is claimed then why stop at switching only 1 per cent of GDP of revenue from one tax base to another? Why not actually replace the tax on labour by a subsidy? Is there not a case for higher taxation of the top ranges of earned income, rather than raising indirect taxes which could fall most heavily on those who are relatively poor? Even approximate estimates of the effects of such changes are very uncertain, since everything depends on the model of the economy that is used. Nevertheless the idea looks a very promising one; possibly it could have a really substantial effect on employment in any country where it was introduced. It illustrates very well the general point we wish to make in this report – that there are areas of the private sector in which the expansion of employment is perfectly possible, and where straightforward government action can help to make it happen.

Expanding employment in the voluntary sector

Before moving on from the private sector to the public sector we should draw attention to the very important sub-sector, which in some senses lies between the two. The 'third sector' as it is sometimes called includes voluntary and charitable activities, organised in a variety of ways, often involving trusts and non-profit companies. Although the activity takes place in the private sector, its funding is a mixture of private donations and public expenditure. There would appear to be scope for expansion here, but it will be necessary to address some of the problems which have arisen in relation to public funding. By 'expansion' we mean an increase in paid employment, jobs which carry similar expectations and similar rewards to those of the other sectors of the economy.

The nature of funding for the voluntary sector has changed considerably over the last twenty years, and with it the kind of work being undertaken and the relationship with the statutory sector. Twenty years ago many voluntary sector organisations (whether large or small) saw their role as providing services which were not provided by the statutory sector, often because there was no statutory requirement to do so. This might be the development of a community-based adventure playground or the provision of group homes for ex-psychiatric patients. Sources such as Urban Aid often provided funding for the initial few years, and where projects were successful they were usually taken onto mainstream funding. (Funders would in these cases provide post-related funding, so that increments and inflation were covered, as were other costs such as maternity cover.)

With the advent of employment-creation schemes such as the Community Programme many voluntary sector organisations became involved in administering 'schemes' of various kinds. The withdrawal of funding regimes such as Urban Aid and the introduction of competitive regimes such as City Challenge (where local authorities have to bid for urban renewal money) meant that it was increasingly difficult for voluntary sector bodies to rely on consistent mainstream funding. In recent years they have had to turn to bidding for contracts to provide services; most grants have now been changed to contracts. Post-related funding is a thing of the past. Some voluntary sector organisations have been ruined by becoming involved in employment-creation schemes with short-term funding dependent on outputs. For others the contractual nature of funding means even more bureaucracy and often extensive annual negotiations to secure funding for the following year.

Many of the areas in which employment could be expanded are covered by the voluntary sector. We see scope for local groups being funded to provide local jobs which are of immediate benefit to local communities. Similarly much work with the most vulnerable in society (such as the homeless and the mentally ill) is done by the voluntary sector and should be expanded. The balance to be struck between creating employment in the public sector and in the voluntary sector is a difficult one. The voluntary sector should not be expected to provide what are effectively statutory services. The voluntary sector should not be seen as a cheap way of providing such services through ever more tightly drawn contracts. Much employment creation in people-related services should be within the public sector. We would, however, favour creating more employment through voluntary organisations in those fields where they have particular expertise, especially in local communities and in innovative social, health and educational projects. Currently, however, many voluntary organisations lack the resources to be good employers, providing proper equipment and training for their staff.

Drawing the borderline between the voluntary sector and the public sector also requires reconsideration of the best means of involving local communities more actively in the planning and provision of services. The Centre for Theology and Public Issues at the University of Edinburgh recently published the report of a conference on *Work, Worth and Community* (edited by John Hughes and Andrew Morton). They concluded both that 'Whatever the scope for locally based measures, they should include close collaboration between the public and the private sectors with strong leadership from the local authorities' (page 59) but also that 'policy making to meet local community needs is a task for the community itself and not for professionals alone'. We agree with both objectives, but also recognise that in some areas of the country they seem to be difficult to reconcile.

Jeremy Rifkin's recent book *The End of Work*, mentioned above, ends up with a chapter on what he calls 'the third sector'. This is the one chapter in which he shows any optimism at all about the expansion of employment. Rifkin has little faith in government expenditure, but he recognises the need for 'community-based organisations' to meet social need and provide worthwhile work opportunities. As he himself acknowledges his solution also involves higher levels of taxation – and he has some imaginative suggestions as to how the revenue should be raised. This provides us with our answer to a question many of our readers may want to ask. Suppose that Rifkin is right, suppose that for many, even most, of the population paid work will not be available in the competitive market sector, what happens then? The answer must be that paid work can still be made available, to meet real needs, but on a not-for-profit basis in the community. It could be financed in part by taxation of the high incomes earned in the competitive market sector. If Rifkin is right the 'third sector' will have to grow vastly bigger than it is now.

Expanding employment in the public sector

Up to this point we have said nothing which is seriously out of line with the 'conventional wisdom' amongst economists who advise governments as exemplified by the European Commission or the OECD Secretariat. Now we do part company. In describing where new jobs could be created the OECD *Jobs Study* said 'new jobs must certainly be generated by the private sector, because in nearly all countries budget deficits and resistance to tax increases rule out significant expansion of the public sector'. We need to ask whether this is really the case. In the OECD report it is asserted rather than argued.

So far as budget deficits are concerned the conventional wisdom may be generally right. The Irish government learnt this lesson in the 1980s. In the long term a country cannot allow its public sector debt to rise indefinitely as a proportion of its national income. Otherwise the interest on that debt will use up more and more of its tax revenue, until ultimately the debt has to be eroded either by an unexpected burst of inflation or else by outright default. In an emergency, for example in wartime, countries always have borrowed in excess of what is prudent in the long term. To meet a temporary crisis of employment similar behaviour would be justified, but the problem of unemployment is not just a temporary one. To counter that problem by unsustainable borrowing might just be to push it into the future.

The case with tax revenue is very different. The OECD Secretariat are right to refer to taxpayers' resistance, but that is a constraint of very different kind to the iron laws of economics or accounting. So far as the economics is concerned, taxes could certainly be increased to pay for a higher level of public spending.

There are two economic arguments against raising taxes to fund employment creation, but neither of them seems to us to be a serious objection. The first is that raising taxes will reduce demand, for example for consumer goods, and hence offset the effect on employment of the increase in public spending. But virtually all the extra public spending will go to expand employment, whilst most of the tax revenue will come out of savings or the purchase of imports, materials and fuels or the profit content of the goods which taxpayers would otherwise have bought. The net effect on employment creation will still be very substantial.

The other argument is about the supply side, about incentives and costs. It would, of course, be very foolish to finance job creation in the public sector with a tax on job creation in the private sector or by taxes which undermine the international competitiveness of the economy. That is not what we propose. Ideally, from the point of view of job creation, all the extra tax would fall on factors of production which compete with private sector jobs, such as income from capital, imports, materials, fuels and so on. That would actually reinforce the expansionary effect on employment of the extra public spending. An increase in general taxation of domestic income and expenditure, if that was the preferred method of finance, would fall in some degree on all factors of production. But, again, this offset to the effect of the extra public expenditure would be relatively small, leaving a substantial net positive effect on employment in total. We believe therefore that the case for extra public spending to raise employment holds good whether it is viewed from the demand side of the economy or the supply. We could put it another way. No one would doubt that an increase in spending on health care in the private sector, paid for by the customers through charges or private insurance schemes, would stimulate employment. Why should the same not be true of a similar increase in spending on health care paid for by society as a whole through the medium of taxation?

Compared with the rest of Europe, Britain has a relatively low ratio of taxation to GDP. In 1994, current receipts of General Government were 36.4 per cent of GDP in the United Kingdom. This compares with only 31.5 per cent in the USA, but as much as 46.5 per cent in Germany and 48.9 per cent in France.

We are not suggesting that taxes should be raised to German or French levels in a one year's Budget. It would be possible, however, to add several percentage points of GDP to taxation in Britain over a run of years, making possible a gradual expansion of labour-intensive public service expenditure. At the same time economies might be found in other areas of public spending which do not have a high direct labour content. We were advised by Andrew Dilnot of the Institute of Fiscal Studies that there is indeed scope to raise that percentage in Britain by judicious changes to the tax system, without causing serious harm to the economy or treating any taxpayers with flagrant injustice. In our view there is scope to widen the tax base to include some categories of expenditure or income which are now untaxed and also to increase the rate of income tax on higher levels of earnings. It would not, of course, be popular with everybody, but that does not mean it could not be done. It seems to us absurd to constrain policy action by saying that it must make no one at all worse off. A great deal could be done without hitting the incomes of people who are already poor. When policies change there will always be winners and losers. If taxes went up there would indeed be some losers – we would hope they were people well able to afford to pay more. If the revenue was used to create jobs there would be some very significant winners as well.

It is worth recalling how the unemployment problems of the 1930s were eventually solved. It was not by making labour markets more flexible, or by tightening the eligibility conditions for welfare benefits. It was by a massive increase in public expenditure, directed at rearmament and ultimately at war. Obviously the economics – and the politics – of different forms of public spending are not the same, but the point is worth making nevertheless.

We have been aware in travelling round the country that the reduction in military spending now under way or in prospect is hitting employment in some localities very hard. We saw this in Belfast, on the Clyde, in the South West and in the Medway towns. The preservation of the armaments industry has been given a particularly high priority by Government and the effective rate of subsidy is very high indeed, according to a recent report by the Campaign against the Arms Trade (*Killing Jobs: The Arms Trade and Employment in the UK*, published April 1996). Politicians and the public seem willing to accept that government expenditure must increase and taxes must be raised when the purpose of that expenditure is seen as essential to national security. Whatever we may think about the morality of defence spending (. . .) there is a lesson here about government spending and employment policy. What is needed today is a similar sense of urgency in relation to the issues of employment and social cohesion which are the subject matter of this report.

It is generally agreed that the greatest scope for employment expansion is in the service sector, especially services which are not subject to foreign competition or technological innovation. It so happens that many such service activities are to be found in the public sector, for example health, education and community care. If we keep these services in the public sector then we will distort the natural growth of activity and employment if they are not adequately funded. Job losses in manufacturing industry or coal mining may be defended as an appropriate, even an inevitable, response to economic change. Job losses in the health service or the care of the environment cannot. Of course the resources devoted to these activities need to be used efficiently with proper accountability and the most effective management techniques. This may mean contracting out work to the private sector or it may mean direct employment by the public sector itself. This is not a matter on which we would claim expertise. The main point is that, by one route or another, employment could be expanded and good work done.

There is no reason to doubt that employment could, indeed, be expanded and good work done by the public sector if more funds were available. We asked some local authority leaders and officials what unmet needs they were aware of in their region and, as we expected, they had no difficulty in providing examples. Moreover some of the examples they gave were tasks which people now unemployed could very readily do with only a limited amount of training. They mentioned for example the imbalance that now arises when new money is made available for high-profile investment projects, but not for the subsequent, less newsworthy but equally necessary, costs of maintenance and repairs. They also mentioned social work where cuts have put an unreasonable burden on both professional and support staff.

It has been suggested to us that giving a green light to the expansion of employment in the public sector would not be compatible with maintaining financial control and accountability within government. We do not accept this criticism at all. We believe in the good use of resources, not least in the public sector – 'stewardship' is the word used for this in the Christian tradition. Moreover, everything we have said about the need to create real work, which makes a real contribution to society, implies that the real value of the work done in the public sector should be subject to continual and rigorous scrutiny. We certainly do not propose signing a blank cheque so that public sector employees can go ahead and spend taxpayers' money on any programmes that they fancy. The point we are making is that taxpayers actually want better services than they have been receiving over the past twenty years and that the drives for economy in the public sector have been conducted in such a way that they are actually preventing taxpayers from getting what they want.

We have referred to 'mismatch' as one of the underlying causes of structural unemployment. Expanding employment in the public services can be seen as a means of tackling that problem. The composition of employment growth in the private sector can only be influenced indirectly and very imprecisely by public policy. If public expenditure is increased, the resulting job growth can be matched much more closely to the skills that are available in the labour force. We are not talking now of special schemes for the long-term unemployed (. . .) but of the level and composition of public spending as part of their normal budgeting process, on a permanent basis and not as a temporary expedient.

In assessing the cost of such expansion it is, of course, important to take account of the resulting saving in social security payments. At the same time society as a whole would benefit from better public services, such as health and education facilities, care for children and the elderly, and so on. There would be real, and very visible improvements in the quality of life for all. The taxpaying public would be getting good value for their money. To win support for tax increases the link with improved services as well as job creation should be made as explicit and direct as possible. The more that tax payers can see and approve the way in which public money is spent the better.

Expanding employment in Ireland

Most of what we have said in this chapter so far is addressed to the situation in Britain. The policy choices faced in the Republic of Ireland are similar in many respects, but different in others. The very rapid growth of the Irish economy illustrates well how an expansion of activity helps create jobs, but also that it does not of itself solve the whole of the unemployment problem. Unemployment in Ireland is falling, but it is still unacceptably high, higher indeed than it is in Britain. Part of the explanation is a reversal of the emigration which took place some years ago before the economic expansion got under way. But there is a further explanation, which indicates a need for policy action: the increase in the demand for labour is failing to reach the regions of the economy and the people whose need for new opportunities is greatest.

The recent history of Ireland illustrates very well the dangers of increasing public expenditure without raising taxation. However, an increase in some areas of public expenditure, properly financed by taxation, could have a part to play in solving the problems of unemployment in Ireland. As we have argued above, the expansion of the service sector, both public and private, provides the best hope of creating more jobs. Moreover in the public sector such expansion can be targeted to the regions and the occupations where the demand for labour is deficient. We also believe that, in Ireland as in Britain, demand for labour in the private sector should be increased by shifting the burden of taxation and insurance contributions away from relatively low-paid labour. Steps in that direction have been taken in Ireland, but we suggest that a great deal more needs to be done before the problem of unemployment is solved.

The Irish government has been imaginative in addressing the issue of financial disincentives to work. (. . . T)hese are more genuinely problematic in Ireland than in Britain as social security provision is more generous. We would emphasise, however, that these financial disincentives do not form the only, or even the most significant, barrier to overcome. Unemployed people need to be aware of what job opportunities are open to them and the various measures that have been introduced in recent years to help the transition back into employment, for example the possibility of retaining some benefits for a period after recommencing paid work. The approach of those helping the unemployed should be active, based on a perception of the right of everyone to appropriate work, as well as the duty of everyone who can to participate in the work of the society to which they belong. It may well be that the approach in Ireland in the past has put too much emphasis on the purely passive task of making sure that people who are unemployed receive the benefits to which they are entitled. This does not mean of course that we favour a policy of 'harassment'. We repeat what we have said in relation to the UK: no one should be written off as unemployable, even if they have few educational qualifications and even if they have been out of work for many years. It is up to the society as a whole to ensure that appropriate and rewarding work is there for everyone to do. To quote the well-chosen words from the Pastoral Letter of the Irish Catholic Bishops' Conference, we believe in 'an economy that needs everyone'.

A question of priorities

We do not think that there is a quick and easy way of expanding employment on the scale which the situation demands. We do believe, however, that such expansion would be possible over a period of time if it were given a much higher priority in the conduct of public policy. We have given some examples, which involve making employment creation an explicit aim and not just the by-product of economic growth.

The Report of the Commission on Social Justice in Britain, published in 1994, was very influential in the formation of Labour Party thinking at that time. It deals with many of the same issues as we have addressed in this chapter and it comes to some of the same conclusions. It recognises the potential of the service sector, both private and public, as the main area for job creation. It also recognises the need for 'the wealth created in a dynamic tradeable sector to be used to employ other people in services which enrich the quality of all our lives'. In other words the parts of the economy which are growing faster and competing successfully in international markets must provide the income which pays for other, less competitive but equally important, parts of the economy like childcare and hospitals. In another passage it refers to finance for such services 'whether through taxes, charges, partnerships or other means'. We agree that charges and 'other means' may be worth exploring, but in practice we think that the main source of funding will have to be taxation. Since so much of the service sector is supported by public spending it is difficult to see how employment creation can take place on a large scale in that sector without increasing the level of taxation. It becomes a question of priorities: job creation as against low taxation. Sacrifice is necessary in seeking the common good. We do not think that the deep running sores of unemployment and poverty can be healed without some sacrifice on the part of those of us who are better off.

It was suggested to us at one meeting that it is becoming increasingly difficult to collect taxes. Certainly there was a scare during the course of our enquiry when government receipts of revenue appeared to be coming in well below forecast. It was suggested to us that both tax avoidance and tax evasion have become more socially accepted. It was also suggested that in a flexible market it may be easier to conceal tax liabilities. If this really is a growing problem – and we are not certain that it is – then the answer is not to reduce taxation, but to devote more resources to collecting it. It may also be necessary to simplify the tax system, removing exemptions which are open to abuse. But it would also help if political leaders were to encourage the belief that paying taxes is a social obligation to the common good and not an arbitrary extortion.

We have argued (. . .) that job creation should be given a very high priority for reasons which are social and spiritual as well as economic. The priority to be given to low taxation is a different question (. . .). One view, with which we sympathise, is that paying taxes is a way of discharging (in some part) our obligation to meet the needs of our national community as a whole, and especially the needs of its less fortunate members. The origin of that obligation can be attributed either to love or to justice – to compassion for those in need or to a duty to share God's gifts more fairly. A case for redistributive taxation can be constructed on either base. These arguments are not heard often enough today.

This does not tell us, of course, what is the optimal rate of taxation, the rate which is neither too low nor too high. Neither does it tell us how the burden of taxation should be shared out between different groups in the community. To answer such questions would involve a review, not just of employment creation but of all the other objectives which public expenditure may serve. Perhaps savings can be made in other programmes. This would take us well beyond the remit of this enquiry. Our plea is simply that the aim of low taxation should not automatically be given the highest priority of all. There are other aims that matter far more than that one.

Note: See References section for Chapter 1, on p. 30.

Chapter 8

Managerializing organizational culture

Refashioning the human resource in educational institutions

Geoff Esland, Karen Esland, Mike Murphy and Karen Yarrow

> Managers themselves and most writers about management conceive of themselves as morally neutral characters whose skills enable them to devise the most efficient means of achieving whatever end is proposed. Whether a given manager is effective or not is on the dominant view quite a different question from that of the morality of the ends which his (*sic*) effectiveness serves or fails to serve. None the less there are strong grounds for refuting the claim that effectiveness is a morally neutral value. For the whole concept of effectiveness is inseparable from a mode of human existence in which the contrivance of means is in central part the manipulation of human beings into compliant patterns of behaviour; and it is by appeal to his own effectiveness in this respect that the manager claims authority within the manipulative mode.
>
> (Macintyre 1985: 74)

Managerial reform in further and higher education

Following the major reforms introduced in further and higher education during the late 1980s and early 1990s, it has become *de rigueur* for the institutions in these sectors to adopt the managerial practices of private business as the chosen method for dealing with the new responsibilities imposed on them (Keep *et al.* 1996). To a considerable extent, the decision to follow this route was dictated by the reforms themselves. The very nature of the organizational changes imposed by the Conservative governments of this period required a set of managerial instruments capable of demonstrating compliance with the new regulatory system of controls. The problem was particularly acute for those further education institutions previously under local authority control, as the necessary management infrastructure was usually much less developed than was the case with the universities. But almost all further and higher education (FHE) institutions have felt the necessity to adopt new forms of management to enable them to cope with the new political demands imposed on them. Under the Education

Reform Act of 1988, some eighty-four HE institutions were removed from LEA control and given independent status. Under the terms of the Further and Higher Education Act of 1992, the former polytechnics were given the right to adopt the title of 'university', and colleges of further education, tertiary and sixth form colleges were required to go through a process of incorporation prior to the granting of independence from local education authorities. From 1 April 1993, the newly constituted governing bodies, or corporations, became formally responsible for the assets, staff and operational management of their colleges.

The sheer scale of these changes, under a Treasury-led financial regime which was demanding annual 'efficiency savings' while student intakes were expected to rise steeply, made it necessary for FHE institutions to invent new forms of strategic management capable of sustaining systems of decision making for the new financial, quality assessment, customer service and staff monitoring requirements set out in the legislation (Warner and Crosthwaite 1995). At the same time, the state's promotion of the 'New Public Management' throughout the public sector made it unlikely that FHE institutions would fail to follow the direction taken by the other public services (Hood 1991; Pollitt 1993; Clarke and Newman 1997). What the government required was a total transformation of FHE institutions, so that they were obliged both to adopt the competitive and customer-oriented culture of the private sector and to make the necessary structural and employment changes to bring this about. The 'management of change' became the dominant discourse in many institutions as they hastened to proclaim their new corporate identity and market presence, reinventing themselves around a new concern for image manufacture and promotion (House and Watson 1995). At the same time, they were unable to avoid the issue of staff management. The requirement that systems of appraisal be installed in each institution coupled with government pressure for the introduction of performance-related pay meant that many institutions felt obliged to upgrade their personnel policies by the introduction of some form of Human Resource Management (HRM) policy. This process was already under way in the former polytechnics after their separation from LEAs in 1988. Reporting on the results of their 1991 survey of senior HE managers, Crosthwaite and Warner (1995) noted that the adoption of an HRM policy was seen as a high priority by almost all of the principals who took part, and that it was second in importance only to financial management.

Although most FHE organizations will of necessity have adopted some form of HRM, there is no suggestion that there is a single standard model which would apply to all. Indeed, it is perfectly possible that in some institutions the term is not used at all and that staffing issues are dealt with as part of a broad management decision-making process. In circumstances such as these, those elements of HRM that are in use may well remain implicit and unsystematized. In many cases, what might be called HRM issues are dealt with by the personnel department, acting as a co-ordinating centre for processes which move between the senior management team and the institution's line managers. In some institutions, elements of HRM have been introduced, but for internal political reasons, their status as such remains unofficially recognized and they tend to exist as a clandestine form of HRM. In its more formal usage, human resource management embraces most of the processes of employee management from recruitment, selection and induction to appraisal, training, promotion and reward. Equal opportunities policies also form part of an HRM brief as do decisions about the type and duration of contracts issued to employees. In its more developed form, HRM becomes sytematized and focused around an organization's strategic planning functions where decisions about the deployment of staff are seen in relation to the financial and market pressures which impact upon it.

Our purpose in this chapter is to examine some of the underlying tendencies and tensions within managerial practice in public sector education and training institutions and to consider their implications for professional identity and working relationships in a context increasingly being characterized as that of 'a self-perpetuating learning society' (FEFC 1997). We look particularly at the significance of the widespread adoption of the principles and methods of HRM and Human Resource Development (HRD) in organizational contexts where the emphasis on unit cost-reduction is often paramount. The research on which our arguments are based has so far focused primarily on the further education sector, but we are aware of similar developments taking place in institutions of higher education.[1] Our central argument is that in spite of its emphasis on employee development and the importance of skill enhancement through training, HRM is often perceived by both managers and those 'managed' as a means of reducing an organization's human resource costs and of increasing 'flexibility' in staffing (Blyton and Morris 1992) – an objective usually achieved in one of two ways. First, HRM enables teaching and curricular inputs to the learning process to be redefined as a variable cost, so that greater output can be achieved for less; and second, it is capable of being deployed as a disciplinary instrument for the identification of 'underperformance' or inadequate commitment among employees, if necessary as a basis for 'downsizing', redundancy or casualization (Cunningham 1997). In effect, HRM operates by defining both the problem in relation to employee skills, attitudes and behaviour and also the solution, and it does so within the terms sanctioned by the organization itself. Thus, usually through a system of staff appraisal, the employee is invited to collude in a process in which he or she accepts the attribution of specific 'deficiencies' in respect of skills and qualities thought to be functional to the organization's success, and takes responsibility for 'correcting' them. Subsequent appraisals provide occasions for assessing whether the employee has met that responsibility. If the transaction is founded on a relatively high-trust relationship, the outcome might well be satisfactory for all parties; but where the organization's culture is perceived as threatening to employee security, and where hidden personnel agendas are seen to be operating among its senior management, then HRM – under its legitimating guise of 'staff development' – can become a major resource in the operation of organizational power politics. By selectively targeting employee attributes – which may or may not have anything to do with their core expertise – HRM can act as a powerful instrument for securing organizational compliance, and, in some instances, for sustaining power structures that are essentially autocratic. In such circumstances, as one author puts it, HRM confirms its reputation as a 'wolf in sheep's clothing' (Keenoy 1990).

Our concern about the potential for HRM to be used in these ways is threefold. In the first place, the nature of the circumstances which gave rise to the demand for HRM among senior managers in FHE institutions makes a close convergence between policies for budgetary and employee management almost inevitable. With staff costs representing an average of 65–70 per cent of an FHE institution's budget, the case for the 'effective management' of staff is undeniable. However, the probability is that under financial pressures, the two management systems become merged and that 'staff development' becomes a euphemism for the harassment, de-skilling and de-professionalization which a number of commentators have argued has been one of the consequences of the further education reforms (Gleeson 1996; Randle and Brady 1997; Yarrow and Esland 1998). As Ainley and Bailey (1997) point out in their analysis of the FE sector since incorporation, the problem has been made particularly acute by the Byzantine complexity of the new funding regime managed by the Further Education Funding Council (FEFC). Here, as with universities, the price mechanism operates with regard both to student enrolment, retention and attainment and to the qualifications for which they enrol, so that teaching inputs and curricula are incorporated within the funding formula. When annual 'efficiency savings', FEFC 'clawbacks' of unfulfilled allocations and the impact of market competition are taken into account – not to mention the fear of going into receivership – the dominance of the financial imperatives is inescapable.

Our second concern is that in their haste to instal new managerial systems following the 1988 and 1992 legislation, FHE professionals – and policy makers, themselves, it has to be said – have shown relatively little inclination to address the contradictions and organizational risks that can arise from cost-driven forms of human resource management. In spite of a significant literature which has examined the double-edged nature of HRM (see, for example, Storey 1989, 1990; Blyton and Turnbull 1992; Townley 1994; Clarke and Newman 1997), there has so far been relatively little engagement by the education community with the potential of HRM to undermine both the professional contribution and commitment of teaching staff and the quality of the student experience within FHE (Gunter 1997). It would appear that in its desire to displace the much-maligned 'producer-interests' in education, the state-as-employer has limited its responsibility to the installation of a set of neo-Taylorist conditions on educational practitioners with little intention of assessing the impact this policy will have on meeting its claimed commitment to establishing what the DfEE has called 'The Learning Age' (DfEE 1998) (see Esland 1996; Randle and Brady 1997). It seems probable that unless the educational community produces its own critical assessments, it will fulfil the fears expressed by Campion and Renner (1995: 74) of the

> potentially negative consequences of an academic community becoming committed to an emasculated professionalism through a half-hearted acceptance of an uncritiqued, imported set of managerial tools from industry.

Part of the explanation for the lack of internal debate about the impact of the new managerial culture on education and training provision lies in the fact that for many employees in the FE sector in particular, the prevailing industrial relations culture has become so negative that consideration of the operational principles of management policy has been overshadowed by the legacy of hostility between staff and management over the FE lecturer's contract. Particularly contentious has been the attempt by the Employers' forum – the Association for Colleges – to revoke the previous conditions of service (the so-called 'Silver Book' contract) and to impose a new contract stipulating longer working hours and shorter annual holidays. In some institutions, this dispute has led to a serious deterioration in management–staff relationships to the point where some of those refusing to sign the new contract have been sacked, and others denied pay increases for more than three years (Ainley and Bailey 1997: 24). Although HE institutions have been largely spared this degree of acrimony in staff–management relationships, they have themselves been involved in an ongoing dispute about the widespread use of fixed-term contracts in HE appointments, an issue to which we will return later.

Another reason for the relative lack of debate in FHE institutions about the impact of the new managerial culture is that for a number of highly placed employees, the managerialism of FHE is seen as a positive development which carries with it opportunities for 're-skilling' and career enhancement into new management roles and responsibilities (Gleeson and Shain 1998). It has also become absorbed within a 'survivalist discourse' in which any questioning of the new managerial regime is discouraged on the grounds that it might undermine an organization's future – particularly in relation to funding providers.

Perhaps even more powerful than survivalism has been the ideology of 'modernization' and the self-identification of senior FE managers with a discourse which denigrates past practice while celebrating a future in which an interventionist management style, a business ethos and a belief in the power of information technology combine to ensure a culture free from the accretions of the past. As with the 1997 British Labour government, the identification of self or organization with a process of 'modernization' establishes political barriers of legitimacy that work to exclude those who wish to subscribe to a different set of values. In a surprisingly short period of time, the 'old' values of public service – represented by the 'archaic' and 'self-serving' LEAs – became politically and culturally discredited while those of private enterprise moved into the ascendant. In the course of our research we found a number of senior and middle managers embracing the new business ethos and enthusiastically supporting the agendas of quality control and the market imperatives of 'meeting customer needs' (Yarrow and Esland 1998). It was significant that the most committed of these 'embracers' of the new culture had been directly recruited from industry, and had had little or no experience of the public education system. In a number of instances the exponents of the new value system expressed impatience with those who perceived the changes to have undermined their professionalism and long-standing commitment to student learning, and it was not uncommon for these 'dissenters' to be characterized as 'dinosaurs' by their more gung-ho colleagues. Between the 'dissenters' and the 'embracers' of the new culture was a group of pragmatists who were prepared to accommodate to the new demands. In many cases, these were middle managers who felt that it was in the best interests of themselves and their students to work with the system. These differing perspectives are, of course, unsurprising and would be replicated in most institutions. Under the previous system, as Ainley and Bailey point out, the main divisions were based on departmental rivalries. But under the post-1992 system the differences are often those of value and educational philosophy. Of necessity, managerialism tends to create divisions within an organization's workforce which derive from differently valued responsibilities and the allocation of differential rewards. The underlying logic of a policy of 'managers being allowed to manage' is that it encourages a polarization between the strategic planning functions of an organization and the 'routine' operations of the professional teacher/lecturer (Ball 1994). According to Randle and Brady (1997: 232), their case study of four merged FE colleges revealed that

> Many lecturers . . . saw management as being obsessed with budgets and business plans against their own concern for the client. In the survey, 85 per cent of respondents believed that the college management did not share the same educational values as staff.

Commenting on the employment relationship in higher education Keep *et al.* (1996: 36) observe that

The irony is that just as cutting-edge practice in the private sector moves towards the 'self-managing' model, UK universities undermine their own version by imposing a fragmented set of practices which are sufficiently intrusive to erode mutual trust but not all-encompassing enough to provide a sustainable alternative.

Our third concern relates to the role played by HRM regimes in the legitimation of narrow and instrumental forms of education and training (Avis *et al.* 1996; Bird *et al.* 1998). There would seem to be at least two aspects to this problem. The first derives from the fact that as its scope expands, human resource management becomes increasingly more influential as a definer of the market for education and training provision. In consequence, as HRM demands for organization-specific education and training increase there is every likelihood that any form of learning which does not match the requirements of such programmes will be excluded, especially if in some ways it is seen as dysfunctional to an organization's core business. There is already some concern that this applies to a good deal of management education, where the normative and value emphases of current business practice are seen as determining much of the content of MBA and management diploma courses (Grey and Mitev 1995; Esland, K., forthcoming). A curriculum focus of this kind is often at the expense of more critical perspectives which might seek to question the ethical basis of certain elements of business practice.

A related problem arises from the fact that HRM performs an important mediating function between an organization's curricular and teaching inputs and assessment outputs, by seeking out and exploiting the flexibilities in each, particularly in circumstances where curricular and staffing policies are dealt with together. This is especially likely to happen where curricular content and assessment outcomes are closely related, as is the case with competence-based NVQs and GNVQs. In effect, what HRM is able to do is to assist the process of scaling down the curriculum resource inputs while seeking ways of reducing the cost of their delivery. An institution adopting this policy is then able to rationalize its outputs in the terms which its own logics have defined. In this way a circular process is created in which curriculum and teaching inputs are specified in terms of the pre-defined outputs – themselves usually based on a mix of assessment and quality measures and completion rates. If the assessment and quality measures are expressed in terms of individual levels of 'competence' – which are themselves linked to output-related funding – there is considerable scope for the process to be rationalized down to its basic, lowest cost level. If this means scaling down the knowledge required from lecturing staff, or reducing teacher–student contact hours, or standardizing assessment procedures then that is no more than a number of respondents claim is happening (Ainley and Bailey 1997; Yarrow and Esland 1998; Bird *et al.* 1998). For example, referring to her responsibilities for teaching GNVQ, a main grade lecturer, one of the respondents cited by Yarrow and Esland, observes that

> The whole GNVQ thing is deprofessionalising. You are reduced to the level of a check list. The old quality assurance guys with their clip boards, the time and motion guys, well they've just done that. All the respect of a lecturer's role becomes diminished with the GNVQ and we become more like manual workers rather than autonomous, professional people who work under their own steam, actually manage their own workload, have that autonomy. I don't feel I have that to the same degree as I used to.

Under a competitive, marketized, cost-driven system in which contracted output-related funding determines both student recruitment and a substantial proportion of the curriculum, HRM can become an effective instrument for bringing about the flexibilization of the professional workforce, by reducing the discretionary areas of the professional role. As such, it plays a significant part in rationalizing curricular and teaching inputs, thereby materially influencing the content of what is taught and learned.

Although some organizations could justifiably claim not to be using a fully developed model of HRM, it is our contention that the current political settlement for education and training makes it extremely difficult for them to avoid at least some of its main features. So pervasive and interventionist has the new regulatory culture become that resort to some form of human resource management is often perceived as a necessary basis of legitimation for the new managerial practice. In the following section, we look more closely at the ways in which HRM is able to change the culture of working relationships within an organization.

HRM and the new managerialism

As a number of commentators have observed, many of the educational reforms introduced by the New Right governments of the 1980s and 1990s are most appropriately described as 'managerialist' in their character and intention (Ball 1994; Avis *et al.* 1996). 'Managerialism' has a number of features, one of the principal ones being that it is usually based on a strong underlying political agenda in which the management practice at its core will be driven by a requirement for control and compliance. At the heart of public sector managerialism is the claim that the objectives of social and educational services can be promoted more efficiently and to a higher standard if the appropriate management techniques are deployed.

The underlying objective of many of the managerial changes introduced by the 1988 and 1992 Acts referred to above was to place limits on the roles of professional employees in education by reducing the discretionary areas of their professional expertise and practice and strengthening the surveillance over the ways in which they performed their jobs. To implement this policy, a series of regulations and methodologies was established capable of exerting powerful constraints over the identities, responsibilities and workloads of professional workers who formerly regarded their working relationships as founded on collegiality and high levels of trust. One of the most significant aspects of this process has been the transformation of the knowledge bases of these groups of employees, which has derived in part from the restructuring of training regimes around the concepts of 'outcomes' and 'competencies'.

In addition to the structural and organizational changes introduced during the 1980s and 1990s, the pressures of cost-cutting and demands for accountability and 'value for money' have resulted in changes in forms of employee management, which have become evident particularly in the widespread installation of human resource management practices and policies. Taking its cue from the private sector, the public sector has adopted practices and strategies which claim to enable organizations to achieve maximum effectiveness through the commitment, flexibility and responsiveness of its staff. Both the shape of organizations and the 'human resources' employed within them have been subject to realignment with the new competitive realities and concomitant drive for cost-effectiveness that have become a central feature within the private and latterly public sectors.

The widespread use of HRM has been part of a shift within management discourse which has occurred since the late 1980s, particularly in the area of employee relations. What was previously known as 'personnel management' has since become 'human resource management'. For some analysts, the change in title is purely superficial (Armstrong 1987), while others consider it to signify a considerable shift in both employee management practices and underlying principles (see Guest 1987: 506).

A number of writers have attempted to analyse the differences between personnel management and human resource management (see Guest 1987; Sisson 1989; Legge 1989). Although as Guest contends, there are considerable problems in making a comparison between personnel management and human resource management, predominantly due to a lack of empirical research on these two modes of management, it is possible to identify a number of assumptions within the literature as to the differences between the two. What is frequently noted as the key difference between the 'old' personnel management and the 'new' human resource management is the emphasis upon a coherence between organizational strategy and the management of employees, and the assumption that employees can make a major contribution to an organization's efficiency and effectiveness if organized, developed and trained in line with organizational goals. Ezzamel et al. (1996) note that underlying personnel management is a philosophy which emphasizes localized problem solving, whereas HRM entails a more systemic approach. The human resource function aims to both deliver and develop the 'human capital' considered to be the source of competitive advantage by increasing employee commitment to and identification with organizational goals (Alvares 1997).

According to Poole (1990), the origins of HRM lie in the human relations school of management, and it is this factor which accounts for its emphasis on teamwork, communications and the importance for an organization of the development of individual talents and skills:

> human resource management is viewed as strategic; it involves all managerial personnel (and especially general managers); it regards people as the most important single asset of the organisation; it is proactive in its relationship with people; and it seeks to enhance company performance, employee 'needs' and societal well-being.
>
> (Poole 1990: 3)

What is striking about this positive formulation of employee relationships is that it sees no contradiction between employee 'needs' and societal well-being, on the one hand, and the enhancement of company performance on the other, and because of that it has to be seen as a highly idealized representation of human resource management in practice – at least for many who work in the public services. For these, it would seem to strike a level of naïveté, as claims about the importance of investing in people as assets have to be set against policies in which the underlying thrust of HRM has been to extract as much labour power as possible from those (diminishing) assets – a process well-captured in the blunt phrase of Sir John Harvey-Jones, former Chairman of ICI, 'making assets sweat'. One of the lecturers quoted by Ainley and Bailey sums up this more realistic view of the HRM ideology:

> I mean, 'human resource development' is a dead giveaway in terms of their attitude towards the staff. Human beings are not people, they're resources to be utilized by the institution.
>
> (op. cit.: 104)

As we suggested earlier, although most FHE organizations have adopted some form of HRM, we would not wish to imply that there is a single standard model which would apply to all. However, it is clear from our research that it is the more strategic approach to employee management that currently prevails in FHE institutions, a situation which owes more to financial pressures on staffing than a desire to enhance the working conditions of professional employees. Further evidence for this judgement lies in the fact that by the time the Labour government published its *Fairness at Work* White Paper in May 1998, the main FE and HE trade unions had embarked upon campaigns of litigation and protest against the growing casualization within the FHE sector. The Association of University Teachers, for example, estimated at the time that across higher education as a whole, no fewer than 44 per cent of academic staff were employed on short fixed-term contracts, and that in some institutions the proportion was over 70 per cent (Wilson 1998). In a large number of cases these contracts were further weakened by the inclusion of waiver clauses depriving their recipients of the right to claim compensation for unfair dismissal in the event of their being made redundant.

HRM: principles and practices

One of the continuing debates within the literature has focused on the issue as to whether human resource management is as widely practised within organizations as the hype surrounding it suggests. As Guest notes, 'there is a danger of confusing "management thinkers" with management practitioners and assuming that because human resource management is being discussed it is also being practised' (1987: 505). Although this may well be the case within the private sector, the managerialist practices which have been introduced within the public sector show all the hallmarks of having been influenced by the principles underlying human resource management.

HRM tends to be considered to comprise a number of heterogeneous techniques and practices, which include human resource planning, recruitment and selection, performance appraisal, 'reward' systems, training and development, and collective employee relations. Townley (1993) notes that despite the apparent heterogeneity of practices falling under the umbrella of HRM, the underlying theoretical model tends to draw upon a systems maintenance or functionalist perspective:

> From this perspective HRM is the black box of production, where organizational inputs – employees – are selected, appraised, trained, developed, and remunerated to deliver the required output of labor.
>
> (Townley 1993: 518)

Human resource management is therefore used as an organizational mechanism for the attainment of specific goals. Within the public sector, organizational goals tend to have been circumscribed and defined by the financial restraints placed upon them by successive governments. The emphasis upon 'economy, efficiency and effectiveness' has made the use of human resource management tools within the public sector a seemingly natural choice, given the emphasis upon raising productivity rates without increasing budgets. Indeed, the utilization of some of these management tools has been identified as a defining characteristic of public sector managerialism:

Target-setting, performance indicators, various forms of activity budgeting, staff appraisal, merit pay – all seem to hang together as complementary elements in a single vision of more tightly focused, financially disciplined, performance-conscious management.

(Pollitt 1993: 113)

The utilization of human resource management policies and practices within the public sector is more a reaction to the structural reorganization which has taken place rather than an integral element of it (Ezzamel *et al.* 1996: 66). The public sector reforms have been characterized by a marked tendency to concentrate on 'inputs' such as cost or employees, due primarily to the fact that until recently most of the 'outputs' of the public services were ambiguous in terms of measurement.

HRM and the appraisal process

One of the key features of both managerialism and human resource management is the extension of appraisal systems to most groups of employees in the public services. With the competitive conditions that the introduction of internal markets has brought – budgetary pressures, governmental demands to demonstrate efficiency and value for money, and a slimmed down, 'lean' workforce – there is little tolerance of under-achievers. Notwithstanding the efforts of some public sector trade unions to secure non-judgemental forms of appraisal, in some institutions appraisals perform the function of ensuring high levels of performance. As such, they constitute a central management instrument for enabling the matching of human resources to the strategies and directions of the organization.

According to Townley (1989), there is an increasing importance placed upon extra-functional, 'social' skills and attributes within appraisal systems. Attitudinal and behavioural criteria are judged alongside technical knowledge and ability, that is, 'those normative and ideological requirements defined as necessary to the task but not related to its technical fulfilment' (Offe 1976: 28, quoted in Townley). By 'measuring' employee performance and encouraging individuals to acknowledge any deficiencies they may have, organizational norms are communicated and employee commitment to them is reinforced. Indeed, Townley argues that alongside their monitoring and disciplinary role, the reinforcement of behavioural norms constitutes a central function of appraisal systems.

The training and development of employees in many organizations is linked to staff appraisals. The employee is supposed to identify weaknessess or gaps in their skill or knowledge bases which can, with the aid of appropriate training or development programmes, be overcome. In this way, what is essentially a management device is presented as a means of employee empowerment: the employee takes responsibility for his or her own training needs and means of occupational advancement. The underlying rationale is that if the quality of the staff is improved then the performance of the organization is also enhanced (Ezzamel *et al*. 1996: 67) Key features of the process of inventorying an individual's skills and weaknesses are competencies and other performance indicators. Boyatzis (1982) defines an occupational competency as an underlying characteristic of a person that is causally related to effective or superior performance. Although he argues that competencies should be seen as distinct from behaviours, he acknowledges that often the two are conflated.

HRM and the 'competence movement'

The concept of competencies has become central to the new organizational landscape, due partly to the influence of agencies such as the National Council for Vocational Qualifications (NCVQ) (now subsumed in the QCA – the Qualifications and Curriculum Authority) and the Management Charter Initiative (MCI). With the emphasis on higher levels of performance along with reduced costs, the use of competencies holds the promise of providing the ability to produce measurable improvements. Notions of 'competence' often feature as part of an overall human resources plan (Schuler and Jackson 1987; Burgoyne 1993; Antonacopoulou and FitzGerald 1996). Competencies are a key mechanism by which organizational strategy becomes operationalized: recruitment, selection, appraisals, and training and development programmes are all articulated in terms of 'competencies'. The attraction of the competence approach is that it appears to offer quantifiable, 'objective' yardsticks against which to assess the level of fit between job requirements and personal characteristics, and the level of compatibility between training programmes and organizational goals and therefore whether they offer 'value for money'.

The concept of competencies forms an important part of management training programmes offered by business schools. A respondent within a research project currently being carried out by one of the authors makes explicit the relationship between organizational performance, competencies and training programmes:

> So very often, a company arrives here with, 'Here is a new strategy, here are the changes we need to implement to achieve that new strategy, here are the capabilities and competencies we believe we need from our management team to deliver those changes, here is an analysis of our own managers in terms of the capabilities and competencies that they've got, here are the gaps, can you fill the gaps?'. . . . [With other companies] we would actually go in, diagnose any needs, devise and agree a set of competencies, diagnose individuals against those competencies, identify the gaps, map the gaps onto our programmes which are them-

selves defined in competence terms, and then show what programmes each individual ought to do to meet the gaps, and then be able to show subsequent to the programme the extent to which that individual has improved his or her performance as a consequence of that gap-filling process.

(Director of Programmes at a major business school)

Burgoyne (1993) argues that the functionalist methodology underlying the competence movement has long been discredited within organizational theory. The assumption of an overarching organizational goal within which skills and behaviours may be identified, which constitute a 'competent' contribution at various stages, Burgoyne characterizes as 'naive' (p. 9). The concept of 'competencies' has been extensively criticized by a number of commentators (see, for example, Hyland 1994, 1995) for privileging behaviour over knowledge and for trivializing the complexities of knowledge creation. Foucault (1991) makes a distinction between two categories of knowledge: *connaissance*, in which the subject or the knower is unchanged by the acquisition of knowledge, and *savoir*, whereby the knower's sense of self undergoes transformation (Marginson 1995). Following from this, the competence movement appears to embrace a 'connaissance' approach to knowledge, with knowledge acquisition being reduced to the progressive accumulation of particular sets of skills and bodies of information. The liberal humanist educational tradition aims towards a more 'savoir' orientated or transformatory approach to knowledge. Competency-based strategies do not tend to concern themselves with processes of education and understanding, but rather place a greater importance upon measurement, assessment and accreditation.

HRM: its relationship to organizational power and discipline

A number of writers (Townley 1993, 1994; Rose 1989; Burrell 1988) have drawn upon the work of Foucault, applying it to an analysis of organizations. Foucault's conceptualizations of power, knowledge and discipline have proved particularly valuable for the analysis of workplace practices. Foucault (1977) makes a distinction between traditional power and disciplinary power, which he identifies as the two modes of domination which have prevailed historically within the Western world. For him, contemporary society is characterized by hidden disciplinary techniques which permeate everyday existence. The example *par excellence* for Foucault of the disciplinary mode of domination is the Panopticon, the prison designed by Jeremy Bentham. The Panopticon has a central observational tower which renders the inmates visible at all times, whilst allowing the observers to remain unseen. Central to its design is the premise that the very act of subjecting the prisoners to such surveillance will ensure they conform regardless of whether they are being watched.

Disciplinary power operates through the process of rendering something or someone visible: as Townley (1993) phrases it, 'before something can be governed or managed, it must first be known'. Foucault referred to this disciplinary system in which knowledge and power are so intimately conjoined, as 'governmentality' (Foucault 1979). For Foucault, power is not a commodity which can be possessed; it is relational. Power resides in a network of relationships, becoming evident only when it is exercised: it lies within practices, procedures and techniques (Townley 1993). Governmentality is dependent upon particular ways of knowing: through the collection and collation of data about populations, groups of people may be ordered, represented, calculated, regulated, administered, supervised and governed in various ways. Knowledge is necessary to the operation of disciplinary power.

Although Foucault did not apply these concepts to a study of work organizations, their relevance is undeniable. Townley (1993: 526) offers a Foucauldian analysis of human resource management:

> HRM serves to render organizations and their participants calculable arenas, offering through a variety of techniques, the means by which activities and individuals become knowable and governable. HRM disciplines the interior of the organization, organizing time, space, and movement within it. Through various techniques, tasks, behavior, and interactions are categorized and measured. HRM provides measurement of both physical and subjective dimensions of labor offering a technology that renders individuals and their behavior predictable and calculable. In so doing, HRM helps to bridge the gap between promise and performance, between labor power and labor, and it organizes labor as a productive force.

Appraisals and the concept of 'competence' construct people as manageable, quantifiable entities. Data about employees and their abilities are able to be collected, and assessments and judgements can be made on the basis of such information. Appraisals are not merely a technical response to problems of governance and accountability, but also actively shape the activities overseen in relation to a specific conception of accountability, in that practices and environments are *made* appraisable, being structured around the need to be monitored (Power 1994).

In tandem with the emergence of the 'enterprise culture' and individualism propagated by the New Right, organizational cultures have also become 'individualized'. The enthusiasm for human resource management is a part of this development. Human resource instruments such as appraisals and competencies tend to operate at the level of the individual: as Townley notes, 'the focus on the productivity of the individual has the result of defining the individual as the *unit* of work'. There has been a shift away from fixed ladders of career progression with merit and remuneration increasingly being decided on an individual basis. Responsibility for training and development has passed to the employee who now seeks to amass a portable portfolio of skills. The individual thereby becomes the analogue of flexible capitalism.

Towards a typology of managerialist organizations

It was suggested earlier that the political agendas which have led to managerialism are underpinned by notions of value-for-money, competition and marketization. Values which put educational organizations at the service of policy become the means by which to produce compliance with political ends. To date, many of these ends have been expressed in terms of targets for student completion rates in specific vocational qualifications as part of an overall policy to create labour market flexibility. To secure these objectives, policy makers have created a system of regulations designed to ensure that educational organizations adhere to policy and do not stray down idiosyncratic pathways.

Managerialism as it has developed in public policy tends to be predicated on a cost-driven, input-output model (see Figure 8.1). The organization receives inputs which are then enhanced by managerial processes to the point where they emerge as outcomes. The outcomes are designed to be in harmony with the stipulations of policy, and to demonstrate this explicitly, and to measure its degree of compliance, the organization is encouraged to devise a corporate plan to show how it proposes to satisfy its stakeholders, chief amongst which are the agencies monitoring policy implementation.

In its basic form, the managerialist system can be represented as a cost-driven, through-put model, where the management processes employed by the organization have to maximize the opportunities afforded by its inputs. It follows, therefore, that if an organization chooses to adhere to the goals implied by the system then it is compelled by its own logic to work to a definition of the management process as being the capacity to use inputs in the most efficient and effective manner in order to achieve low-cost outcomes. Such a definition is forced, or determined, by the very nature of a cost-based approach to the educational process.

According to this model, all internal process, including the managerial process itself, is to be treated as a cost, and in this ideal–typical form, the rationale for the organization is measured wholly by its capacity to generate acceptable outcomes. It follows, therefore, that any internal process has no intrinsic value except in so far as it directly contributes to low-cost outcomes.

In practice, of course, there will be alternative objectives and values in

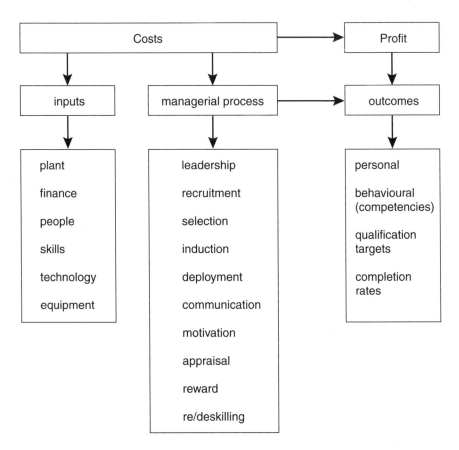

Figure 8.1 A cost-driven model of the managerial process

play, arising from the different perspectives of an institution's employees towards their own role as teachers and that of their institution. However, it is our contention that under the 'hard' versions of HRM currently demanded by the regulatory systems operating on FHE institutions that managerial practice will be obliged to find ways of politically disarming or neutralizing the influence of dissenting voices.

The problem of fixed costs

Under the highly regulated conditions we have described, teaching is treated as an operational process, and, like all other processes, is a cost in the service of outcomes. It follows, therefore, that by reducing the cost of teaching, say, then it is possible to achieve more outcomes for a fixed unit of resource. Traditionally, as we suggested earlier, teaching costs have represented roughly 65–70 per cent of overall fixed costs. But the enemy of any cost-driven organization is fixed cost. Immovable fixed costs undermine management choice and flexibility. Chief executives are, therefore, forced to attack fixed costs and have little alternative but either to reduce the organization's fixed costs directly or to shift some of them into the category of variable costs. This shifting of costs from fixed to variable has enormous consequences for how the organization views itself – for its strategic development and for its corporate culture, structures and operational management. Attitudes to cost and their management provide the ideological rationale underpinning labour flexibility in terms of the relationship between 'core' and 'peripheral' workers and the use of casualization. Each of these employment options is a corporate expression of the drive to control fixed salary costs, and the identification of an increasing proportion of salary costs as *variable* which operate according to market demand, student numbers, and shifts in funding. But once an item is defined as a variable cost it is difficult to convert its status back into that of a fixed cost. To manage an organization as if its cost base were mostly variable inevitably means that its size, in terms of the numbers it employs, its operational and quality assurance processes must adapt accordingly.

HRM as a form of superstructure

The shift from a view of operations based on fixed as distinct from variable costs can materially change organizational culture. In this scenario, financial control becomes a sub-structure, which, because of its threats to the organization's culture, requires a justificatory superstructure – a rationale for change in the form of mission statements, corporate values, and the encouragement of new behaviours and beliefs. In short, a new guiding culture becomes necessary, one strong enough to produce acceptance of the powers which now manipulate organizational sub-structures based largely on considerations of service cost and accountancy measures of outcomes. It is at this point that the public sector cost-driven organization subsumes private sector values of productivity and competition based on price – a new orientation which has to be 'sold' to the teaching staff. A successful superstructure operating inside the organization will work to convince staff to 'buy into' the input–output way of working. To accommodate this process a variety of cultural agents (some internally and some externally devised) are deployed: most notably HRM and HRD.

These two approaches to staff development assume their place in an expositional superstructure designed to justify why an organization's costs are to be perceived as variable and not as fixed. HRM and HRD encourage employees to collude in legitimating the dominance of variable over fixed costs and, therefore, work to achieve a substantial shift in perception away from the structural inflexibility associated with organizations dominated by fixed costs. Indeed, such organizations are castigated for their assumed weaknesses: formal differentiation of roles and tasks, lack of responsiveness to customer relations, high overheads and job security; but, worst of all, inflexibility.

To overcome the supposed burden of inflexibility, superstructural devices such as HRM and HRD are put in the service of change management, and employees, often unaware that they are now regarded as a variable cost, are actively encouraged to procure their place in the new flexibility, and to ignore the paradox that long-term employment is now based on an ability to move from one insecure job to another in a never-ending series, and possibly all the way to retirement. The new flexibility is legitimated by the need to be competitive, highly productive and, on the organization's behalf, innovative. Indeed, 'competitiveness' is defined in terms of an organization's capacity to achieve productivity and innovation at all levels and in all business processes. HRM and HRD are then directed at these two key areas.

Generally, HRM is considered to be a long-term process of development, applied in a continuous and consistent fashion (through the transmission of information, staff meetings, evaluation and performance review, for example), whilst HRD usually comes into operation only after the strategic objectives have been set. The current trend amongst those involved in private sector management training is that HRM works to support HRD so that HRD is resourced and fine-tuned to the point at which corporate strategy has been set by line managers with direct knowledge of markets, technologies, operational procedures, etc, and not by chief executives and boards, whose role is normally focused on the control of resources. Senior management then enters into a dialogue with the organization's line managers as to how best to resource their strategic ambitions: a collegial approach to strategy.

Whether FHE institutions are able to so orient themselves towards collegial strategy development is problematic. It is clearly possible in theory and intention, but, as Ainley and Bailey indicate, many of the lecturers in their case studies felt marginalized from the strategic decision making of senior management – a situation also applying to the lecturer respondents involved in our research. In view of the financial pressures to secure successful student throughput, it is more probable that institutions will rely on a variety of human resource approaches designed to accommodate predetermined strategies set by senior management, and in this respect will be used *post hoc* to help consolidate changes announced, rather than discussed – a phenomenon characteristic of mechanistic, top-down decisional styles prevalent in managerialist organizations. Rarely are HRM and HRD used to render an organization more collegial – rather the opposite.

In its own terms, HRM is at its most effective as a socialization process – a persuasive and educative preparation for human resource development.

The support which each gives to the other draws on a common value system which is intended to service an input–output view of the educational process. In such a context there is pressure to bring an individual's public persona into line with the organization's corporate values, a process which equates individual autonomy with corporate responsibility. It follows, therefore, that within training and staff development programmes, critical sources of knowledge and learning are likely to be treated, at best, as an expensive and wasteful luxury discordant with corporate values. The result is that intellectual enquiry, critique and diversity are neglected in favour of expediency and pragmatism, and education is replaced by training and skills development.

A worst case scenario?

In its basic, ideal–typical form, the managerialist organization can be perceived as being dedicated to the control of resources which in turn are dedicated to servicing outcomes. Under such a regime, an organization's value to society is measured largely in terms of the number and quality of the outcomes it can produce from the resources available to it. Competition between organizations creates demands for higher levels of productivity and innovation, and resource utilization has to adjust accordingly. The ends (outcomes) determine the means (the use of resources), and human resource management and development service the ends by manipulating the means. Under managerialist regimes there is progressively less discussion about means: it is as if, by being separated from discussion about ends, educational professionals also lose their rights with regard to influencing the best means. With cost as a pressure point, power is re-allocated, and roles and tasks re-designed to ensure that the lowest cost means minister to the demand of outcomes. Driven as it is by its adherence to the input–output mode of operation, the managerial organization must both originate and supervise key areas of control. It will most probably seek to remove from professional employees areas of discretion which were once fundamental and axiomatic and substitute refinements and redefinitions so that values are brought into harmony with the concerns of the cost-conscious corporation. As means change so values are also required to adapt, decisions and operational procedures bend to the moment, and when the moment demands low-cost flexibility whatever stands in the way is liable to be treated as antiquated practice, best forgotten. History and tradition become the enemy of the forward looking corporation as it attaches itself to its low-cost outputs.

Although we have characterized the *managerial organization* in its basic, ideal–typical form, the model we have described accords in most of its characteristics with the perceptions of many of the respondents in our research interviews (Yarrow and Esland 1998). Along with other researchers in the FE sector, we have found a substantial amount of evidence confirming the view that lecturing staff are experiencing the reforms in ways which accord with our depiction of the 'managerialization' process in further education institutions. The experiences reported include work intensification and overload, casualization, and for some, deskilling and de-professionalization – a view particularly prevalent among those who have been moved from more 'advanced' courses to those offering GNVQ and NVQ accreditation. There is also a widely reported sense of polarization between the strategic decision making of the senior management teams and the work environment of rank-and-file teachers.

As far as the impact of the reforms on the quality of provision is concerned, there are doubts particularly about the forms of measurement used in its assessment. Randle and Brady (1997) report, for example, that many of their lecturer respondents were sceptical about the systems of quality assurance put in place in their case study institutions:

> Lecturers felt that their judgment and control over the educational process was being displaced by that of managers. Of our survey, 80% of respondents felt that organisational changes had not improved the quality of services to students, and 95% thought that the changes as a whole had not enhanced student learning.
>
> (ibid.: 233)

They also indicate a concern about the concept of 'quality' used by the senior managers which, the authors felt,

> conforms not with the common understanding of goods or services of a superior standard but with the 'conformance to requirements' definitions of the quality gurus. Thus, however 'inferior' a product may be in absolute terms, as long as it consistently meets the standards that beat the competition within its market niche, goods or services can be regarded as having quality.
>
> (ibid.: 234)

Ainley and Bailey sum up many of their respondents' concerns in the following terms

> The effect [of the policies of the FEFC] has been to reduce the space and scope for the exercise of teachers' professional autonomy . . . a common element in [the] statements by teachers is the loss of control over much of their working lives and the feeling that they are increasingly regulated either from outside (as by the NCVQ) or indirectly by systems locally created in response to the requirements of the FEFC.
>
> (1997: 72)

Perhaps more seriously they cite one of their respondents as speaking for many in claiming that

> I would say that the actual quality of teaching and therefore the quality of what we offer has declined dramatically . . . The curriculum offer for students is far worse. It is narrower in some ways because the actual range of the offer has decreased. We've withdrawn from many vocational areas of course. In terms of staff/student contact that has reduced fairly dramatically and because of the engine of the funding mechanism the college is recruiting inappropriately to courses thereby affecting retention. Students are joining courses, finding that their course is not appropriate, above their level of ability – it's just not the thing for them – and they are then withdrawing or just dropping out, occasionally transferring to another course but very little transfer goes on.
>
> (ibid.: 71)

Beyond determinism?

While not disputing the force and accuracy of these and similar assessments, Gleeson and Shain (1998) draw attention to the fact that the management culture currently prevailing in the FE sector is itself open to contestation. Simply to underline the polarization of interests is to understate the ways in which internal policy decisions will often reflect compromise and negotiation. Particularly important in their view is the role of the 'middle manager' who is often a mediating agent between senior management and the teachers. As Gleeson and Shain put it, one of their key functions is to engage in 'the tricky task of constructing the *art of the possible* in translating policy into practice in ways which are acceptable and make sense to both groups'. In terms of the *realpolitik* of the FHE institution, therefore, it would be a mistake to overemphasize the monolithic nature of the managerial culture.

A similar view of the managerial process in FHE institutions is taken by Winter (1995: 137), who, while recognizing the totalizing ambitions of management practices such as HRM and Total Quality Management underlines the point that

> industrialised labour processes are structured by managerial *attempts* at controlling the methods and procedures at work which are only partially successful, generating antagonisms which are nevertheless limited by management's need to maintain consent and creativity on the part of workers.

While Winter may be correct in the broader scheme of things, there are many who have been unable to prevent the exercise of managerial will within their own institutions and who have paid the price in terms of their job, livelihood and self-respect.

Conclusion

We have set out in this chapter to examine the ways in which human resource management in its various forms – both explicitly and implictly – has become a major instrument for the management of change imposed by the 1992 legislation on FHE institutions. Although the state has retained overall control through its devolved regulatory system, each institution has had to take responsibility for its own management solutions, in which the compounding of financial, curricular and staffing demands has found in HRM an adaptable instrument enabling each to be calibrated against the others within the total equation for driving down costs. So intrusive have the processes of HRM become that it is now probable that the ambiguities noted by commentators in its early years of use have been resolved by its widespread promotion by the state in further and higher education. The ferocity of its application in organizations which have a claim to be involved in 'learning for life' may well come to be viewed as a tragic irony. While in the FEHE Act of 1992 the immediate political objectives of the New Right may have been met, it could well come to be seen as a Pyrrhic victory.

The authors

Geoff Esland is Director of the Centre for Sociology and Social Research in the School of Education at the Open University.

Karen Esland is a researcher in the School of Education at the Open University.

Mike Murphy is Senior Lecturer in Corporate Strategy, Nottingham Business School, Nottingham Trent University.

Karen Yarrow is a researcher in the School of Education at the Open University.

Note

1   The research on which this paper is based is currently being carried out within the School of Education's Centre for Sociology and Social Research. The focus of the research is the direction and impact of managerial reform in the institutions of further and higher education. The two projects on which this paper draws are 'The impact of the 1992 FE and HE Act on the Roles and Identities of FE Professionals' (Karen Yarrow), and 'Business Schools and the Construction of Management Knowledge' (Karen Esland).

References

Ainley, P. and Bailey, B. (1997) *The Business of Learning: Staff and Student Experiences of Further Education in the 1990s*, London: Cassell.

Alvares, K.M. (1997) 'The business of human resources', *Human Resource Management* 36(1): 9–15.

Antonacopoulou, E. and FitzGerald, L. (1996) 'Reframing competency in management development', *Human Resource Management Journal* 6(1): 27–48.

Armstrong, M. (1987) 'Human resource management: a case of the emperor's new clothes?', *Personnel Management* August.

Avis, J., Bloomer, M., Esland, G., Gleeson, D. and Hodkinson, P. (1996) *Knowledge and Nationhood: Education, Politics and Work*, London, Cassell.

Ball, S.J. (1994) *Education Reform: A Critical and Post-structural Approach*, Buckingham: Open University Press.

Bird, M., Esland, G., Greenberg, J., Sieminski, S. and Yarrow, K. (1998) 'The implementation of GNVQ in Further Education: the impact on the role of the professional', in M. Flude and S. Sieminski (eds) *Education, Training and the Future of Work II: Developments in Vocational Education and Training*, London: Routledge.

Blyton, P. and Morris, J. (1992) 'HRM and the limits of flexibility', in P. Blyton and P. Turnbull (eds) *op. cit.*

Blyton, P. and Turnbull, P. (eds) (1992) *Reassessing Human Resource Management*, London: Sage.

Boyatzis, R.E. (1982) *The Competent Manager: A Model for Effectiveness Performance*, New York: Wiley.

Burgoyne, J. (1993) 'The competence movement: issues, stakeholders and prospects', *Personnel Review* 22: 6–13.

Burrell, G. (1988) 'Modernism, post modernism and organizational analysis 2: the contribution of Michel Foucault', *Organization Studies* 9(2): 221–35.

Campion, M. and Renner, W. (1995) 'Goal setting, domestication and academia: the beginnings of an analysis', in J. Smyth (ed.) *Academic Work: The Changing Labour Process in Higher Education*, Buckingham: SRHE and Open University Press.

Clarke, J. and Newman, J. (1997) *The Managerial State: Power, Politics and Ideology in the Remaking of Social Welfare*, London: Sage.

Crosthwaite, E. and Warner, D. (1995) 'Setting the scene', in D. Warner and E. Crosthwaite (eds) *op. cit.*

Cunningham, B. (1997) 'The failing teacher in further education', *Journal of Further and Higher Education* 21(3): 365–71.

Department for Education and Employment (DfEE) (1998) *The Learning Age: A Renaissance for a New Britain*, Cm 3790, London: HMSO.

Esland, G.M. (1996) 'Knowledge and nationhood: the New Right, education and the global market', in J. Avis *et al. op. cit.*

Esland, K. (forthcoming) *Business Schools and the Construction of Management Knowledge*.

Ezzamel, M., Lilley, S., Wilkinson, A. and Willmott, H. (1996) 'Practices and practicalities in Human Resource Management', *Human Resource Management Journal* 6(1): 63–80.

Foucault, M. (1977) *Discipline and Punish: The Birth of the Prison*, Harmondsworth: Penguin.

Foucault, M. (1979) 'Governmentality', *Ideology and Consciousness*, 6(5): 5–21.

Foucault, M. (1991) *Remarks on Marx* (trans. R.J. Goldstein and J. Cascaito) New York: Colombia University.

Further Education Funding Council (FEFC) (1997) *Learning Works: Widening Participation in Further Education* (Kennedy Report), Coventry: FEFC.

Gleeson, D. (1996) 'Post-compulsory education in a post-industrial and post-modern age', in J. Avis *et al. op. cit.*

Gleeson, D. and Shain, F. (1998) 'Managing ambiguity: between markets and managerialism: a case study of 'middle' managers in further education', unpublished paper .

Grey, C. and Mitev, N. (1995) 'Management education: a polemic', *Management Learning* 26(1): 73–90.

Guest, D.E. (1987) 'Human resource management and industrial relations', *Journal of Management Studies* 24(5): 503–21.

Guest, D.E. (1991) 'Personnel management: the end of orthodoxy?', *British Journal of Industrial Relations* 29(2): 149–75.

Gunter, H. (1997) *Rethinking Education: The Consequences of Jurassic Management*, London: Cassell.

Hood, C. (1991) 'A public management for all seasons', *Public Administration*, 69: 3 19.

House, D. and Watson, D. (1995) 'Managing change', in D. Warner and E. Crosthwaite (eds) *op. cit.*

Hyland, T. (1994) *Competence, Education and NVQs: Dissenting Perspectives*, London: Cassell.

Hyland, T. (1995) 'Behaviourism and the meaning of competence', in P. Hodkinson and M. Issitt (eds) *The Challenge of Competence: Professionalism through Vocational Education and Training*, London: Cassell.

Keenoy, T. (1990) 'HRM: a case of the wolf in sheep's clothing' *Personnel Review* 19(2): 3–9.

Keep, E., Storey, J. and Sisson, K. (1996) 'Managing the employment relationship in higher education: quo vadis?', in R. Cuthbert (ed.) *Working in Higher Education*, Buckingham: SRHE and Open University Press.

Legge, K. (1989) 'Human resource management: a critical analysis', in J. Storey (ed.) *New Perspectives on Human Resource Management*, London: Routledge.

Macintyre, A. (1985) *After Virtue: A Study in Moral Theory*, London: Duckworth.

Marginson, S. (1995) 'Markets in higher education: Australia', in J. Smyth (ed.) *Academic Work: The Changing Labour Process in Higher Education*, Buckingham: SHRE and Open University Press.

Offe, C. (1976) *Industry and Inequality: The Achievement Principle in Work and Social Status*, (trans. by James Wickham), London: Edward Arnold.

Pollitt, C. (1993) *Managerialism and the Public Services*, Oxford: Blackwell.

Poole, M. (1990) 'Editorial: HRM in an international perspective', *International Journal of Human Resource Management* 1(1): 1–15.

Power, M. (1994) *The Audit Explosion*, London: Demos.

Randle, K. and Brady, N. (1997) 'Further education and the new managerialism', *Journal of Further and Higher Education* 21(2): 229–39.

Rose, N. (1989) *Governing the Soul: The Shaping of the Private Self*, London: Routledge.

Schuler, R. and Jackson, S. (1987) 'Linking competitive strategies with human resource management practices', *Academy of Management Executive* 1(3): 207–19.

Sisson, K. (1989) 'Personnel management in transition', in K. Sisson (ed.) *Personnel Management in Britain*, Oxford: Basil Blackwell.

Storey, J. (1989) 'Human Resource Management in the public sector', in *Public Money and Management* 9(3): 19–24.

Townley, B. (1989) 'Selection and appraisal', in J. Storey (ed.) *New Perspectives on Human Resource Management*, London: Routledge.

Townley, B. (1993) 'Foucault, power/knowledge, and its relevance for human resource management', *Academy of Management Review* 18(3): 518–45.

Townley, B. (1994) *Reframing Human Resource Management: Power, Ethics and the Subject at Work*, London: Sage.

Warner, D. and Crosthwaite, E. (eds) (1995) *Human Resource Management in Higher and Further Education*, Buckingham: SRHE and Open University Press.

Wilson, T. (1998) 'United front aims to end casual labour', *Times Higher Education Supplement* 17 July: 9.

Winter, R. (1995) 'The University of Life plc: the 'industrialisation' of higher education?', in J. Smyth (ed.) *Academic Work*, Buckingham: SRHE and Open University Press.

Yarrow, K. and Esland, G. (1998) 'The changing role of the professional in the new further education', paper presented to the BERA Conference, September 1998.

Yarrow, K. (forthcoming) *The impact of the 1992 FE and HE Act on the Roles and Identities of FE Professionals*.

Chapter 9

The University of Life plc[1]

The 'industrialization' of higher education?

Richard Winter

Introduction

The increasing subjection of public institutions to the reductive rigours of monetarist economics has gradually, over the past 15 years or so, produced a crisis of confidence in certain quarters. No longer does it seem generally plausible to prescribe the forms and values required for public welfare on the basis of institutionalized expert authority, i.e. that of civil servants, politicians, professionals in general or (in particular) educators. Instead, cultural authority is now projected on to 'the market' and a bereft humanity seems to be condemned for the time being to organize *all* its affairs within the general parameters of capitalism, whose apparent claim is that matters of value and priority must be adjudicated simply by the forces of supply and demand. In other words, since there can be no welfare without profitability, the former can be subsumed under the latter: the good may be equated with the profitable. Faced with this ideological challenge, higher education staff, who have traditionally raised their own serious claim to cultural authority, are called upon to formulate a response which is both critical and constructive, neither retreating into a merely rhetorical expression of lost ideals nor colluding with a social system whose disorders are plain to see. The problem is, as always, one of articulating an explorative, critical, yet practical understanding of the various forces and processes involved.

It is to this end that the argument of this chapter is addressed. The contemporary university is inevitably bound up with the political and economic forces of capitalism, which threaten to submit the integrity of educational and academic values to the forms and priorities of market-oriented production. Fortunately, however, these threats are mitigated by the contradictions within the managerial ideology which tries to implement them. Hence, although we are indeed faced by *attempts* to impose an industrial, profit-oriented logic on to higher education, this situation is not without real educational opportunities, both to shed some of the oppressive practices enshrined in higher education's traditional forms and to begin to realize some innovative and progressive possibilities. In other words, contradictions do not only generate 'problems' (injustices, evasions and suffering), but they also generate spaces within which power can be contested and reforms can be won. Let us begin, therefore, by looking at the *ambiguities* underlying current pressures for change in the UK higher education system.

Pressures for change: education *and* economic development

A significant aspect of current higher education initiatives in the UK is that they emanate not from the government Department for Education but from the Employment Department (Employment Department 1990; Duckenfield and Stirner 1992). This, of course, may serve to confirm the worst suspicions of academics, that education is now officially equated with labour force training, having noted that the government's 1985 consultative document *The Development of Higher Education into the 1990s* begins 'The economic performance of the UK since 1945 has been disappointing' (DES 1985: para. 1.2), and immediately continues 'The societies of our competitors are producing ... more qualified scientists, engineers, technologists, and technicians than the UK' (para 1.3).

Although some HE staff may feel antagonized when the Employment Department introduces accounts of its higher education initiatives by announcing, frankly, its concern 'to support economic growth by promoting a competitive, efficient, and flexible labour market' (Employment Department 1990: 5; Duckenfield and Stirner 1992: 3), the relationship between educational values and economic development is not a simple opposition. The list of headings under which the Employment Department presents its funded projects includes not only 'employer relevance' and 'high level skills supply' but also such acceptable educational concepts as 'increased learner responsibility' and 'continuing professional development' (Employment Department 1990: 88 ff.). It also challenges the restrictive elitism of HE institutions through headings such as 'wider accessibility' (i.e. 'access for non-traditional students'), 'alternative admissions mechanisms' and 'accreditation of prior experiential learning' (*ibid.*).

The latter themes provide an obvious managerial issue, which is frequently presented as higher education's most urgent current problem: how can restricted, elitist HE be extended to become open access HE available to the mass of the citizenry without a loss in 'quality'? (see Ball 1990). But beneath this issue lies another, one which managerial rhetoric takes for granted and at the same time ignores. It is neatly symbolized by Ball's reference to 'UK plc' (1990: 3–4), which subsumes the entire nation state within the conceptual field of commerce. The issue here is the relationship between a theory of decision-making based entirely on market forces, competitive profitability, etc. (as in 'UK plc') and decision-making supposedly based on the direct analysis and judgement of human need, which has traditionally been the province (or at least the claim) of the various professions, including educationists. This is the real challenge currently facing higher education, a challenge which many current initiatives both conceal and render more acute (e.g. the nature of 'personal skills': Employment Department 1990). The first step, then, is to explore the nature of this ideological challenge: how should we articulate the relationship between higher education institutions and those embodying commerce and industry?

(. . .)

Changes in higher education and the industrialization of the labour process

Let us begin with an interpretation of the broad historical context, namely Mandel's argument that the fundamental historical pressure of a capitalist economy is a general drive to extend the logic of the market into more and more areas of social activity (Mandel 1978: 47), which, therefore, is now affecting universities, along with schools, hospitals, ambulance services, prisons, the civil service, etc. Mandel's argument is as follows. At any point in time (since the Middle Ages at least) areas of economic activity have been structured in one of two ways: (a) as the investment of capital (seeking dividends) in order to manufacture goods for a market (seeking profits); (b) as the primary organization of available resources in order to produce goods through craft labour in direct response to cultural definitions of social need. The superior dynamism of the former (due to the possibility of dividends and profits, leading to the rapid accumulation of capital for further developmental investment) means that it has tended to supersede the latter: gradually, but (it would seem) inexorably, craft work has yielded to highly capitalized production (Mandel 1978: 46–8). The increasing pace of technological innovation (*ibid.*: Chapter 8) is dictated by the fact that it is the creativity of workers, not machines themselves, that creates profits (because machinery must be bought at a price which has already made a profit for the seller). Consequently, the higher the component of capital expenditure in the costs of production (i.e. with advancing technology), the lower is the *rate* of profit per unit of cost. Hence we see the continual seeking of new domains in which capital can be invested, advanced technology applied and profits created, i.e. in such areas as research and development (*ibid.*: 249), the provision of services (transport, power utilities, accounting, stock control) and thus, finally, for the purposes of our analysis here, education. 'Far from representing a "post-industrial" society, late capitalism thus constitutes *generalized universal industrialization* for the first time in history' (*ibid.*: 387).

From the perspective of Mandel's argument, therefore, higher education may be seen as a sector currently dominated by craft processes and now due for 'industrialization'. The new initiatives and rationales already referred to are thus not simply the imposition of a political dogma, as a set of arbitrary, barbarous and implausible metaphors, but an expression of the inherent developmental logic of capitalism. The next question is, therefore, if this is the nature of the underlying historical forces at work, what does this imply in terms of the actual experience of university staff? What is entailed in a move from craft work to 'industrialized' production in the context of higher education?

Harry Braverman's account of the changing labour process in manufacturing contexts offers various chilling suggestions (Braverman 1974). Braverman looks back to a period of craft labour in which 'the worker was presumed to be the master [sic] of a body of traditional knowledge, and methods and procedures were left to his or her discretion' (ibid.: 109, 443), and argues that the process of industrialization has entailed a sustained and successful attempt by management (inspired by Frederick Taylor's theories and exhortations) to impose rigid control over the production process by subdividing the complex ensemble of craft work into simple stages, none of which allows the worker to comprehend or to take responsibility for the overall process. Decisions about the production process are taken centrally by management, through their control of the complex equipment which in turn dictates the 'methods and procedures' required. From the point of view of the worker, therefore, work becomes fragmentary, and its meaning is displaced from an awareness of its contribution to human needs on to its function within a determined production process over which the worker has no control. This displacement of the meaning of the labour process corresponds to the displacement of the meaning of the product of labour, from its value in meeting human needs ('use value') to its ability to command a profitable price on the market ('exchange value'). In other words, the labour process and the product of labour become mere 'commodities', whose value is defined solely by their capacity to generate profits. This in turn means that the worker is subjected to unmitigated control by management, since management is in charge of decisions affecting the profitability of the enterprise, i.e. concerning the disposition of resources.

Let us see how far Braverman's analysis can be applied to higher education, i.e. to teaching and research. One of the most important current educational initiatives, strongly endorsed by the UK government, is 'competence-based vocational education', in which curricula (in vocational areas) are cast in the form of competence statements that guide students in presenting work-derived evidence to be assessed mainly by staff employed in the students' workplace. These competences (which function rather like curriculum objectives) are established by consortia consisting mainly of employers ('industrial lead bodies'). Attempts are currently being made to apply this curriculum model to professional education within universities, especially in the field of management (see MCI 1991). It appears to entail a reduction in the role of the teacher to that of a supportive tutor: the setting of objectives and the design and sequencing of learning has been on the one hand appropriated by the industrial lead body and on the other hand delegated to the students, and responsibility for assessing students' work is redistributed from HE staff to (a) workplace assessors and (b) university quality control procedures.

Similarly, university courses are increasingly being recast into integrated systems of 'modular' units, allowing students to construct their own 'customized' courses by selecting their own combination of modules. This means that HE staff no longer have responsibility for designing a sequence of learning experiences which might profoundly affect student identities; instead they merely make available a circumscribed fragment of expertise within a computerized system of options. Gone is the general authority of the individual 'educator' (parent-figure or cultural crusader); instead HE staff are purveyors of commodities within a knowledge 'supermarket', which may or may not be selected by the student-as-customer. Responsibility for the overall coherence and progression of students' education is assumed not by the staff who teach individual modules but by the academic managers who design the modular system and by the academic counsellors who guide student choice of modules.

Parallel expressions of the loss of formerly comprehensive responsibilities occur in the context of research. Sandra Harding proposes the rejection of 'industrialized' forms of social inquiry (capital intensive, hierarchically managed) in favour of a return to an earlier model of the scientist as a 'craft worker', who is responsible for the whole process of inquiry, from the selection of problems and methods to the interpretation of results, and thus requires a 'unity of hand, brain and heart' which is the antithesis of the modern labour process (Harding 1986: 248). (See also Julius Roth's (1965) strictures on 'hired hand research'.)

Is this link between the alienation of the assembly line worker and the alienation of the contemporary university lecturer/researcher merely a plausible emotive analogy, or does it also have a theoretical basis? Let us now consider, in more detail, the sense in which the 'products' of education and those of manufacturing industry are comparable, i.e. the nature of the 'commodity' form.

Commodities, knowledge and qualifications

Many would wish to restrict the analogy between the labour process in manufacture and the labour process in education by maintaining a theoretical distinction between 'productive' and 'non-productive' labour. The original basis for this distinction, however, is between labour which *produces* commodities (thereby adding value to raw material) and labour involved merely in the *circulation* of commodities (e.g. transport) (Mandel 1978: 401). But Mandel then generalizes the notion of 'unproductiveness' from the sector of circulation to services in general, and continues: 'The logic of late capitalism is therefore necessarily to convert idle capital into service capital and simultaneously to replace service capital with productive capital, in other words, services with commodities: transport services with private cars, theatre and film services with private television sets, tomorrow television services and educational instruction with video cassettes' (*ibid.*: 406).

However, the theoretical significance of this latter step is not clear: services begin to be incorporated into the relationships of an industrialized market economy when the provision of what is *needed* is converted into the provision of what can be profitably marketed, without necessarily requiring that the consumption of services take the form of purchasing an object. Production and consumption are complementary halves of the same circle of supply and demand (Samuelson 1980: 41); and 'services' are one form of all those 'goods' that can be produced and supplied, demanded and consumed. Thus, in a university context, although there is indeed pressure upon staff to create products that can be *sold* (videos, computer software, patentable technology), it is also recognized that profits can be made through *franchising* other types of product (course units, quality assurance procedures) and by *hiring out* facilities (human and material) for research and 'consultancy'. In the same way, some enterprises *sell* cars and TVs while others hire or lease them. In other words, following Burrell (1990: 292), it can be argued that surplus value can be created and realized wherever a market exists, and that commodities may be 'material or non-material'.

The essence of a commodity, then, is not that it actually is a 'thing', but that its *value* is determined by its capacity for being marketed for profit, rather than by its usefulness in contributing to 'genuine' human need. Its form therefore must be such that its profitability may be calculated, and for this reason it must be considered *as if* it were a 'thing' (with calculable properties). This thing-like quality disguises the fact that these properties are merely constructs necessitated by the social relationships embodied in the structure of the market, within which alone the commodity has value and meaning. The commodity form is thus a *displacement* of meaning: the market acts as a self-justifying decision-making mechanism, prioritizing social activities according to a systematically limited reality, in which the meaning and value of artefacts, actions and people are reconstructed in terms of the restrictive logic of profit generation.

According to this 'market logic', the relationship between teacher, student and curriculum is reconstructed as a relationship between producer, consumer and commodity. This might be seen in two ways. First, knowledge is packaged into pedagogical units ('modules') which correspond to numerical units of academic credit, based on average learning time. Second, academic qualifications constitute a currency with exchange value in relation to employment. The argument would then be as follows. Higher education staff and institutions will promote those pedagogical units and qualifications which have marketable value and students may be expected to attempt to acquire academic credit and profitable credentials at an advantageous 'price' (i.e. for relatively little effort). Clearly, such an analysis is not convincing as a *description* of current educational realities; rather, it delineates the form of an ideological *pressure*, with which HE staff will need to come to terms, a set of *metaphors* whose new-found plausibility may be used to legitimate (in the name of supposedly universal and inescapable market forces) the subjection of educational processes to specific political interests.

However, it is important to recognize that this type of analysis (economic imperatives leading to the commodification of culture) can easily lapse into yet another form of determinism, whose pretensions are always undermined by its lack of reflexivity: if culture in general has succumbed to commodification, then this very piece of writing itself must have the status of a commodity; and if so, what credence can be given to it? I must emphasize, therefore, that the increasing influence of the ideology of market relationships does not mean that human experience is about to be wholly encapsulated in commodity form, as Baudrillard and Wernick, for example, would have us believe (Baudrillard 1988; Wernick 1991). More precisely, an increase in the tendency towards the commodity formulation of knowledge, research and academic qualifications must not lead us (in an excess of melodramatic and self-important pessimism) to deny the possibilities for critical under-standing and innovative practice (see Willmott 1990: 358). Indeed, the argument in the next section is that the managers of market-oriented educa-tional institutions will not wish *simply* to restrict the scope of staff responsibility in order to achieve the commodification of the educational process; that (on the contrary) managers appear to have their own reasons for defining workers as possessing the capacity for critical, innovative autonomy.

The contradictions of 'management'

Higher education as the craft work of individual academic staff has always operated under some sort of institutional regulation and sanction, originally that of the Church and latterly that of the university bureaucracy, itself regulated by the state. What is new is the subjection of teaching, curriculum design and research to detailed management processes imitated from those of market-oriented manufacturing enterprises. How far will these new management processes interfere with that freedom of creation, interpreta-tion and criticism which academic staff would wish to claim (following Newman, perhaps) as traditionally characteristic of their work, but which they now see as being under threat (see Thompson 1970)?

Braverman's pessimism concerning management's inexorable domination of the labour process has been criticized as oversimplified (Littler 1990; Wardell 1990). Instead it is suggested that industrialized labour processes are structured by managerial attempts at controlling the methods and procedures of work which are only partially successful (Thompson 1990: 100), generating antagonisms which are nevertheless limited by management's need to maintain consent and creativity on the part of workers (*ibid.*: 101). This is the contradiction at the heart of the management role, reflecting, of course, the continuing contradictions at the heart of capitalism (Mandel 1978: 472), which necessitate 'the huge machinery of ideological manipulation' designed to 'integrate the worker into late capitalist society as a consumer, social partner, or citizen' (*ibid.*: 485). However, ideology is not an integrated, rationalized structure of illusions, but a series of fragments, reflections of the contradictions it seeks (with only partial success) to disguise (see Winter 1989). Management theory, therefore, in presenting its insistently harmonious view of the aims and processes of commercial enterprises cannot help accidentally revealing the contradictions it wishes to ignore and thus cannot address.

Hence arise the manifold inconsistencies of Peter Drucker's perpetually reprinted classic text on management (Drucker 1974, reprinted 1991). For example, we are told that 'the ultimate test of management is performance', and that performance must be measured against objectives, but that no one knows how to measure or even conceptualize objectives: even profitability is only measured with 'a rubber yardstick'. Similarly, he emphasizes that managers must live with uncertainty but that their decision-making must above all be 'systematic'. In other words, management is formulated both as the necessity for control and as an understanding of the impossibility of control. Hence, there is an emphasis that every job has to focus on the company's objectives and thus on the need for 'clear decision authority', and, at the same time, that workers are colleagues, not inferiors, who 'make genuine decisions' and 'take on the burden of responsibility', so that 'rank and file jobs are potentially managerial, or would be more productive if made so'. (Except that we don't know how to 'define, let alone measure productivity'.)

The analytical power of management theory is thus undermined by its own ideology. On the one hand it promotes a self-justificatory portrayal of the senior executive as the organizational 'brain', activating the enterprise by imposing objectives for all staff on the basis of management's exclusive understanding of the organization's relationship with its economic and political environment (Garratt 1987: 74–81) (which would seem to justify Braverman's nightmare of a triumphant Taylorian hierarchy). On the other hand there is total quality management (TQM), inspired by the work of Kaoru Ishikawa, which emphasizes that *every* worker can (and must) take responsibility for the overall purpose of the organization and for the continued improvement of the quality of its work – *their* work. The TQM model was explicitly developed as a rejection of Taylorian theories, which Ishikawa (like Braverman) saw as responsible for the alienation of workers from the objectives and results of their work (Hutchins 1988: 148–9).

However, the TQM focus on management's responsibility to establish 'commitment' on the part of the whole workforce (Hakes 1991: 66–8) is itself, as one would expect, highly contradictory. The commitment to 'never ending improvement' which provides the motivation for staff involvement in their 'quality circles' is based on supposed efforts to make their 'organization the best in its field' (Hutchins 1988: 23) within a competitive market whose main rationale for efficiency is that failure will be widespread. Hence, workers' sense of 'responsibility' is constructed (through organizational procedures) as a state of mind which management aims to manipulate: 'People have an innate loyalty to their group and to their company, even when their needs are not satisfied and even when they are unsuccessful' (*ibid.*: 132). (The expectation of an absolute loyalty to a specific organization must bring profound professional dilemmas for higher education workers, who will rather subscribe to an *academic responsibility* towards the wider critical community of their discipline.)

TQM's confidence in its vision of no faults, no delays and the harmonization of all organizational interests rests on a failure to address the contradictions between manipulation and responsibility, between customer sovereignty and pre-empting markets by anticipating and creating demand, between 'quality' as 'conformance to requirements' and the continual raising of targets (Hakes 1991). There are therefore grounds for hope: the inherent contradictions of the management role formulated by the model and, in particular, its commitment to the criticism of decisions by those to whom they have been delegated will ensure that industrialized educational institutions will, like their predecessors, afford conceptual and political space in which to formulate alternative practices to those anticipated in managerial rhetoric.

Conclusion: educational possibilities

Let us recapitulate the argument so far. The initiatives currently being urged upon higher education may be explained in terms of the ideological forces of fundamental historical developments. It is not helpful, therefore, to react with nostalgia, contrasting the malign logic of the market (mediated through the power of a profit-oriented management) with a supposed 'golden age' when the craft of the academic was simply the direct expression of moral value, educational need and the search for truth: traditional university culture has its own ambivalent involvement with oppressive social and political power (Bourdieu 1977, 1988). It is also important to note that there is a real sense in which a market decision-making structure can liberate citizens from subjection to elitist cultural authority by enfranchising them as consumers with 'money votes'. But it is equally clear that a market orientation (for educational processes as for anything else) involves not simply a rational functional relevance but a systematic distortion of meaning, an evasion of questions of value, need and ultimate purpose. To acquiesce completely in the commodification of knowledge would thus be, at the very least, a cultural disaster. It might also threaten the continued existence of humanity, since the purposes of market-oriented organizations are limited to the tiny period over which accountants can claim to be able to calculate profitability while their ecological effects are immense and hardly calculable at all. Management theory is too pragmatic, too self-serving, to acknowledge its contradictions, its inadequacies. Hence, for higher education institutions (as for other organizations) it is essential (for justice, for understanding, even for planetary survival) that managerial perspectives be challenged; and it is the accidental merit of modern management theory that its unacknowledged inconsistencies offer scope for such challenges. In the light of these considerations, then, let us consider how higher education institutions might formulate a critical response to a market-oriented ideology, through the redefinition of some key concepts.

Theory

'Theory' is linked etymologically with the idea of the spectator, and we have seen how Newman, for example, tried to formulate HE as insulated from worldly practices. As universities are drawn by market forces into a structured relationship with economics and politics, theory will no longer be a refuge from the world, and will have to protect itself against commodification by identifying its 'use value'. The separation of theory and practice will then not only be a matter for repeated lament, but will have to be addressed, not only in theory but in practice (Winter 1991). Theory may thus finally cease being merely abstraction (and thus as readily transmuted into commodity form as money itself: Sohn-Rethel 1978) and become (essentially, not merely as an option) intellectual critique, political challenge and a moment in the development of practice.

Scholarship

The scope of decision-making within market-oriented organizations is inherently limited: (i) by the priority given to the objectives of the organization, (ii) by the priority given to profitability, and (iii) by the exclusive focus on the current accounting period. Scholarship's concern with the preservation, collection and mastery of bodies of knowledge will thus be needed to expand the intellectual resources which can be brought to bear to inform (and hence to challenge) the limitations of market decision-making. It will offer the possibility of assembling a tradition and a multifarious range of understandings, from which alternatives can be derived and authorized. It will thus make available a variety of resources for disputing the legitimacy of managerial ideology.

Intellectuals

One aspect of the legitimating ideology of late capitalism is a general belief in 'technical rationality', which claims that fundamental antagonisms (i.e. other than those of 'opinion') have been abolished through rational organizational procedures and the application of innovative technology, thereby rendering obsolete any value systems beyond the calculation of instrumental means and functions (Mandel 1978: 501–2). We can assume that this ideology will come to exercise increasing influence in the debates over educational knowledge, and will need to be contested. Thus, in formulating principles and objectives for the curricula offered by HE institutions, the conceptions of 'the intellectual' to be found in the work of Gramsci (1971) and Gouldner (1979) will be an essential complement to the purely technical specifications which will be promoted by employers. Gramsci's work focuses on the general critical and integrative understandings which are potentially available to all citizens because they can be created upon those 'general conceptions of the world' which are already 'implicitly contained . . . in their practical activity' (Gramsci 1971: 344). Whereas Gramsci is explicitly outlining an educational programme for the future, Gouldner describes a certain aspect of (middle class) culture as though it were already achieved (which is doubtful). But his analysis of the 'culture of critical discourse', with its emphasis on reflexivity, self-monitoring, metacommunication and problematic justification (Gouldner 1979: 28–9) is none the less relevant for planners of HE curricula and assessment criteria. In other words, the ambition of HE staff should be that those who emerge with qualifications from our courses should not only be 'employees', possessing technically relevant knowledge, but should also be (in ways derivable from the ideas of Gramsci and Gouldner) 'intellectuals', and thus equipped to exploit to the full the opportunities for autonomy which the organizations in which they work are likely (following TQM principles) to make available.

The educative workplace

Reference has already been made to the increasing introduction of educational curricula based on evidence gathered and assessed in the workplace, led in the UK by the National Council for Vocational Qualifications (NCVQ). In many ways the current format for this work, based on prespecified 'competences', follows the organizational rationality of 'management by objectives' (Drucker 1974: 38); but it also rests explicitly on a learner-centred educational theory (Jessup 1991: Chapter 1), and this permits reinterpretations of the competence format aimed at reintroducing educational principles, such as critical reflection upon values, into the purely market-oriented version (Winter 1992). The work of the NCVQ evokes the possibility of the 'educative workplace' as an institutional form for the decentralization of knowledge creation, one of the progressive aspects of the 'postmodernist' epistemology (Winter 1991) which, together with the 'technical rationality' previously noted, constitutes the complex ideological underpinning of late capitalism (Jameson 1984). This will pose an interesting challenge to the current institutional structure of higher education. However, where work is structured by the processes and relationships of capitalism there are contradictions inherent in the very phrase 'educative workplace', and these are already beginning to appear. The construction industry is complaining about the narrowness of the competence-based curriculum, suggesting that managements do, in some ways, take seriously the need to increase the scope of workers' responsibilities (Callender 1992); and evidence from the initial phases of our own workplace-focused honours degree in social work suggests that staff find the pressures of the workplace so intense that finding genuine 'space' for reflection is a major problem (Winter and Maisch 1992: 11, 16–17, 29).

In conclusion, higher education institutions are already (and unavoidably) caught up in the contradictions of capitalist development. But for higher education staff this ought not to signify the doleful ending of a sacred tradition; rather, it should constitute the current challenge to our understanding of our role in a historical process which it would be futile to ignore, and which (like earlier phases of the process) offers not only threats but also opportunities.

Note

1   plc: public limited company. A company whose shares are quoted, bought and sold on the commercial stock market, like Unilever and Ford, but unlike a small family business, a charity or a public service institution.

References

Ball, C. (1990) *More Means Different.* London, Royal Society of Arts.

Baudrillard, J. (1988) The system of objects, in *Selected Writings.* Cambridge, Polity Press.

Bourdieu, P. (1977) *Reproduction in Education, Society, and Culture.* London, Sage Publications.

Bourdieu, P. (1988) *Homo Academicus.* Cambridge, Polity Press.

Braverman, H. (1974) *Labor and Monopoly Capital.* New York, Monthly Review Press.

Burrell, G. (1990) Fragmented Labours, in D. Knights and H. Willmott (eds) *Labour Process Theory.* Basingstoke, Macmillan.

Callender, C. (1992) *Will NVQs Work?* London, Institute of Manpower Studies.

Department of Education and Science (1985) *The Development of Higher Education into the 1990s.* London, HMSO.

Drucker, P. (1974) *Management.* Oxford, Butterworth/Heinemann.

Duckenfield, M. and Stirner, P. (1992) *Learning through Work.* Sheffield, Employment Department.

Employment Department (1990) *The Skills Link.* Sheffield, Employment Department.

Garratt, B. (1987) *The Learning Organization.* London, Fontana.

Gouldner, A. (1979) *The Future of Intellectuals.* London, Macmillan.

Gramsci, A. (1971) *Selections from the Prison Notebooks.* London, Lawrence and Wishart.

Hakes, C. (1991) *Total Quality Management.* London, Chapman & Hall.

Harding, S. (1986) *The Science Question in Feminism.* Milton Keynes, Open University Press.

Hutchins, D. (1988) *Just in Time.* Aldershot, Gower.

Jameson, F. (1984) Postmodernism, or the cultural logic of late capitalism, *New Left Review*, no. 146.

Jessup, G. (1991) *Outcomes.* London, Falmer Press.

Littler, C. (1990) The labour process debate, a theoretical review, in D. Knights and H. Willmott (eds) *Labour Process Theory.* Basingstoke, Macmillan.

Mandel, E. (1978) *Late Capitalism.* London, Verso.

MCI (1991) *Occupational Standards for Management.* London, Management Charter Initiative.

Roth, J. (1965) Hired hand research, *The American Sociologist*, 1, 190–6.

Samuelson, P. (1980) *Economics*, 11th edn. Tokyo, McGraw-Hill.

Sohn-Rethel A. (1978) *Intellectual and Manual Labour.* London, Macmillan.

Thompson, E.P. (1970) *Warwick University Ltd.* Harmondsworth, Penguin.

Thompson, P. (1990) Crawling from the wreckage: the labour process and the politics of production, in D. Knights and H. Willmott (eds) *Labour Process Theory.* Basingstoke, Macmillan.

Wardell, M. (1990) Labour and labour process, in D. Knights and H. Willmott (eds) *Labour Process Theory.* Basingstoke, Macmillan.

Wernick, A. (1991) *Promotional Culture.* London, Sage Publications.

Willmott, H. (1990) Subjectivity and the dialectics of praxis, in D. Knights and H. Willmott (eds) *Labour Process Theory.* Basingstoke, Macmillan.

Winter, R. (1989) Some notes on ideology and critique, in *Learning from Experience.* Lewes, Falmer Press.

Winter, R. (1991) Postmodern sociology as a democratic educational practice – some suggestions, *British Journal of Sociology of Education*, 12(4), 467–82.

Winter, R. (1992) 'Quality management' or 'the educative workplace': alternative versions of competence-based education, *Journal of Further and Higher Education*, 16(3).

Winter, R. and Maisch, M. (1992) *Accrediting Professional Competences, the Final Report of the ASSET programme.* Chelmsford, Anglia Polytechnic University.

Chapter 10

Economic restructuring and unemployment

A crisis for masculinity?

Faith Robertson Elliot

Over the past thirty years Western societies have experienced the development of labour-intensive technologies, increasing competition from the
expanding economies of the Third World, the decline of traditional heavy
manufacturing industry and the growth of service sector activity. This
massive restructuring of the economy has had as a major outcome the
contraction and increasing casualisation of labour markets. At the same
time, married women are increasingly economically active and the labour
force has grown in size. These processes have produced a shift from full-
time, secure and pensionable employment to part-time and casual
employment, from male labour to female labour and from full or nearly
full employment conditions to high levels of unemployment and sub-
employment.

The consequences of these changed labour market conditions are far
reaching and corrosive. Unemployment and sub-employment undermine the
economic status of individuals and their families and, in the view of some
authorities, have increased poverty, widened the gap between the financially
comfortable and the poor and contributed to the growth of an underclass.
Further, these employment conditions are widely perceived as threatening
the traditional organisation of masculinity, disrupting expected transitions
from dependent childhood to independent adulthood, putting at risk the
independence women have achieved through increasing economic activity,
challenging the work ethic and undermining everyday understandings of
what is fair and just. They may lead not only to physical and psychological ill-health and conflict between family members but also to lawlessness
and self-destructive deviance.

(. . .)

This chapter explores the consequences of these labour market conditions
for gender and family relations.

(. . .)

(I)t is generally agreed that employment and unemployment categorisa-
tions are problematic, that unemployment statistics are uncertain guides to
unemployment trends and that their overall effect is to mask the extent of

unemployment. Nevertheless, it is clear that unemployment levels have risen markedly.

The available data show that, during the early post-war period of economic expansion, all the major industrial societies of the Western world enjoyed full or nearly full employment. In Britain, for example, unemployment rates stood at less than 2 per cent of the labour force throughout most of the 1950s and 1960s. However, in the 1970s and 1980s the development of labour-intensive technologies, competition from the expanding economies of the Third World and the decline of traditional manufacturing industries combined, as has already been indicated, to produce contracting and casualised labour markets. (. . .)

(I)n-depth studies suggest that most families now experience the unemployment or sub-employment (part-time and/or casual employment), at some point in their life course, of one or more of their members. For example, in Allatt and Yeandle's study of youth unemployment in Newcastle in the early 1980s only seven of forty young people had been in continuous employment since leaving school and only seventeen had had only one job (Allatt and Yeandle, 1992, pp. 49–57). Thirteen had never had a job and ten had had twenty-six jobs between them. In addition, many new jobs are part-time jobs and increasingly men, like women, are in part-time employment. (. . .) Nearly one in every fifteen men and one in every two women is now in part-time employment.

Unemployment and sub-employment are not evenly distributed across the population but vary in four major ways. First, it has been consistently found that class disadvantage is associated with increased vulnerability to unemployment. (. . .) (M)anual workers are more likely to experience unemployment than white-collar workers and, within these broad occupational categories, semi-skilled and unskilled workers are more likely to be unemployed than skilled workers and junior intermediate workers than professional workers. Second, differences between ethnic groups in the incidence of unemployment have been extensively documented. In Britain, the 1991 Census shows not only that unemployment rates are considerably higher in ethnic minority populations than in the 'white' population, but that there is variation between ethnic minority groups. Levels are significantly higher among Pakistani, Bangladeshi, Black African and Afro-Caribbean men than among men in other ethnic minority groups. (. . .) Third, levels of unemployment among young people are higher than in older age groups and have increased at a faster rate. In Britain in 1992, nearly one in four young men aged 16–19 and one in six young men aged 20–29 were unemployed. (. . .) The comparable figures for young women were approximately one in six and one in ten respectively Further, part-time and temporary work and recurrent unemployment have increased proportionately more among young people than among older workers (Allatt and Yeandle, 1992, pp. 18–19). On the other hand, unemployed young people seem to have a better chance of obtaining employment than unemployed older people and are less likely to experience long-term unemployment (Payne and Payne, 1994). Fourth, (. . .) unemployment rates are higher and durations of unemployment longer among men than women. These gender differences are particularly marked among unskilled and semi-skilled workers (. . .). They reflect the fact that the sectors of the economy in which men were heavily concentrated (namely heavy manufacturing industries) have contracted sharply, whereas the service sector of the economy, in which women have conventionally been concentrated, expanded in the 1970s and, though also subject to recessionary troughs, continues to offer more employment opportunities than manufacturing industry.

(. . .)

Unemployment and family life

Contemporary Western images of unemployment and sub-employment are based on the belief that employment plays a critical and positive role in structuring social life. In a now classic analysis, Jahoda (1982, pp. 22–6) argues that employment does not provide the individual only with a livelihood. Employment, she maintains, provides a time structure for the day, the week and the year, enforces regular activity, establishes structured social networks outside the family, links the individual to goals and purposes that transcend his/her own, and is the basis of personal identity and status. Conversely, unemployment brings not only poverty, dependence and powerlessness, but it also places the unemployed and their families outside the taken-for-granted structures of everyday life.

However, images of the deleterious consequences of unemployment and sub-employment are largely concerned with the fracturing of men's lives. In the dominant strands of academic and everyday thought, family breadwinning is presumed to be of secondary importance in women's lives, but to be men's primary responsibility, to be the basis of masculine identity and to be central to men's status and authority in family life and the wider society. Contracting and unsettled labour market conditions thus tend to be interpreted as a crisis for masculinity, but not for femininity. Moreover, the unemployment of young men is the source of considerable concern and alarm. It is widely seen as jeopardising an orderly transition to adulthood, undermining the work ethic and creating a lawless and aggressive masculinity. It has been linked with vandalism, theft, violence, racial conflict and self-destructive deviance and with the emergence of an impoverished, marginalised and nihilistic underclass.

Feminist analysis provides a different perspective on unemployment. It suggests that employment is significant for women as well as men and seeks to show that unemployment denies women an independent source of income and an occupational identity. Further, many feminist writers construe men's unemployment as presenting opportunities for reworking the conventional sexual division of labour through role sharing and role reversal, an opportunity which, it is argued, is not being realised.

This section examines these issues by looking at accounts of the consequences of unemployment and sub-employment for (i) men, (ii) women and (iii) young people.

Married men, unemployment and family life

Most studies of male unemployment are studies of unemployment among the 'white' working class. They have focused on three sets of issues: (i) the erosion of family living standards; (ii) the erosion of a work-based masculine identity and the psychological and relationship problems of unemployed men and their families; and (iii) disruptions to, and the possibility of renegotiating, the conventional sexual division of labour. The first issue has in general been discussed from Left-wing political perspectives and tends to be linked with a critique of state income support policies. Discussion of the second issue is dominated by individualistic social psychological perspectives. Discussions of the third issue reflect feminist concerns and are based on critiques of the conventional sexual division of labour.

(i) The erosion of family living standards

Male unemployment deprives families of their primary means of economic support, the male wage, and leaves them with redundancy payments, the earnings of their partners and sometimes their children, unemployment insurance benefits and various forms of means-tested state benefits as their major alternative sources of income. However, these income sources are, in the view of most observers, poor substitutes for the male wage.

The research literature shows that only a small proportion of unemployed men have substantial redundancy payments (Daniel, 1990), that women's earnings are low relative to men's (. . .) and that unemployment insurance benefits are lower than earnings, are available only for a limited period, have been cut back as high unemployment levels persisted and, in any case, are available only to those who have been in employment long enough to have built up sufficient national insurance contributions. Means-tested benefits, the fourth source of income, are intended only to enable those whose income falls below an officially defined poverty level to have a basic income. Yet, with the persistence of high levels of unemployment and the reduction of unemployment insurance benefits, the families of unemployed men have become increasingly dependent on this meagre income source. In Britain, official data show that the proportion of unemployed men who are either wholly or partly dependent on means-tested supplementary benefit/income support rose from 31 per cent in 1961 to 70 per cent in 1992 (*Social Trends*,

1994, Table 5.8). Official data also demonstrate the sharpness with which incomes fall following unemployment. A Department of Social Security survey shows that the average disposable income of families in which the household head is unemployed (and had been in full-time work) is only 59 per cent of what it had been during employment (Heady and Smyth, 1989).

Moreover, some of the research literature suggests that any period of unemployment has long-term disadvantaging effects on family life. It has been found that men who experience unemployment typically take a pay cut in order to return to employment (Daniel, 1990, p. 232), when they return to employment are more likely to be in low-status, part-time or temporary jobs than men of comparable skill levels who have not experienced unemployment (Payne and Payne, 1993), are at risk of subsequent spells of unemployment (Daniel, 1990, p. 232; Gershuny and Marsh, 1993) and lose out on derivative forms of welfare such as occupational pensions and health insurance (Rodger, 1992). (. . .)

Predictably, researchers have found that the material hardship experienced during unemployment varies with its duration, stage in the life course, number of dependants, availability of supportive kin networks and class position. However, and again predictably, the living standards of both long-term and short-term unemployed men and their families are in general lower than the living standards of the poorest families in work (Bradshaw et al., 1983). Studies of their expenditure patterns show that they economise on all the major components of everyday living – food, clothing and social activity – as well as on consumer durables and holidays (Heady and Smyth, 1989; Gallie and Vogler, 1993), are more likely than the employed to be living in council housing and are likely to be in poor quality council housing (Gallie and Vogler, 1993), may be in arrears with their fuel bills and rents or mortgages (Hakim, 1982) and are likely to be more dissatisfied with their family income, standard of living and position relative to others in the community than any other group in work (Daniel, 1990, p.88).

Feminist research, like studies of unemployment during the depression of the 1930s, shows that women bear the brunt not only of managing household expenditure on reduced incomes but also of the sacrifices made (The Pilgrim Trust, 1938; Komarovsky, 1940; McKee and Bell, 1985, 1986; Morris, 1985, 1990). Much of this research literature suggests that women's skill, resourcefulness and effort in 'stretching' the available money is a critical factor in the family's ability to survive men's unemployment. Further, women may protect both their children and their husbands or partners from the worst effects of 'life on the dole' by concealing their own worries, or prioritising their children's and their husband's or partner's needs. The overall effect is twofold and in a sense contradictory. On the one hand, women may fare less well than other members of the household in the distribution of household resources. On the other hand, men's status in the household may be weakened and the intensity and importance of women's sphere of activity strengthened (Morris, 1990, pp. 28–9).

(ii) The psychological and relationship costs

Whereas most early accounts of the psychological consequences of unemployment assumed that its effects are *sui generis* and more or less uniform, recent studies emphasise that its consequences vary over time, between social class and ethnic groups, with the circumstances of unemployment and from individual to individual (Madge, 1983; Morris, 1990). Duration of unemployment, age and stage in the life course, the availability of supportive social networks and ideologies and the modest independence provided by casual earnings in the 'black' economy are among the variables commonly identified as mediating factors. Moreover, the positive nature of employment – and the negative nature of unemployment – are no longer taken for granted: it has been shown that employment may take place in polluted and health-injuring conditions, may be psychologically stressful, may be poorly paid and of low status and may leave little time for family life. Unemployment may therefore bring improvements in health (Allan, 1985), relief from stress (Fineman, 1983, 1987) and time for involvement in child-rearing (Coyle, 1984, p. 113; Salfield and Durward, 1985, p.14)

Nevertheless, from the 1930s onwards psychological research has consistently documented clear statistical correlations between unemployment and various indicators of stress and sociological research has provided vivid accounts of its disruptive effects (see, in particular, Komarovsky, 1940; Jahoda *et al.* 1972; Marsden, 1982; Warr and Jackson 1985; Warr 1987; Gershuny, 1993). Recently, a marked relationship between insecure employment and stress, has also been demonstrated (Burchell, 1993). This research literature points to the erosion of personal, social and working skills, to high levels of anxiety, depression and irritability, to loss of self-esteem and self-respect and to demoralisation, isolation and stigmatisation. (. . .) For men, Coyle (1984, pp. 114–15) argues, being at home during the day is 'a daily confrontation with the fact that they are not doing what men are supposed to do; not simply to work, but to be the breadwinners.' She writes:

> Work and masculinity are so entangled that in unemployment men are not only workless, they are seemingly unsexed. They have lost the very point of their existence as men, to work to support a family.
>
> (Coyle, 1984, p. 94).

The impact of the economic and psychological stresses of men's unemployment on their wives or partners and on the marriage relationship is (. . .) a major concern of recent feminist research (McKee and Bell, 1985, 1986; Morris, 1985, 1987). These studies point to women's empathy with the wounded pride and punctured self-respect of their men but they also show that anxiety, resentment and marital conflict are pervasive. It seems that men's unemployment stigmatises the wives of unemployed men, as well as the men themselves, and undermines their status and identity (Komarovsky, 1940; Jackson and Walsh, 1987). Further, women's participation in social networks and leisure activities outside the home seems to be constrained by the financial stringencies of unemployment while their informal socialising with other women in the home may be inhibited by the husband's presence or even actively discouraged by husbands (Morris, 1985; McKee and Bell, 1986; Jackson and Walsh, 1987). Isolation and loneliness may therefore be experienced. In addition, the struggle to 'make ends meet' on reduced incomes may lead to conflict over spending priorities and may be a major source of anxiety (McKee and Bell, 1985, 1986; Morris, 1985). Finally, it seems that the unemployed husband about the home, though sometimes a source of companionship and support in childrearing, disrupts domestic routines, unsettles customary divisions of household labour and generates tension and conflict (Komarovsky, 1940; Marsden, 1982; McKee and Bell, 1985, 1986; Morris, 1985). (. . .)

The end result of the tensions and stress associated with men's unemployment may be marital breakdown and dissolution – as evidenced by the apparently increased vulnerability of the marriages of unemployed or irregularly employed men to divorce (Lampard, 1993). However, unemployment may be the catalyst rather than the cause of marital break-up. Kelvin and Jarrett (1985) suggest that it brings to breaking point relationships that are already stressed but reinforces those that are strong: it polarises rather than transforms marital relationships.

Most of the available literature on the impact of male unemployment on children dates from earlier periods and is probably of limited relevance to the present situation. For what it is worth, this literature shows that the children of unemployed men feel the stigma and stress of their father's unemployment. Madge's (1983) review of the psychological literature points to disturbed feeding and sleep patterns, vulnerability to accidents, undue dependence, inappropriate sexual behaviour and play patterns involving irritable fathers, overworked mothers and financial hardship. Further, children perform relatively badly at school. Truancy, absence from school because of poor health, reading difficulties and referrals to education psychologists seem to be recurring problems where fathers experience long-term unemployment (Hakim, 1982). (. . .)

Most researchers hesitate to assert a direct and unambiguous causal link between male unemployment and the difficulties children experience. Madge (1983, pp. 316–17) argues that, while it is probable that economic hardship, parental stress, changes of routine and insecurity about the future affect children, the effects are complex and are mediated by a number of factors. She emphasises that the unemployed are disproportionately drawn from groups who are already disadvantaged so that the difficulties children experience may be determined by their class status rather than by unemployment itself. (. . .)

(iii) Male unemployment and the sexual division of labour

Contracting labour markets provide an opportunity for reworking the sexual division of labour through role-sharing strategies (whereby women and men share available jobs by working part-time and assume joint responsibility for the work of the household) or negotiated role reversals (whereby women assume responsibility for breadwinning and men for the work of the household). Feminist studies of male unemployment focus on this issue – and have unambiguously concluded that high levels of male unemployment are not effecting any significant change in conventional definitions of masculinity and femininity.

Role sharing seems to have received little support from trade unions, employers and the government, and labour force statistics suggest that it is not widespread. Where it is found, it seems to have been adopted as a means of enabling women to combine a work role with motherhood through job sharing between women rather than as a solution to unemployment. There is also little evidence of extensive role reversal. Evidence from a variety of sources shows conclusively that the wives of unemployed men are in fact more likely to be economically inactive than the wives of employed men (Martin and Roberts, 1984; Moylan *et al.*, 1984; *GHS*, 1992, (. . .) Davies *et al.*, 1993). (. . .)

Three main explanations for the absence of any significant trend to role reversal have been advanced. First, Joshi (1984) points out that where male unemployment levels are high, employment opportunities for women may also be limited. Secondly, McKee and Bell (1985) argue that the opportunity for primary breadwinning by the partners of unemployed men is bound up with, and limited by, women's location in a specifically female and disadvantaged labour market. They point out that the jobs available to married women with young children are not the equivalent in status and pay of the jobs available to men and, when reductions in benefits and job-related expenses such as travelling and childcare are taken into account, may not result in a significant improvement in the family's living standards. McKee and Bell find that few women opt for employment in these circumstances. Moylan *et al.* (1984), Kell and Wright (1990) and Davies *et al.* (1993) provide further, and quantitative, evidence of the disincentive impact of the benefit system on the labour force participation of the wives of unemployed men. Third, a number of studies suggest that both women and men are convinced of the impropriety of women taking on the male breadwinning role and resist role reversal even where it would make economic sense (Marsden, 1982; Cragg and Dawson, 1984; Coyle, 1984;

McKee and Bell, 1985, 1986; Morris, 1985, 1987). It seems that women perceive masculine authority, identity and pride, as well as marital stability as depending on a man's right to provide for his family, and regard the jobs available in a recession as a male prerogative. Thus, although women's part-time or temporary employment may be accepted, there are few families for whom women's primary breadwinning is an appropriate or easy solution. (. . .)

When we turn to accounts of the division of domestic labour during periods of male unemployment, we find evidence of a shift in, but not of a fundamental reworking of, traditional patterns. The work of Laite and Halfpenny (1987), Wheelock (1990), Gallie *et al.* (1993) and others shows that unemployed men are more involved in the work of the household than employed men. However, the level of their participation varies depending on whether or not their wives or partners are in full-time employment (where there may be a distinct shift to a more or less equal sharing of the work of the household), in part-time employment (where men's household labour tends to vary according to the number of hours their wives work) or are not in employment (where change may be modest). (. . .)

The limited participation of unemployed men in the work of the household seems to reflect, on the one hand, men's resistance to domestic incorporation and, on the other, women's defence of their traditional terrain. Morris (1985), for example, finds that while many of the men in her sample see domestic labour as a means of dealing with the boredom and disorientation of unemployment, they also perceive it to be unmanly, take exaggerated precautions not to be seen doing it and, in some cases, react strongly against it. Resistance, she suggests, is particularly intense where men are involved in a predominantly male social network. Conversely, women may value men's moral support and increased involvement in childcare, but may nevertheless feel that they perform domestic tasks more quickly and thoroughly than men, may re-do tasks done by men to their own standards and may actively discourage male domestication (Coyle, 1984, p. 114; McKee and Bell, 1985, 1986; Morris, 1985, 1987).

Confronted with these data, some researchers have argued that male breadwinning and female domesticity are so deeply embedded in masculine and feminine identities by a lifetime of conditioning that recession and unemployment cannot readily effect change. McKee and Bell (1986) maintain that men feel that they have a public profile and purpose, despite their severance from the labour market. This legitimates their preoccupations outside the home and provides a justification for a limited contribution within the home. Women, for their part, relate the level and standard of male participation in the work of the home to men's incompetence and women's skill and expertise, and experience male domesticity as a disruption of their routines and a threat to their identity. (. . .)

Women, unemployment and family life

Until quite recently, unemployed women usually 'appeared only as fleeting shadows in the literature on unemployment' (Marshall, 1984, p. 237). Their shadowy presence reflected the everyday assumption that women are primarily wives, mothers and carers and only secondarily workers. The public image of women's unemployment was thus one of its relative unimportance.

Feminist writers challenge this construction of women's employment and unemployment. They seek to demonstrate the importance of employment in the lives of partnered and unpartnered women and to show that unemployment has economic and psychological costs for women and for their families.

The economic costs

Feminist accounts of women's employment depict women's earnings not as 'pin money', but as a significant element in family budgets and as integral to their role as mothers. They have shown that financial necessity is an important element in married women's participation in the labour force, that women's earnings may lift families out of poverty where men's wages are low and that, at all income levels, desired living standards are now commonly built around two incomes (McNay and Pond, 1980; Martin and Roberts, 1984; Wallace, 1987). Further, they (like some critical social policy analysts) have emphasised that lone mothers constitute a growing proportion of women, receive little support from their former partners, experience considerable hardship where they are dependent on state benefits (Bradshaw and Millar, 1991; Millar, 1992) and are less likely to be in poverty where they are in full-time employment than where they are not ((. . .) Mitchell and Bradshaw 1991).

Conversely, feminist accounts of women's unemployment are concerned to show that family living standards are significantly affected when women are unemployed. This body of literature shows that women's unemployment has particularly severe consequences for women on their own and – because their wages play a critical part in keeping families out of poverty where men's earnings are low – for poor families (Coyle, 1984; Morris, 1990, p. 137; Callender, 1992). However, there is general agreement that women's unemployment spells financial difficulty for all families. Martin and Roberts (1984, pp. 89–91) say that one-third of all unemployed women, compared with less than 10 per cent of employed women, find it 'very difficult to manage' or 'are not managing at all'. Callender (1992, pp. 142–4) finds that women's redundancy leads to economies that begin with cutbacks on their own personal needs and then range from cutbacks on savings to cutbacks on essentials like food. About half of the women in this study were struggling to meet basic financial commitments. Yet, Callender reports, many husbands realised the importance of their wives' wages to the family economy only with its loss. Similarly, Coyle (1984) finds that redundancy confronts women with what they had always known: that a man's wage is not enough to live on.

The psychological costs

Feminist accounts of the housewife role suggest that it is characterised by monotonous and meaningless work, economic dependence, low status and social isolation (Oakley, 1974, 1976). Full-time housewifery would thus seem to present women with a structural condition that has much in common with that of the unemployed. At the same time, feminist researchers have consistently argued that employment provides women with a way out of the dependence and isolation of full-time housewifery. This research literature suggests that marriage and motherhood remain the primary focus of women's lives but that women nevertheless value employment as a means to economic autonomy and incorporation into the public world (Coyle, 1984; Cragg and Dawson, 1984; Martin and Roberts, 1984).

Women's experience of unemployment seems to be the mirror image of the value they place on both family life and employment.

Studies of women's unemployment, such as Coyle (1984), Cragg and Dawson (1984), Martin and Wallace (1984) and Callender (1992), show that unemployment cuts women off from the social relationships of the workplace and leaves them without the resources to finance social activity. It thus radically curtails their social contacts and horizons, accentuates the privatised nature of their lives, gives rise to loneliness and boredom and may lead to depression and poor health. In addition, these studies show that unemployment deprives women of the modicum of autonomy, freedom and economic independence that employment had given them. (. . .)

(M)arried women's experience of unemployment seems to differ from that of unmarried women and of men. Data on the experiences of unmarried women are slender but those that are available suggest that unmarried women, like men, feel redundant and displaced, tend to be particularly isolated and are subject to a high level of demoralisation (Morris, 1990). In contrast, married women seem to elaborate their domestic roles to fill the vacuums left by un-employment, may even be glad of some relief from the double burden of employment and domesticity and do not in general experience the sense of social redundancy and crisis of identity that men and unmarried women experience. (. . .)

(S)tudies show that unemployed married women perceive their own situation as radically different from that of unemployed men. They may want to return to work and may affirm women's right to employment, but they also perceive the work of the household as work in its own right and tend not to define themselves as unemployed though they may be looking for work. Commenting on such findings, Morris (1990, p.133) suggests that, despite the dissatisfactions of the housewife–mother role, women do not see employment as an alternative to domesticity but as a source of relief from domesticity and as another dimension to life. Femininity is thus not threatened by unemployment in the way that masculinity is.

Coming of age unemployed

Young people are at greater risk of unemployment and sub-employment than older workers (. . .). Moreover, the government-sponsored youth training schemes into which they may be propelled provide a respite from the dole queue, but do not appear to provide either effective training for employment or a permanent structural solution to the collapse of youth labour markets (Muncie, 1984; Bates and Riseborough, 1993). In addition, young people's entitlements to social security have been eroded (and their parents' responsibility extended) with, *inter alia*, the removal of income support for 16–17-year-olds and its reduction for those under 24. In the view of some commentators, young people are the primary victims of contracting and casualised labour markets. According to Coffield (1987), they have become the most expendable section of the labour force and are marginalised and stigmatised as an unemployed and unemployable 'lumpenproletariat'. He writes:

> In little more than ten years the economic crisis in Western societies has transformed the golden age of youth into a massive social problem . . . In the 1960s young people were celebrated as the embodiment of sexuality, freedom, health and progress; before the end of the 1970s they had again become economically marginalised and began to be treated in the same way as other stigmatised groups . . .
>
> (Coffield, 1987, pp. 87–8).

Sociological accounts of the problematisation of youth unemployment rest on the proposition that in Western societies employment is critical to the transition from childhood to independent, responsible and law-abiding adulthood. (. . .) Allatt and Yeandle (1992, pp. 60–94) argue that employment brings young people the achieved status and prestige of 'worker', the power of an independent income and social relationships which are beyond the control of parents. It thus provides the basis for renegotiating rights and obligations with parents and for pushing back the boundaries of parental control. Further, Allatt and Yeandle argue that 'being settled' in a 'proper job' – meaning a steady job with a fair wage – is widely perceived as necessary, albeit in gender-specific ways, to marriage and the establishment of an independent family unit. They find that the construction of paid work as (in the words of one of their respondents) men's 'whole purpose in life, what they function for' means that graduation to full adult masculinity is predicated on family breadwinning. For young, working-class women, on the other hand, graduation to full adult femininity (married motherhood) is dependent on access, through marriage, to a male wage and thus on men's access to employment. Their own employment is an opportunity to 'live a bit' between childhood and marriage and domesticity (Wallace, 1987).

Unemployment jeopardises this orderly progression through the 'normal' stages of the life course. Unemployed young people, say Allatt and Yeandle, are without an occupational status, have only the limited and 'less deserved' income which state benefits provide, and are deprived of those work relationships which would teach them about work identities and work itself. Their position in the family does not mature into the independence of adulthood, and marriage and parenthood may be deemed unwise. In addition, Allatt and Yeandle (pp. 85–110) argue that, because the daily use of time and space is structured and synchronised by the time schedules of paid work, unemployed young people are literally 'matter out of time, out of place'. They have no reason for getting up at the 'normal time', cannot share in the leisure activities of their peer groups, disrupt domestic routines by their presence in the household and are oppressed by an overabundance of time. They are outside the work-structured patterns and routines of the everyday world – and in the way of those who must conform to these routines.

Young people's reactions to this situation have been characterised in two broadly opposing but overlapping ways. They have been depicted as (i) rebellious, lawless and/or nihilistic and as (ii) troubled but resigned and broadly conforming.

(i) Rebellious, lawless and nihilistic images

Images of a rebellious, lawless and nihilistic journey through an unemployed youth dominate the media and much of the political rhetoric of the Left and Right.

Media and political commentary depict the unemployed young as poorly educated and unskilled, as effectively excluded from the welfare system and as the victims of family breakdown and homelessness. They document, and attribute to unemployment and sub-employment, trends towards unmarried parenthood among young women, and rising crime, rioting and racial violence, drug and alcohol abuse and suicide among young men. Representations of unemployed young 'black' people (and in particular of unemployed young Afro-Caribbean men) as hanging about street corners, at risk of drifting into crime and of becoming alienated from society, occupy a distinctive and salient place in this imagery of unemployed youth and, according to Solomos (1985), sharpen perceptions of ethnic minority groups as threatening dominant cultural values and institutions.

These images of unemployed young people draw on various social science research findings. Research in both Britain and the USA shows that property crimes rise sharply during recessions (Hakim, 1982; Dickinson, 1994), that significant proportions of young people who come before the courts are unemployed or sub-employed (Hakim, 1982) and that neighbourhoods with relatively high levels of youth unemployment and sub-employment are characterised by a high incidence of vandalism, property crime, racial violence and generalised lawlessness. Some researchers also point to links between unemployment and suicide in young adulthood. One report suggests that in England and Wales the suicide rate among men aged 14 to 24 increased by 78 per cent between 1980–90 (Hawton, 1992).

In a speculative analysis of this response to unemployment and sub-employment, Willis (1984a, 1984b) argues that whereas older unemployed people are workers without work, wage earners without the wage and consumers without money, young people are in a state of 'suspended animation'. They are without the golden key to the separate households, couple relationships and consumer power of adulthood. Willis maintains that working-class young men are confronted with a 'crisis' of masculinity and may react with anger and an aggressive assertion of masculinity, while working-class young women may opt for unmarried motherhood. Young women thus escape the parental home and the failure of trying to find work while achieving a clear role, a limited independence and adult status, but young men have only the collective solace of young male peer groups and the boastful and aggressive fantasies of thwarted masculinity.

This imagery of unemployed young people depicts unemployment as leading to unmarried mother families and the marginalisation of young men and is reminiscent of accounts of the development of the Afro-Caribbean and Afro-American woman-headed family (. . .). It fuels beliefs in the growth of an underclass, a social category separated from other classes by its poverty and its lifestyle. (. . .)

(ii) Troubled but conforming images

Media images of lawless and nihilistic unemployed young people contrast with the images of a troubled but stoical acceptance of unemployment which are to be found in a number of sociological studies of youth unemployment. These studies include Allatt and Yeandle (1992), McRae (1987), Wallace (1987) and Hutson and Jenkins (1989).

Allatt and Yeandle, like Willis (above), see the unemployed young as 'in danger of being socially dislodged and disconnected' and as troubled and in some measure troubling. However, unlike Willis, they depict a resigned and broadly conforming response to unemployment. They document loss of faith in educational qualifications, youth training schemes and careers services, anger at the exploitative practices of employers and a widespread feeling that the government and society have opted out of their responsibilities and obligations to the young. They show that bewilderment, anxiety, depression, a sense of unfairness and feelings of marginalisation are commonplace. Nevertheless, the young women and men in their sample see dependence on social security as an unsatisfactory state of affairs, regard having a job, however poor, as a good thing and do not appear to be either losing the motivation to work or drifting into criminality.

McRae, in a study of the social and political attitudes of unemployed young people in four English cities, finds that young women and men are fairly evenly divided between those who feel cheated and angry and those who do not. Some express a deep sense of resentment about lost opportunities, most believe that something could and should be done to improve the situation and many are in principle supportive of collective protest. However, the idea that one must work for one's money seemed to be general, the aspirations of the majority differed little from those in work and political activism was minimal. McRae maintains that most young people expect to be in work in the future and see themselves not as 'the unemployed', but as 'unemployed at present'. Unemployment, says McRae, has not created a pool of hostile young people desirous of overthrowing society, but a pool of unhappy young people waiting their turn to join society.

The unemployed young people in Wallace's (1987) Isle of Sheppey study bear some resemblance to the young people described by Willis (...). However, Wallace points to ultimate conformity with traditional expectations of male breadwinning. She reports that on leaving school young people find personal relationships, status and identity in local youth sub-cultures and are ambivalent about employment. They are dismissive of jobs they regard as boring or insufficiently rewarded, are prepared to wait for the right job to turn up rather than to take any available job and sometimes deliberately adopt self-images which are antithetical to those required by employers. Seeing unemployment as a fact of life and a period of unemployment after leaving school as a break between school and work, they hardly consider themselves unemployed.

However, Wallace shows that reactions to unemployment vary with gender and status and change during the journey through youth. She finds that unemployed young women are more likely than unemployed young men to pursue home-based pastimes and to participate in the work of the household. They are more isolated from their peers, but they have a more secure sense of belonging somewhere. Further, she finds that young men in the 'respectable' strata of the working class also spend their time in home-based pastimes and parentally approved hobbies. In contrast, young men in the 'rough' strata of the working class assert a masculine identity by exaggerating the symbols of masculinity. They identify with romantic rebels, prize survival skills that embody an independent individualism and clever if shady deals, and tell highly embellished and dramatised stories of confrontations with authority in which humiliating incidents are transformed into personal triumphs. Some take to pill-popping, drinking binges, fighting and other masochistically 'heroic' activities.

Wallace thus sees unemployed young women as drawn into domestic servitude within the parental home and low-status young men as seeking to redeem their impoverished masculinity through fantasy and an aggressive but destructive 'macho' male youth sub-culture. However, she finds that most young men reject the scenario of starting families on the dole, that most young women envisage being married to conventionally employed young men and that the adoption of alternative identities is experimental and short-lived. Five years after leaving school, the unemployed young people in her sample were less involved in local youth cultures and feel unemployment severely. Aspirations had been revised downwards, orientations to work had become instrumental and jobs that would have been rejected at sixteen are tolerated. Wallace attributes this change of attitude to recognition of the lack of viable alternatives, acclimatisation to the jobs they are able to get and the assumption of family responsibilities.

Hutson and Jenkins (1989) provide a relatively optimistic picture of the journey to adulthood through an unemployed youth. First, they argue that unemployment affects young people to different degrees and in all probability severely damages only a minority. Second, they point out that adulthood, before it is anything else, is a legal status which is defined by citizenship rights (such as the right to vote and the right to marry without parental consent) which are not dependent on employment status. Third, they argue that social security benefits, though now reduced, give young people some economic independence. Finally, Hutson and Jenkins argue that adulthood has an important moral dimension based on ideas of 'responsible' behaviour which parents seek to sustain and on the basis of which young people claim adult rights whatever their employment status. Hutson and Jenkins thus seek to qualify the emphasis that most writers have placed on employment as the key to adulthood and to show that there are niches within which the unemployed young can make successful claims to some degree of independence. Adulthood, they say, is a robust, multi-dimensional identity and is not destroyed, though it is impoverished, by unemployment.

All these researchers suggest that parental support and surveillance – and in particular maternal support and surveillance – play an important part in sustaining the morality of work and independence, and in protecting young people from the more brutal consequences of recession. According to Allatt and Yeandle, parents fear not so much that the young cannot survive without employment but that they may be content to do so and may drift into a lifetime of dependence on state welfare and criminality. Fearing this, they seek to succour and control the young. Allatt and Yeandle (as well as Wallace, and Hutson and Jenkins) show that parents insist on active and continued job hunting, draw on their knowledge of the job market to guide job-seeking, define social security benefits as degrading and provide emotional support in the face of despondency. Further, parents seek to prevent their sons and daughters sliding into 'bad ways' by 'nagging' about long hours spent in bed and personal untidiness, encouraging participation in the work of the household, fostering the pursuit of home-based hobbies and promoting the skilful management of money. At the same time, parental subsidies enable young people to finance job hunting, to continue with their hobbies and to have a lifestyle that may not be very different from that of their employed contemporaries. These studies show that parental reactions are not without their ambivalences and may veer from affection and the desire to ease the child's life to harshness stemming from the belief that young people should be earning. Where conflict is severe, the young may leave home. Nevertheless, these studies suggest that parental support is an important resource in confronting unemployment. They demonstrate the enduring strength of traditional parental relationships.

However, they also point to the erosion of traditional family bonds in that they show that uncertain and declining employment opportunities are an obstacle to marriage and the formation of new conjugal family units. Allatt and Yeandle, Hutson and Jenkins, and Wallace report that most young men feel that they must be breadwinners in order to marry – and most young women and their parents view unemployed young men as unsuitable prospective husbands. In this situation, young men may lose interest in 'girls', may adopt a predatory lifestyle or may move down-market and seek partners among schoolgirls whose own limited resources and expectations are unthreatening (Hutson and Jenkins, 1989). Young women may drift into lone motherhood (Wallace, 1987). Couples may opt for unmarried cohabitation; in Wallace's study, nearly half of the young men in cohabiting relationships were unemployed while nearly all the married young men were employed. It seems that cohabitation, as a relationship based on flexibility and impermanence, may be preferred to marriage where unemployment prevents young men from assuming a breadwinning role.

Two recent studies of cohabitation McRae (1993, p. 29) and Kiernan and Estaugh (1993, p. 15) also find that the partners of cohabiting mothers are more likely than the partners of married mothers to be unemployed.

(. . .)

References

Allan, G. (1985) *Family Life*, Oxford, Blackwell.

Allatt, P. and Yeandle, S. (1992) *Youth Unemployment and the Family: Voices of Disordered Times*, London, Routledge.

Bates, I. and Riseborough, G. (eds) (1993) *Youth and Inequality*, Buckingham, Open University Press.

Bradshaw, J., Cooke, K. and Godfrey, C. (1983) 'The Impact of Unemployment on the Living Standards of Families', *Journal of Social Policy*, 12, pp. 433–52.

Bradshaw, J. and Millar, J. (1991) *Lone Parent Families in the UK*, Department of Social Security Research Report No. 6, London, HMSO.

Burchell, B. (1993) 'The Effects of Labour Market Position, Job Insecurity, and Unemployment on Psychological Health', in D. Gallie, C. Marsh and C. Vogler (eds) *Social Change and the Experience of Unemployment*, Oxford, Oxford University Press.

Callender, C. (1992) 'Redundancy, Unemployment and Poverty', in C. Glendinning and J. Millar (eds) *Women and Poverty in Britain: the 1990s*, London, Harvester Wheatsheaf.

Coffield, F. (1987) 'From the Celebration to the Marginalisation of Youth', in G. Cohen (ed.) *Social Change and the Life Course*, London, Tavistock.

Coyle, A. (1984) *Redundant Women*, London, The Women's Press.

Cragg, A. and Dawson, T. (1984) *Unemployed Women: A Study of Attitudes and Experiences*, Department of Employment Research Paper No. 47, London, HMSO.

Daniel, W. W. (1990) *The Unemployed Flow*, London, Policy Studies Institute.

Davies, R. B., Elias, P. and Penn, R. (1993) 'The Relationship Between a Husband's Unemployment and his Wife's Participation in the Labour Force', in D. Gallie, C. Marsh and C. Vogler (eds) *Social Change and the Experience of Unemployment*, Oxford, Oxford University Press.

Dickinson, D. (1994) *Crime and Unemployment*, mimeo, Department of Applied Economics, Cambridge University.

Fineman, S. (1983) *White Collar Unemployment: Impact and Stress*, Chichester, Wiley.

Fineman, S. (1987) 'Back to Employment: Wounds and Wisdoms', in D. Fryer and P. Ullah (eds) *Unemployed People: Social and Psychological Perspectives*, Milton Keynes, Open University Press.

Gallie, D. and Vogler, C. (1993) 'Labour Market Deprivation, Welfare, and Collectivism', in D. Gallie, C. Marsh and C. Vogler (eds) *Social Change and the Experience of Unemployment*, Oxford, Oxford University Press.

General Household Survey (1992) Office of Population Censuses and Surveys, London, HMSO.

Gershuny, J. (1993) 'The Psychological Consequences of Unemployment: An Assessment of the Jahoda Thesis', in D. Gallie, C. Marsh and C. Vogler (eds) *Social Change and the Experience of Unemployment*, Oxford, Oxford University Press.

Gershuny, J. and Marsh, C. (1993) 'Unemployment in Work Histories', in D. Gallie, C. Marsh and C. Vogler (eds) *Social Change and the Experience of Unemployment*, Oxford, Oxford University Press.

Hakim, C. (1982) 'The Social Consequences of High Unemployment', *Journal of Social Policy*, 11, pp. 433–67.

Hawton, K. (1992) 'By Their Own Hand', *Journal of Social Policy*, 11, pp. 433–67.

Heady, P. and Smyth, M. (1989) *Living Standards during Unemployment*, London, OPCS/HMSO.

Hutson, S. and Jenkins, R. (1989) *Taking the Strain: Families, Unemployment and the Transition to Adulthood*, Milton Keynes, Open University Press.

Jackson, P. R. and Walsh, S. (1987) 'Unemployment and the Family', in Fryer, D. and Ullah, P. (eds) *Unemployed People: Social and Psychological Perspectives*, Milton Keynes, Open University Press.

Jahoda, M. (1982) *Employment and Unemployment: A Social–Psychological Analysis*, Cambridge, Cambridge University Press.

Jahoda, M., Lazarsfeld, P. F. and Zeisel, H. (1972) *Marienthal: The Sociography of an Unemployed Community*, London, Tavistock (first published in 1933).

Joshi, H. (1984) *Women's Participation in Paid Work: Further Analysis of the Women and Employment Survey* (Research Paper No. 45, Department of Employment), London, HMSO.

Kell, M. and Wright, J. (1990) 'Benefits and the Labour Supply of Women Married to Unemployed Men', *Economic Journal*, 100, Supplement, pp. 119–26.

Kelvin, P. and Jarrett, J. E. (1985) *Unemployment: Its Social and Psychological Effects*, Cambridge, Cambridge University Press.

Kiernan, K. and Estaugh, V. (1993) *Cohabitation: Extra-Marital Childbearing and Social Policy*, London, Family Policy Studies Centre.

Komarovsky, M. (1940) *The Unemployed Man and His Family*, New York, Octagon Books.

Laite, J. and Halfpenny, P. (1987) 'Unemployment and the Domestic Division of Labour', in Fryer, D. and Ullah, P. (eds) *Unemployed People: Social and Psychological Perspectives*, Milton Keynes, Open University Press.

Lampard, R. (1993) 'An Examination of the Relationship Between Marital Dissolution and Unemployment', in D. Gallie, C. Marsh and C. Vogler (eds) *Social Change and the Experience of Unemployment*, Oxford, Oxford University Press.

McKee, L. and Bell, C. (1985) 'Marital and Family Relations in Times of Male Unemployment', in B. Roberts, R. Finnegan and D. Gallie (eds) *New Approaches to Economic Life*, Manchester, Manchester University Press.

McKee, L. and Bell, C. (1986) 'His Unemployment, Her Problem: The Domestic and Marital Consequences of Male Unemployment', in S. Allen, A. Waton, K. Purcell and S. Wood (eds) *The Experience of Unemployment*, Basingstoke, Macmillan.

McNay, M. and Pond, C. (1980) *Low Pay and Family Poverty*, London, Study Commission on the Family.

McRae, S. (1987) 'Social and Political Perspectives Found Among Unemployed Young Men and Women', in M. White (ed.) *The Social World of the Young Unemployed*, London, Policy Studies Institute.

McRae, S. (1993) *Cohabiting Mothers: Changing Marriage and Motherhood?*, London, Policy Studies Institute.

Madge, N. (1983) 'Unemployment and its Effects on Children', *Journal of Child Psychology and Psychiatry*, 24, pp. 311–19.

Marsden, S. (1982) *Workless: An Exploration of the Social Contract between Society and the Worker* (2nd edn.), London, Croom Helm.

Marshall, G. (1984) 'On the Sociology of Women's Unemployment, Its Neglect and Significance', *Sociological Review*, 32, pp. 234–59.

Martin, J. and Roberts, C (1984) *Women and Employment: A Lifetime Perspective*, Report of the 1980 DE/OPCS Women and Employment Survey, London, HMSO.

Martin, R. and Wallace, J. (1984) *Working Women in Recession: Employment, Redundancy and Unemployment*, Oxford, Oxford University Press.

Millar, J. (1992) 'Lone Mothers and Poverty', in C. Glendinning and J. Millar (eds) *Women and Poverty in Britain: the 1990s*, London, Harvester Wheatsheaf.

Mitchell, D. and Bradshaw, J. (1991) *Lone Parents and Their Incomes: A Comparative Study of Ten Countries*, Unpublished Research, University of York.

Morris, L. D. (1985) 'Responses to Redundancy: Labour Market Experience, Domestic Organisation and Male Social Networks', *International Journal of Social Economics*, 12, pp. 5–16.

Morris, L. D. (1987) 'Domestic Circumstances', in Harris, C. C. (ed.) *Redundancy and Recession*, Oxford, Blackwell.

Morris, L. D. (1990) *The Workings of the Household: A US–UK Comparison*, Cambridge, Polity Press.

Moylan, S., Millar, J. and Davies, R. (1984) *For Richer, For Poorer? DHSS Cohort Study of Unemployed Men*, DHSS Research Report No. 11, London, HMSO.

Muncie, J. (1984) *The Trouble with Kids Today: Youth and Crime in Post-war Britain*, London, Hutchinson.

Oakley, A. (1974) *The Sociology of Housework*, London, Martin Robertson.

Oakley, A. (1976) *Housewife*, Harmondsworth, Penguin Books.

Payne, J. and Payne, C. (1993) 'Unemployment and Peripheral Work', *Work, Employment and Society*, 7, pp. 513–34.

Payne, J. and Payne, C. (1994) 'Recession, Restructuring and the Fate of the Unemployed: Evidence in the Underclass Debate', *Sociology*, 28, pp. 1–19.

Pilgrim Trust (1938) *Men Without Work*, Cambridge, Cambridge University Press.

Rodger, J. (1992) 'The Welfare State and Social Closure: Social Division and the "Underclass"', *Critical Social Policy*, 35, pp. 45–63.

Salfield, A. and Durward, L. (1985) '"Coping, but Only Just" – Families' Experiences of Pregnancy and Childrearing on the Dole', in Durward, L. (ed.) *Born Unequal: Perspectives in Pregnancy and Childrearing in Unemployed Families*, London, Maternity Alliance.

Social Trends (1994), Central Statistical Office, London, HMSO.

Solomos, J. (1985) 'Problems, But Whose Problems: The Social Construction of Black Youth Unemployment and State Policies', *Journal of Social Policy*, 14, pp. 527–54.

Wallace, C. (1987) *For Richer, For Poorer: Growing Up in and out of Work*, London, Tavistock.

Warr, P. (1987) *Work, Unemployment and Mental Health*, Oxford, Clarendon Press.

Warr, P. and Jackson, Paul (1985) 'Factors Influencing the Psychological Impact of Prolonged Unemployment and of Reemployment', in *Psychological Medicine*, 15, pp. 795–807.

Wheelock, J. (1990) *Husbands at Home: The Domestic Economy in a Post-industrial Society*, London, Routledge.

Willis, P. (1984a) 'Youth Unemployment: A New Social State', *New Society*, 67, pp. 475–7.

Willis, P. (1984b) 'Youth Unemployment: Ways of Living', *New Society*, 68, pp. 13–15.

Chapter 11

Social change *and* labour market transitions

Andy Furlong and Fred Cartmel

In the past transitions were shorter and simpler . . . By the 1980s . . . there were no longer any clear, normal career patterns from which most individuals could deviate. In this sense, individualisation had become the norm.

(Roberts *et al.* 1994: 44)

Introduction

(. . .) With a sharp decline in demand for unqualified, minimum-aged, school-leavers, young people are remaining at school for longer periods of time, partly due to the lack of opportunities to engage in paid work. As a result of these changes, the transition from school to work tends to take longer to complete and has become much more complex; this has implications for domestic and housing transitions as well as for other life experiences (. . .).

The transition from school to work is often regarded as an important phase in the life cycle which holds the key to a greater understanding of the ways in which social advantages and inequalities are passed from one generation to the next. In the 1970s young people tended to make fairly direct transitions from school to full-time jobs; the situation in the mid-1990s is very different. We suggest that short, stable and predictable transitions are characteristic of a Fordist social structure in which the life experiences of the masses are relatively standardized and homogeneous. Over the last three decades, transitions have changed in a number of ways. The transition from school to work has become much more protracted (Roberts *et al.* 1987; Roberts and Parsell 1992a), increasingly fragmented and in some respects less predictable.

As Giddens suggests, social life in the modern world takes place in settings which are increasingly 'diverse and segmented' (1991: 83). Employment in manufacturing industry continues to decline, while the service sector has become increasingly significant. For some commentators, these changes represent a significant development in capitalist societies. Whereas the industrial revolution was accompanied by a sharp decline in agricultural employment, post-industrial society is characterized by a shrinking manufacturing sector and the dominance of the service sector (Bell 1973). Alongside these changes, there has been a growth in part-time working and non-standard employment, employment in smaller work units, an increased demand for technical skills and 'flexible specializations' which together have been taken as characteristic of post-Fordist economies (Kumar 1995). In late modernity, individual skills and educational attainments are of crucial importance in smoothing labour market entry, while the collectivized transitions which were once central to an understanding of social reproduction have weakened.

For Beck (1992) these changes underpin the emergence of the risk society. Individuals are forced to assume greater responsibility for their experiences in the labour market and to constantly assess the implications of their actions and experiences. Life in the modern world involves a global insecurity of life (Jansen and Van der Veen 1992) and while successful labour market integration is achieved by some, others find themselves marginalized. Indeed, the increasing complexity of the skill market and the segmentation of labour means that young people can become vulnerable to long-term exclusion at an early stage in their lives.

In this chapter we describe the main changes in the youth labour market and in transitions from school to work and consider their implications for our understanding of processes of economic integration and the reproduction of inequalities based on class and gender. While there is strong evidence that school to work transitions have become more protracted, complex and differentiated, we are sceptical about the tendency to regard these changes as indicative of a new era in which social structures have become fragmented. However, we argue that structures have become more obscure as individuals have been made more accountable for their labour market fates. It is argued that two somewhat contradictory processes can be observed within modern societies: on the one hand a trend towards differentiation and diversity that reflects the economic transformations, which some interpret as leading to a post-industrial society, and on the other, the maintenance of stable, predictable transitions which help ensure that those occupying advantaged social positions retain the ability to transmit privileges to their offspring (Olk 1988, quoted in Chisholm *et al.* 1990). Finally, in the context of the risk society thesis, it is also important to examine the extent to which the greater protraction of transitions have led to growing unease and uncertainty as young people try to make sense of a world in which their future is perceived as risky and difficult to predict.

The changing youth labour market

Some of the key changes affecting the experiences of young people in Britain stem from the collapse of the youth labour market during the early 1980s and the restructuring of employment opportunities within a policy framework which placed priority on increased training, flexibility and securing a reduction in relative labour costs. With an increase in all-age unemployment caused by the economic recession, minimum-aged school-leavers increasingly faced difficulties securing work and by the mid-1980s, the majority of 16-year-old leavers were spending time on government sponsored training schemes (Furlong and Raffe 1989). These changes led to a fundamental restructuring of the youth labour market (Ashton et al. 1990) and had a radical impact on transitions from school to work. As a consequence, the number of young people leaving school to enter the labour market at age 16 declined sharply; in 1988, around 52 per cent of the school year cohort entered the labour market at the minimum age, compared to 42 per cent in 1990 and just 34 per cent in 1991 (Payne 1995).

The magnitude of these changes is highlighted through the evidence collected as part of the England and Wales Youth Cohort Study (YCS) and the Scottish Young People's Surveys (SYPS). Among the 1991 England and Wales cohort, less than one in five 16–17-year-olds (18 per cent) were in full-time employment more than six months after reaching the minimum school-leaving age (Courtenay and McAleese 1993), a decline of 9 percentage points since 1985. Conducted biennially between 1977 and 1991, the SYPS can be used to provide information about changes in the destinations of young people over a longer period of time. By focusing on the declining group of young Scots who left school at the minimum age, the surveys show that in 1977, 72 per cent were in full-time jobs by the spring after leaving school; by 1991 this had declined to just 28 per cent.

In line with changes occurring throughout the industrialized world, the restructuring of the British economy has involved a continued decline in the manufacturing sector and the growth of employment in the service sector. Between 1970 and 1995, the total number of employees working in manufacturing industries fell from around 8.6 to around 3.8 million (Maguire 1991; DfEE 1996). During the 1980–83 recession, around a third of the jobs in the engineering industry were lost, a trend which affected the large number of young males who traditionally found employment in this sector (Maguire 1991). Over the same period, employment in the service sector increased from 11.3 to 16.2 million (Maguire 1991; DfEE 1996). Whereas school-leavers in many industrial centres once made mass transitions from school to manufacturing employment, today they tend to work in smaller scale service environments and are less likely to be working with large numbers of other young people or sharing work experiences with their peers. By 1991, nearly half of the 18–19 age group were working in firms with less than 24 employees. Yet school-leavers with the highest qualifications tend to work in large firms, while the least qualified tend to be concentrated in small firms (Park 1994). In this respect the work situations of low-attaining youth have become more individualized.

Associated with these changing employment contexts, there has been a weakening of collectivist traditions manifest in the decline of the trade unions which has been reinforced by legislation to curb their powers. Between 1979 and 1993 the number of trade unions fell from 453 to 254 (DfEE 1995), and membership fell equally dramatically. In 1977, around half of the workforce were members of trade unions; by 1994 this had declined to around 30 per cent. Moreover, rates of union membership tend to be lowest in the growing sectors of the economy in which young people are heavily represented (sales and personal and protective services) (Maguire 1991; DfEE 1996). In the hotel and restaurant sector and in sales, for example, only around one in ten employees are members of trade unions, while among professionals around one in two are members (CSO 1996).

As trade unions once provided young people with an introduction to working-class politics and collective action, the decline in union membership has implications for political socialization (. . .). While there have been few studies of young people and trade unions, Spilsbury and colleagues (1987) argue that levels of unionization among young people are primarily determined by overall patterns of union activity within an industry or firm. As a result of recent industrial changes, young people are increasingly finding employment in small firms and in areas where union activity has traditionally been weak. However, in a study of firms in the Swindon area, Rose noted that even in manufacturing industries, young employees displayed a 'sheer lack of interest' in trade unions (1996: 126).

One particularly significant change in the youth labour market is that which stems from the development of 'flexible' employment practices. The recession of the 1980s provided employers with an incentive to seek ways of reducing labour costs and one of the ways in which this was achieved was through the increased use of part-time and temporary workers (Ashton *et al.* 1990). Indeed, during the 1980s, many firms reduced their core workforces and created a periphery of workers, many of whom were females working part-time hours or provided through government funded schemes (strategies which relieved employers of a number of financial obligations, such as the provision of sick pay or the payment of national insurance contributions) (Atkinson 1984). The concentration of women in certain sectors of the labour market has led to the argument that women's labour market prospects are restricted both by horizontal segregation (by occupation) and vertical segregation (with upward mobility chances being restricted in all occupational sectors) (Hakim 1979).

In this context it is important to note that young service workers tend to be concentrated in the lower tier services (Krahn and Lowe 1993), frequently have little control over their working environment and often have poor job security. Among 18–19-year-olds in 1991, nearly eight in ten young women (76 per cent) and nearly three in ten young men (28 per cent) worked in lower tier services such as clerical, personal service and sales work (Park 1994). The poor working conditions of young service workers have been highlighted in the British press where attention was drawn to part-time employees at Burger King who were apparently forced to clock out at those times during the day when customer demand was low. Krahn and Lowe (1993) report that Burger King in Toronto restricts shifts to three hours so as to avoid having to provide workers with breaks.

With a shortage of job opportunities for young people, some survive through marginal employment, described by MacDonald (1996) as 'fiddly jobs'. According to MacDonald, young people become engaged in the marginal economy as a survival strategy, and they take up 'fiddly jobs' because of the shortage of mainstream job opportunities and because of the difficulties in surviving economically on benefits (MacDonald 1996). Although self-employment among young people has risen, most of those who become self-employed have few academic qualifications and their businesses have a high failure rate (Park 1994; MacDonald 1996).

Unemployment and schemes

For young people, unemployment and the threat of unemployment has had a strong impact on recent labour market experiences. As Mizen (1995: 2) argues,

> today, in the 1990s, far from being easy, finding a job directly from school has been the exception rather than the rule and many young workers are now forced to confront realities of a hostile labour market in a way unimaginable even 20 years ago.

Youth unemployment increased fairly steadily from the late 1970s to the mid-1980s, declined over a period of about three years and then from 1989 began to increase again. Unemployment among the 16–17 age group increased from 9 per cent among males and females in 1977, to 13 per cent of males and 14 per cent of females in 1993 (OPCS 1995). Among the 18–24 age group unemployment increased from 7 per cent of males and 6 per cent of females in 1977, to 18 per cent of males and 11 per cent of females in 1993 (Figure 11.1).

For young people leaving school at age 16 and 17, the introduction of government training schemes must be regarded as one of the most significant changes affecting transitional patterns. From the mid-1970s, as levels of youth unemployment increased, youth training schemes were introduced. The first scheme specifically aimed at young people (the Job Creation Programme) was introduced in 1975 in order to provide temporary work experience for school-leavers without jobs. At this stage, a small minority of young people experienced schemes, but with the introduction of the Youth Opportunities Programme (YOP) in 1978 providing six months of

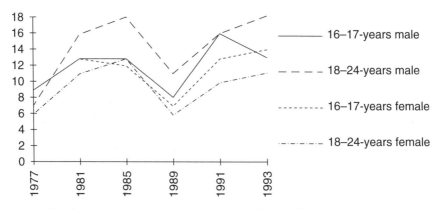

Figure 11.1 Proportion of age group unemployed. *Source:* OPCS (1995)

work experience for those who had been unemployed for six weeks, levels of participation grew. In 1981, YOP was succeeded by the year-long Youth Training Scheme (YTS) and in 1986 YTS became a two-year programme (subsequently renamed YT and, more recently, Skillseekers).

By the mid-1980s, with a majority of minimum-aged school-leavers having had experience of YTS (Furlong and Raffe 1989), schemes had become central to an understanding of the transition from school to work. In 1985, 20 per cent of males and 14 per cent of females in England and Wales were on YTS in the spring after reaching the minimum school-leaving age (Courtenay 1988). By 1989, participation had increased to account for the spring destinations of 27 per cent of males and 20 per cent of females, but thereafter started to decline (as educational participation grew). In spring 1992, 16 per cent of males and 13 per cent of females were on YT (Courtenay and McAleese 1993). With the collapse of the youth labour market and the subsequent withdrawal of social security and unemployment benefit, today's 16-year-olds tend to face a choice between remaining in full-time education or finding a place on a scheme. In some areas the range of training opportunities has been limited; young people have been sceptical about the value of the programmes and hostile towards the low allowance provided (Raffe and Smith 1987; Raffe 1989).

Despite government claims that YT has helped increase the skill level of young people, subsequent employment prospects are not good. Official statistics for 1994 show that in England and Wales only 42 per cent of trainees were awarded NVQs *(Times Higher Educational Supplement* 1994) and just 56 per cent of ex-trainees were in jobs six months after completing their schemes (DE 1995). Other commentators are even more pessimistic about the labour market benefits of youth training; some going so far as to argue that YT has 'virtually no impact' on young people's employment chances

(Times Educational Supplement 1989). Moreover, there is strong evidence to suggest that those who fail to find a job immediately after leaving their schemes find it difficult to escape long-term unemployment (Furlong 1993). Indeed, it has been argued that when it comes to securing jobs, the *context* of youth training (which includes contact with internal labour markets and informal recruitment networks) is much more significant than the *content* of the training (including the skills and competencies gained) (Raffe 1990). Roberts and Parsell (1992b) also argue that the stratification of youth training results in a diversity of experiences with some young people (primarily working-class trainees with few qualifications and members of ethnic minorities) being trained in contexts where the chances of employment are virtually nil.

Although the government (. . .) tried to make political mileage out of the claim that it (. . .) helped raise training standards among young people, there is clear evidence to show a continued decline in apprentice training stretching back to the mid-1960s. In 1964, there were 235,000 male apprentices and 5,400 female apprentices in manufacturing industries. By 1989 this had declined to 49,700 and 3,900 respectively (Layard *et al.* 1994). Moreover, these figures do not simply reflect the general decline in manufacturing. As a proportion of all employees in manufacturing, apprentices fell from 3 per cent to 1 per cent over the same period (Layard *et al.* 1994). Despite the rapid growth of the service sector, the number of apprentices in all industries has declined in recent years (from 332,000 in 1984 to 191,000 in 1995) (CSO 1996; Deakin 1996).

Discouraged workers

While government investment in training schemes has been justified by the need to increase skill levels in order to provide a labour force which can compete in a global economy, Ashton and colleagues have argued that the measures introduced by governments during the 1980s actually produced a 'mismatch between the supply flow of young people entering the labour market and the demands of employers for a highly educated labour force' (1990: 2). Effectively, government intervention during this period strengthened a national system of training geared towards 16- and 17-year-old school-leavers which discouraged continued educational participation. Ironically, increases in educational participation, which have the potential to deliver highly qualified workers, occurred primarily through a lack of consumer confidence in the product (YT) being offered by the government.

(. . .) With a rapid decline in the number of jobs available to minimum-aged school leavers and the growth of a 'surrogate labour market' (Lee *et al.* 1990) involving the introduction and development of various youth training schemes, remaining in full-time education has provided young people with a credible alternative and has been perceived by some as involving less risk than direct entry into a contracting labour market. Recent work in Scotland, England and Wales has highlighted this relationship between labour markets and post-compulsory educational participation. Using Scottish data Raffe and Williams (1989) argued that in labour markets with above average rates of unemployment, fewer young people leave school at the minimum age, the effect being strongest among those with mid-range qualifications who may have been on the margins of deciding whether to leave or stay. However, in an attempt to replicate the Scottish analysis using data from England and Wales, Grey and colleagues (1992) failed to find a comparable 'discouraged worker' effect; indeed, they found that in England more young people stayed on at school in low unemployment areas. In a subsequent analysis, Paterson and Raffe (1995) reconsidered their earlier conclusions. In this new analysis, they concluded that the 'discouraged worker' effect seemed to be weaker among more recent cohorts of young people and they explained this change in terms of a general weakening of the pull from the labour market on young people as job opportunities continued to decline for all young people.

In sum, the significant changes which have occurred in the youth labour market during the 1980s and early 1990s provide some support for the idea that Britain is becoming a post-industrial society. Young people are increasingly finding work in the service sector while skill development and 'flexible specialization' have become necessary for young workers in the struggle to avoid long-term unemployment and economic and social marginalization. These changes can be seen as arising from economic rather than political processes (Green 1989; Ashton et al. 1990). While Thatcherite policies helped strip away legislative frameworks developed in the Fordist era, the main changes in the youth labour market were undoubtedly caused by changes in the global economy following the recession of the early 1980s (Green 1989; Ashton et al. 1990). The decline in union power, for example, was accelerated by legislation and confrontation, yet the root cause was to be found in the decline of employment in large-scale industrial units and the growth of the small private firms.

The diversification of labour market transitions and the maintenance of structured inequalities

Changes occurring over the last decade appear to have radically altered the nature of young people's labour market participation. Transitions to employment now tend to take longer to complete, while the diversification of routes means that experiences have become more individualized. Indeed, many researchers have highlighted the increasing complexity of the transition from school to work with young people finishing school at different stages and following a variety of overlapping routes into the labour market (Clough et al. 1986; Furlong and Raffe, 1989). Between the ages of 16 and

18, young people build up a far greater range of experiences than previously; they embark on different courses of study, receive training in a number of contexts, and spend time both out of work and in employment. From the stage that they leave school until they obtain their first full-time jobs, few young people share identical sets of experiences and most encounter situations where they are able to select between competing sets of alternatives (Roberts 1995). In this context Roberts suggests that a process of individualization has occurred in so far as these changes have involved a reduction in the number of young people with closely matching transitional patterns.

Differentiated experiences

However, the existence of individualized or diversified routes should not be taken as an indication that structural determinants of transitional outcomes have weakened. On a number of different levels, young people's transitional experiences can be seen as differentiated along the lines of class and gender. Indeed, we suggest that in many crucial respects, continuity rather than change best describes the trends of the last two decades.

Despite an apparent increase in the possibilities to continue full-time education or embark on a course of training, young people from advantaged positions in the socioeconomic hierarchy have been relatively successful in protecting privileged access to the most desirable routes. Although young people from working-class families are increasingly likely to remain at school beyond the age of 16, they continue to be overrepresented among early labour market entrants; in 1992 around 6 per cent of the children of professional workers were in full-time jobs at the age of 16–17 compared to more than one in five of those from the manual classes (Courtenay and McAleese 1993). Moreover, there is no evidence to suggest that class-based differentials have declined over the last decade ((. . .) Furlong 1992; Marshall and Swift 1993), although those from ethnic minorities are becoming more likely than their white counterparts to avoid early labour market entry (Courtenay and McAleese 1993).

The timing of entry to full-time jobs has also continued to be strongly affected by gender: while girls tend to stay on at school, boys are more likely to have entered full-time jobs by the age of 16–17. Of those reaching the minimum leaving-age in 1991, for example, 22 per cent of boys but just 14 per cent of girls were in full-time jobs by the following spring (Courtenay and McAleese 1993). This differential has increased since the mid-1980s, reflecting an increased tendency for young women to remain in full-time education which is partly explained by the demands of service sector employers for educated female workers. The increased demand for female service workers has also been reflected in narrowing wage differentials. At age 18–19 women still tend to earn less than men (92 per cent of the male wage in 1991), yet they work fewer hours and once these differences have been taken into account, the difference between male and female workers is in the order of 2 per cent (Park 1994). However, there is evidence to suggest that wage inequalities increase with age ((. . .) Dex 1985).

Similarly, experiences of youth training have remained highly stratified by class, gender and 'race'. Those from working-class families have always been more likely than middle-class youths to join training schemes (Furlong 1992; Roberts and Parsell 1992b; Courtenay and McAleese 1993), and quality training tends to be reserved for those with strong academic credentials (who are often from the more advantaged class positions). A number of writers have noted the ways in which the most disadvantaged young people and those from ethnic minorities tend to be concentrated in certain schemes with low rates of post-training employment (Lee *et al.* 1990; Roberts and Parsell 1992b). These second-rate training schemes have been variously described as 'sink schemes' or the 'warehousing' schemes (Roberts and Parsell 1992b). It has also been argued that schemes serve to reinforce gender stereotypes in the labour market (. . .) and that scheme employers often lack an awareness of equal opportunities issues (Lee *et al.* 1990).

While levels of unemployment have increased in a general sense, again most young people who spend significant periods of time out of work come from working-class families and are located in parts of Britain which have been badly hit by recession and by the restructuring of labour markets ((. . .) Roberts *et al.* 1987; Furlong and Raffe 1989; (. . .)). Among those who reached the minimum school-leaving age in 1991, just 2 per cent of those with parents in professional occupations were unemployed the following spring, compared with around one in ten of those with parents in manual occupations (Courtenay and McAleese 1993). Moreover, while 7 per cent of white respondents were unemployed at this stage, 12 per cent of black respondents, 8 per cent of Asians and 14 per cent of those from other ethnic groups reported themselves as unemployed (Courtenay and McAleese 1993). Differences in levels of unemployment among various ethnic groups are even more significant among older age groups. Between the ages of 16 and 24, unemployment is significantly higher among Afro-Caribbeans (40 per cent), Pakistanis and Bangladeshis (35 per cent) while the unemployment rate among the Indian population is similar to that of the white population (20 per cent) (DfEE 1994).

Although all young people have become increasingly vulnerable to unemployment, in recent years there has been a disproportionate increase in male unemployment which has been observed in a number of European countries (. . .). Whereas in the late 1970s unemployment rates among the 18 to 24 age group were similar for both sexes, by 1993 the male unemployment rate was 4 percentage points above the female rate. Among graduates, the unemployment rate is also higher among males; a year after graduation, 12 per cent of males are unemployed, compared to 8 per cent of women (*Sunday Times* 1995). Males are also likely to be unemployed for longer periods of time than females; in 1995, around 127,000 males in the 18 to 24 age group had been unemployed for a year or more compared to 38,000 women (*Sunday Times* 1995). These differences are partly explained by the decline in the manufacturing sector (traditionally an important source of employment for males) and the growth of the service sector (in which many jobs traditionally performed by females have been located). Yet differential patterns of labour market withdrawal among the unemployed are also significant.

Of those who experience unemployment after completing education or training, some young people subsequently withdraw from the labour market. Most of those who withdraw have substantial experience of unemployment, with young women being twice as likely to withdraw than males (Furlong 1992). Once a young person gives up hope of finding a job, labour market withdrawal may represent an option which provides positive psychological benefits. Indeed, for young women, especially those who are married or have children, withdrawal may be a socially acceptable alternative to long-term unemployment.

Reconceptualizing transitions

The changes in the youth labour market described in this chapter have been reflected in the different ways in which sociologists have conceptualized the transition from school to work. In the 1960s and 1970s, the predictability of transitional routes tended to be stressed (Carter 1962; (. . .) Ashton and Field 1976; Willis 1977). Within these models, social class and gender were seen as powerful predictors of school experiences and educational attainment, which in turn helped determine the nature of the transition and the positions young people entered in the labour market. Ashton and Field (1976), for example, identified three main routes which young people followed from school to work: 'extended careers' involving higher education and access to the graduate labour market; 'short-term careers' involving short periods of training or post-compulsory education and leading to skilled manual or routine white collar employment; and 'careerless' routes which involved leaving school at the minimum age to take up semi-skilled or unskilled employment. With young people being allocated to distinct routes at an early age, this model corresponds to the train journey metaphor (. . .). In a context of collectivized transitions, young people were provided with clear messages about their destinations and the likely timing of their journeys and tended to develop an awareness of likely sequences of events.

With the transition from school to work tending to become much more complex during the 1980s, it became increasingly difficult for minimum-aged school-leavers to secure jobs immediately after leaving school and routes into work tended to become more diverse. Yet despite this diversification of routes, sociologists tended to argue that transitional outcomes remained highly structured (Roberts *et al*. 1987; Bynner and Roberts 1991; Banks *et al*. 1992). This structural emphasis was underlined by the use of the term 'trajectory', implying that individuals had little control over their destinations (Evans and Furlong 1997).

Reflecting the theoretical influence of Beck and Giddens, transitional models introduced during the 1990s have tended to place a greater emphasis on the ways individuals actively negotiate risk and uncertainty, referred to by Evans and Furlong (1997) as a 'navigation' model and loosely corresponding to the analogy of a switch from rail transport to road travel (. . .). In the age of high modernity, the range of possibilities open to individuals means that people are constantly forced to engage with the likely consequences of their actions on a subjective level. Indeed, Beck highlights the extent to which 'reflexive modernization' involves an ongoing 'self-confrontation with the effects of risk' (1994: 5).

The emphasis placed on subjective perceptions of risk and uncertainty represents an important break with earlier traditions. Prior to the 1990s, the predominant theme was that having followed well-trodden and predictable routes or trajectories from the family, through the school and into the labour market, the transition from school to work tended not to be associated with a subjective unease or discomfort (Carter 1962; Ashton and Field 1976). Although we remain sceptical about the extent to which changes in the youth labour market have affected underlying patterns of social reproduction, we recognize that processes which appear stable and predictable on an objective level may involve greater subjective risk and uncertainty.

During the 1960s and 1970s, as a consequence of following highly structured trajectories from school into the labour market, young people tended to develop sets of assumptions which helped make their experiences seem natural and normal. After spending their formative years in socially restricted networks, young people usually developed an awareness of the range of opportunities likely to be available to people like themselves and the nature of the associated lifestyles. Consequently Ashton and Field (1976) maintained that the transition from school to work, generally being a confirmation of earlier experiences and expectations, was a smooth and relatively untraumatic event in the lives of most young people.

In many ways, processes of social reproduction which are smooth and predictable on a subjective level can be regarded as characteristic of a traditional social order in which children, following in the footsteps of their parents, may not give very much consideration to a wider range of jobs or careers. In communities with a limited range of job opportunities young people may tailor their expectations to the main types of jobs available. In the mining communities of the Northeast and in the Welsh valleys, boys often grew up expecting to follow their fathers down the pits (Dennis *et al*. 1956). In the West Midlands, Willis (1977) highlighted subjective continuities among working-class males who celebrated the masculine culture represented on building sites and the factory floor. The strength of these assumptions in traditional working-class communities is also emphasized by Carter (1962) who found a widespread expectation that boys would enter the steel trade. Similar patterns have been identified among females. Westwood (1984), for example, argued that working-class girls expected to enter the textile factories of the East Midlands before withdrawing to become involved in full-time domestic labour.

The restructuring of the adult labour market and the decline of the youth labour market have important implications for the way young people experience the transition to work on a subjective level. These changes, which stem from the continued decline in demand for low skill labour, have led to a demand for a better educated, more skilled labour force in advanced industrial societies. But the speed of change has meant that the current generation of young people are making their transitions to work in a period of turmoil and, as a consequence, may lack the clear frames of reference which can help smooth transitions. In this respect, entry to the world of work in the 1990s is characterized by a heightened sense of risk.

Having parents who experienced very different transitions, young people often perceive the process as filled with risk and uncertainty. Many, fearing the consequences, shelter from the labour market as long as possible by remaining in education (Biggart and Furlong 1996). Yet it is important to stress that subjective perceptions of risk can be present even among those whose routes appear relatively safe to the outside observer; even young people from privileged social backgrounds and with excellent academic credentials frequently worry about failure and about the uncertainty surrounding future events and experiences (Lucey 1996).

Conclusion

In this chapter we have highlighted the extent to which labour market experiences of young people have changed over the last two decades. The types of jobs which young people enter and their experiences of the transition from school to work have changed quite significantly, largely as a result of global economic changes in the demand for labour. Although greater opportunities for advanced education and training are available to all young people, existing social disadvantages seem to have been maintained. Indeed, young people from working-class families and ethnic minorities face a new set of disadvantages which stem from the development of a labour market periphery. New forms of flexible working have reduced job security and many of the least qualified young people have become trapped on the labour market periphery and are vulnerable to periodic unemployment. Moreover, the creation of opportunities in small service environments has been associated with a decline in collective traditions and union membership for working-class youth, while the professional and technical middle classes have become more organized and increasingly unionized (Lash and Urry 1987). In this respect, we agree with Jessop and colleagues who argue that post-Fordism is characterized by a 'division between a skill-flexible core and a time-flexible periphery, which is now replacing the old manual/non-manual division' (1987: 109).

While the demand for flexible, skilled workers in the new information society creates advantages for some young people, the continued segmentation of labour markets helps ensure that traditional privileges are protected. Yet despite the maintenance of traditional lines of inequality, subjectively young people are forced to reflexively negotiate a complex set of routes into the labour market and in doing so, develop a sense that they alone are responsible for their labour market outcomes. It is in this context that (. . .) a transitional metaphor based around car journeys reflects the pattern of change. Young people are forced to negotiate a complex maze of potential routes and tend to perceive outcomes as dependent upon their individual skills, even when the objective risks of failure are slim. In turn, the perception of risk can lead to subjective discomfort. The evidence we have presented in this chapter provides some support for Beck and Giddens. Transitions have become more individualized and young people from all social backgrounds perceive their situations as filled with risk and uncertainty. At the same time, there is also evidence that, on an objective level, risks are distributed in an unequal fashion and correspond closely to traditional lines of disadvantage based on class and gender.

References

Ashton, D. N. and Field, D. (1976) *Young Workers*, London, Hutchinson.

Ashton, D. N., Maguire, M. J. and Spilsbury, M. (1990) *Restructuring the Labour Market. The Implications for Youth*, Basingstoke, Macmillan.

Atkinson, J. (1984) 'Manpower strategies for flexible organizations', *Personnel Management*, August, pp. 28–32.

Banks, M. H., Bates, I., Breakwell, G., Bynner, J., Emler, N., Jamieson, L. and Roberts, K. (1992) *Careers and Identities*, Buckingham, Open University Press.

Beck, U. (1994) 'The reinvention of politics. Towards a theory of reflexive modernization' in U. Beck, A. Giddens and S. Lash (eds) *Reflexive Modernization. Politics, Tradition and Aesthetics in the Modern Social Order*, Oxford, Polity.

Bell, D. (1973) *The Coming of Post-industrial Society*, New York, Basic Books.

Biggart, A. and Furlong, A. (1996) 'Educating "discouraged workers". Cultural diversity in the upper secondary school', *British Journal of Sociology of Education*, 17, pp. 253–66.

Bynner, J. and Roberts, K. (eds) (1991) *Youth and Work. Transitions to Employment in England and Germany*, London, Anglo-German Foundation.

Carter, M. P., (1962) *Home, School and Work*, London, Pergammon.

Chisholm, L., Büchner, P., Krüger, H.-H. and Brown, P. (1990) 'Childhood and youth in the United Kingdom and West Germany'. An introduction, in

Chisholm, L., Büchner, P., Krüger, H.-H. and Brown, P. (eds) *Childhood, Youth and Social Change. A Comparative Perspective*, London, Falmer.

Clough, E., Gray, J., Jones, B. and Pattie, C. (1986) *Routes Through YTS*, Youth Cohort Studies No. 2, Sheffield, Manpower Services Commission.

Courtenay, G. (1988) *England and Wales Youth Cohort Study. Report on Cohort 1, Sweep 1*, Sheffield, Manpower Services Commission.

Courtenay, G. and McAleese, I. (1993) *England and Wales Youth Cohort Study. Report on Cohort 5, Sweep 1*, Sheffield, Employment Department.

CSO (Central Statistical Office) (1996) *Social Trends*, London, HMSO.

Deakin, B. M. (1996) *The Youth Labour Market in Britain. The Role of Intervention*, Cambridge, Cambridge University Press.

DE (Department of Employment) (1995) *Labour Market Quarterly Report*, November, London, Department of Employment.

Dennis, N., Henriques, F. and Slaughter, C. (1956) *Coal is Our Life*, London, Eyre and Spottiswoode.

Dex, S. (1985) *The Sexual Division of Work. Conceptual Revolution in the Social Sciences*, Brighton, Wheatsheaf.

DfEE (Department for Education and Employment) (1994) *Employment Gazette*, 102, London, HMSO.

DfEE (Department for Education and Employment) (1995) *Employment Gazette*, 103, London, HMSO.

DfEE (Department for Education and Employment) (1996) *Employment Gazette*, 104, London, HMSO.

Evans, K. and Furlong, A. (1997) 'Metaphors of youth transitions. Niches, pathways, trajectories or navigations', in J. Bynner, L. Chisholm and A. Furlong (eds) *Youth, Citizenship and Social Change in a European Context*, Aldershot, Avebury.

Furlong, A. (1992) *Growing Up in a Classless Society*, Edinburgh, Edinburgh University Press.

Furlong, A. (1993) 'The youth transition, unemployment and labour market disadvantage. Gambling on YTS', *Youth and Policy*, 41, pp. 24–35.

Furlong, A. and Raffe, D. (1989) *Young People's Routes into the Labour Market*, Edinburgh, Industry Department for Scotland.

Giddens, A. (1991) *Modernity and Self Identity. Self and Society in the Late Modern Age*, Oxford, Polity.

Green, F. (1989) 'Evaluating structural economic change. Britain in the 1980s', in F. Green (ed.) *The Restructuring of the UK Economy*, Hemel Hempstead, Harvester Wheatsheaf.

Grey, J., Jesson, D. and Sime, N. (1992) 'The discouraged worker. Post-16 participation in education south of the border', *Sociology*, 26, pp. 493–505.

Hakim, C. (1979) *Occupational Segregation. A Comparative Study of the Degree and Patterns of Differentiation Between Men's and Women's Work in Britain, the United States and Other Countries*, London, Department of Employment.

Jansen, T. and Van der Veen, R. (1992) 'Reflective modernity, self-reflexive biographies. Adult education in the light of the risk society', *International Journal of Lifelong Learning*, 11, pp. 275–86.

Jessop, B., Bonnett, K., Bromley, S. and Ling, T. (1987) 'Popular capitalism, flexible accumulation and left strategy', *New Left Review*, 165, pp. 104–22.

Krahn, H. J. and Lowe, G. S. (1993) *Work, Industry and Canadian Society*, Scarborough, Ontario, Nelson.

Kumar, K. (1995) *From Post-Industrial to Post-Modern Society*, Oxford, Blackwell.

Lash, S. and Urry, J. (1987) *The End of Organised Capital*, Cambridge, Polity.

Layard, R., Mayhew, L. and Owen, G. (1994) *Britain's Training Deficit*, Aldershot, Avebury.

Lee, D., Marsden, D., Rickman, P. and Duncombe, J. (1990) *Scheming for Youth. A Study of YTS in the Enterprise Culture*, Milton Keynes, Open University Press.

Lucey, H. (1996) 'Transitions to womanhood. Constructions of success and failure for middle and working class young women', conference paper, University of Glasgow, British Youth Research: The New Agenda, 26–28 January.

MacDonald, R. (1996) 'Youth transitions at the margins', conference paper, University of Glasgow, British Youth Research: The New Agenda, 26–28 January.

Maguire, M. (1991) 'British labour market trends', in D. N. Ashton and G. Lowe (eds) *Making Their Way. Education, Training and the Labour Market in Canada and Britain*, Milton Keynes, Open University Press.

Marshall, G. and Swift, A. (1993) 'Social class and social justice', *British Journal of Sociology of Education*, 44, pp. 187–211.

Mizen, P. (1995) *The State, Young People and Youth Training. In and Against the Training State*, London, Mansell.

Moore, R. (1984) 'Schooling and the world of work', in Bates, I., Clarke, J., Cohen, P., Finn, D., Moore, R. and Willis, P. (eds) *Schooling for the Dole*, Basingstoke, Macmillan.

OPCS (Office of Population Censuses and Surveys) (1995) *General Household Survey 1993*, London, HMSO.

Park, A. (1994) *England and Wales Youth Cohort Study Cohort 4. Young people 18–19 years old in 1991. Report on Sweep 3*, London, Employment Department.

Paterson, L. and Raffe, D. (1995) 'Staying-on in full-time education in Scotland. 1985–1991', *Oxford Review of Education*, 21, pp. 3–23.

Payne, J. (1995) *Routes Beyond Compulsory Schooling*, Youth Cohort Paper No. 31, London, Employment Department.

Raffe, D. (1989) 'Longitudinal and historical changes in young people's attitudes to YTS', *British Educational Research Journal*, 15, pp. 129–39.

Raffe, D. (1990) 'The transition from school to work. Content, context and the external labour market', in C. Wallace and M. Cross (eds) *Youth in Transition. The Sociology of Youth and Youth Policy*, London, Falmer.

Raffe, D. and Smith, P. (1987) 'Young people's attitudes to YTS. The first two years', *British Educational Research Journal*, 13, pp. 241–60.

Raffe, D. and Williams, J. D. (1989) 'Schooling the discouraged worker. Local labour-market effects on educational participation', *Sociology*, 23, pp. 559–81.

Roberts, K. (1995) *Youth and Employment in Modern Britain*, Oxford, Oxford University Press.

Roberts, K., Clark, S. C. and Wallace, C. (1994) 'Flexibility and individualisation. A comparison of transitions into employment in England and Germany', *Sociology*, 28, pp. 31–54.

Roberts, K., Dench, S. and Richardson, D. (1987) *The Changing Structure of Youth Labour Markets*, London, Department of Employment.

Roberts, K. and Parsell, G. (1992a) 'Entering the labour market in Britain. The survival of traditional opportunity structures', *Sociological Review*, 30, pp. 727–53.

Roberts, K. and Parsell, G. (1992b) 'The stratification of youth training', *British Journal of Education and Work*, 5, pp. 65–83.

Rose, M. (1996) 'Still life in Swindon. Case-studies in union survival and employer policy in a 'Sunrise' labour market', in D. Gallie, R. Penn and M. Rose (eds) *Trade Unionism in Recession*, Oxford, Oxford University Press.

Spilsbury, M., Hoskins, M., Ashton, D. N. and Maguire, M. J. (1987) 'A note on trade union membership patterns of young people', *British Journal of Industrial Relations*, 25, pp. 267–74.

Sunday Times (1995) 'Angry young men', 2 April.

Times Educational Supplement (1989) 'A less than flattering spot', 29 January.

Times Educational Supplement (1994) 'Youth training fails the grade', 2 September.

Westwood, S. (1984) *All Day Every Day. Factory and Family in the Making of Women's Lives*, London, Pluto.

Willis, P. (1977) *Learning to Labour*, Farnborough, Saxon House.

Chapter 12

Big pictures and fine detail

School work experience policy and the local labour market in the 1990s

John Ahier and Rob Moore

Introduction

Our aim in this paper is to question how work experience for school pupils, which has now become a standardized and universal national policy in England and Wales, fits with some recent developments in labour markets, work conditions and the lives of young people. We shall do this by looking at a range of rationales given for the policy over recent years at national level by government, educators and employers. These will be compared with the reactions of those directly involved in providing, or, indeed, refusing to provide work experience in one local labour market.[1] Because of changes in the conditions of work in certain sectors and in the employment position of many students, new reasons are emerging for the involvement of some employers in the policy and the non-involvement of others. Such changes may come to make difficulties for the policy of work experience for all secondary school pupils just as it has become almost universal.

There is a simple commonsense way in which work experience can be seen and justified as part of the transition to adulthood. It introduces young people to the workplace, the routines and disciplines of employment and the nature of life in a public institution very different from home and school. Such a view forms the bedrock of everyday, shared understandings between educators, parents, and employers. (. . .) But at least one conclusion of this research is that the notion of different worlds, based on a series of dualities, such as the private and public, production and consumption, school and work, has become more difficult to maintain.

Over the years, the provision of work experience has been justified at national level by appeals to the self-interest of employers and also to more general concerns for the national economy and visions of its future. Central to the debate has been the way in which national, general economic interests have been combined with the particular interests of educators on the one hand, and local employers on the other. For example, the practical short-term interests of many employers in recruiting and maintaining young workers could easily cohere with educational commitments to giving young people

er, non-academic contexts for learning. In turn, these
r' under very general political concerns about the prob-
y youth, or Britain's declining manufacturing base and
dustrial culture of the educators.

course, the promotion of work experience generally has
cique of the enclosed, divided, school curriculum. For
n of a progressive 'outgoing' of the curriculum via the
ser links between school and industry is used by Jamieson
to make sense of, and periodize, a success story from the
of work experience for *some* pupils (1973–82), to 'work
(1983–92). (. . .)

ucationalist's) critiques of the divided curriculum are not,
likely to persuade local employers to co-operate with schools
ng work experience places for thousands of school pupils. (. . .)
ve have to look at how public justifications for the growth and
n of work experience to all pupils have been developed in terms of
more global, all-encompassing narratives of national economic and social
imperatives and at how these 'big pictures' provide sufficient scope to appropriate rationales of a more particular and sectional character. A central
concern in the research discussed in this paper was with how far (or in
what way) these global justifications at the level of national rhetoric and
policy formation inform local thinking about WE for pupils, teachers and
employers.

The contextualization of work experience within a broader socio-economic
narrative parallels the dominant technique for justifying educational change
in general in the post-war period. Typically, 'the nation' (or more specifically, the nation's economy) is presented in a particular way that defines a
set of needs that constitute change as an imperative – a general national
problem with a particular educational solution. Although the story-line
remains much the same, the central character changes with time. In the
1950s, 'the nation' was described in terms of 'advanced industrial society',
later, in the sixties (under the influence of Daniel Bell's book *The Coming
of Post-Industrial Society* (1973) it became 'post industrial society' and today
a variety of characterizations compete to provide the leading persona: 'post-
fordism', 'post-modern society', 'late-modern society', etc.[2] A significant
feature of the changing persona of 'the nation' as the leading character in
these successive meta-narratives is the move from the proactive nation-state
of the Keynsian socio-democratic 'advanced industrial society' to the more
passively reactive governments of post-modernity, diminished and emascu-
lated by globalization.[3]

Whereas these 'big pictures' of socio-economic change framed the process
of educational change, the problems they constructed tend to be focused
upon a particular issue that is foregrounded by the rhetoric of policy. For
instance, 'youth' is frequently presented as a key character facing particular

types of problems, suffering particular deficits and requiring particular educational remedies. Another enduring cause for concern has been the national culture typically presented as outmoded and out of step with the developing economic trends (Ahier 1996; Hickox 1995). (. . .)

We will address two sets of inter-related issues. The first is to trace these 'big stories' of socio-economic change into the specific local labour market contexts within which work experience is operative. The question is: do the rationales constructed at the national level of policy rhetoric inform and structure the ways in which those involved participate in work experience? Secondly, we will examine how different sectors of the local labour market reflect change in contrasting ways and the implications for work experience. Finally, we will focus upon those sectors that most successfully approximate the conditions emphasized by current rationales and examine how far they sustain and promote work experience. In short: is it the case that the dominant 'big picture' of socio-economic change provides the rationale for work experience at the local level and is it the case that those sectors and trends promoted by the big picture support the policy locally?

Economic rationales for work experience – the big pictures

In this section we will review some of the 'big picture' scenarios of socio-economic change that have informed work experience policy over recent years and will look in detail at the current position as represented in official policy documents. Although the meta-narrative of *economic* change is the central theme, as we observed above, other issues are frequently brought into play: the problem of 'youth' (e.g., as citizens as well as workers), the 'national culture', etc. We will briefly cover some of these additional concerns within policy problematics.

The Trident Trust has been concerned with the organization of work experience for more than twenty years. (. . .) The original overall rationale for what was then called Project Trident in 1971 was couched in the style and concepts of social democracy, consistent with the social studies literature of the time. There was an acknowledgement of social difficulties; '. . . the problem of youth is, in fact, the problem of our modern urban society . . .' (Project Trident 1971). The fear was of a generation 'developing without proper motivation or clear purpose . . .', which can be blamed on 'the speed of change in modern society' leading to the 'weakening of the traditional patterns in society . . .' (p. 3).[4] The answers were to be found in closing the gap between young people's lives in school and the world beyond. But Trident has always accepted that firms would be motivated to provide placements for various instrumental reasons. Involvement might develop their image in the local community, boost their own employee development and training, as well as aiding them in recruitment. (. . .)

Of course, the ways in which the self-interest of employers is presented by promoters of WE has changed over the years. For example, in the late 1980s much was made of the so-called demographic time bomb. (. . .) By the mid-1990s, when that time-bomb was meant to explode, we heard nothing of it.

Over recent years, central government has attempted to articulate the longer term self-interest of employers and employees in terms of improving national competitiveness (e.g. DFEE 1995) and persuaded employers to participate by suggesting it is in both the national and their individual interest. By providing opportunities for work experience, 'employers can help improve the quality and preparedness of young people coming onto the labour market' (DFEE 1995, p. 6) and it was said to be a good way of 'raising the profile of career opportunities with their organisation, and, in some cases, of dispelling unwarranted stereotyped views'. A full appreci-ation of the way school-based work experience is inserted in a general picture of national self-improvement can be gained by looking at two publications which appeared during the planning and execution of this research project: the Consultative Document from the DFEE entitled *Equipping Young People for Working Life* (DFEE 1996) and the Government White Paper, *Learning to Compete: Education and Training for 14–19 Year Olds* (December 1996, subsequently referenced here as HM Government 1996).

The scene is set by characterizing the current economic situation as one of rapid change and 'unprecedented challenges, both social and economic' (HM Government 1996, p. 6), arising from changes in technology and the openness to international competition. (. . .) In the face of such uncertainty there is an emphasis on individualization as the only way forward, because old structures cannot be relied upon; 'The changing nature of work will mean that people of all ages need to manage their own futures, develop in new directions, and acquire and use new knowledge and skills flexibly' (p. 17). Lifelong learning is a necessity. In view of this picture of the contemporary scene, work experience at school is presented as part of the preparation for learning, not just preparation for work (p. 16). Recording such work experience in the proposed new National Record of Achievement (NRA) will be an important part of an individual's self-management (HM Government 1996, p. 17; DFEE 1996, p. 18).

In common with many other publications concerning the future of national education, the promotion of any policy depends upon an identification of personal and mental qualities which have been, hitherto, in short supply, and a conviction that the institutional changes proposed or supported will nurture such qualities. These two publications seek to promote changes which develop the qualities for employability deduced from the general picture of economic change. Throughout these publications two themes and two concepts reoccur. The first theme concerns the need for individuals to make employment choices. Because of the rapid changes, young people's decisions must be more related to the world of work. For this to be possible they need to be aware of the 'needs of the labour market' (HM Government 1996, p. 4 and p. 21; DFEE 1996 p. 5). The intention is to, 'provide them with the information and guidance necessary to improve the quality of their choices and their relevance to the needs of employment' (HM Government 1996, p. 6; DFEE 1996, p. 17). A second theme refers to the need for flexibility, making 'foundation skills' a vital part of learning by 14 to 19 year-olds for the transition to work. These skills include the 'ability to adapt and respond, quickly and confidently, to rapid change' (HM Government 1996, p. 6). (. . .)

The two concepts which, by repetition, provide the imagined dynamics to the whole process of 'learning to compete' are those of 'progression' and 'integration'. Concepts used over the years in educational discourse to attack 'artificial boundaries', rigid distinctions and, apparently, false notions of completeness, are used here as part of what is claimed to be 'a shared vision' (HM Government 1996, p. 8). The central features of this vision are 'high participation, high attainment, and effective *progression* (our italics) into work and further learning through life' (HM Government 1996, p. 8; DFEE 1996, pp. 12–16). To facilitate this progress the world of work must be *integrated* into the world of education (p. 14), with work experience being seen as an important place where such integration can be developed (HM Government 1996, pp. 18 and 24).

Against this background, Government publications such as these have to seek to persuade what is called 'the employer community' (DFEE 1996, p. 5) to get more involved in work experience and other links with education. It is acknowledged that, 'Work experience placements represent a considerable investment of both time and resources . . . ' and this may make for problems with smaller companies. The answer is to ensure that 'this investment pays proper dividends' (DFEE 1996, p. 19). The White Paper ends with a series of challenges to employers, schools, colleges and young people themselves. The employers are addressed as 'key beneficiaries' of 14–19 learning and are asked to get more involved in education on governing bodies, working in Education–Business Partnerships, etc., and to provide work experience placements (HM Government 1996, p. 50). The education and training providers are challenged to work with employers, TECs and the Careers Service to improve the employability of young people (HM Government 1996, p. 51). Young people are encouraged to develop 'the skills, knowledge and understanding needed as a basis for further learning throughout life and work' (HM Government 1996, p. 52), via pursuing qualifications, 'regular reviewing and recording personal achievement', part-time employment, voluntary work and 'structured work experience' (HM Government 1996, p. 52).

Central government thinking about work experience and related policies appears as a mix of old and new. The old concerns with young people making a smooth transition from school to work and some appreciation of a new situation in which both the national economy and the young find themselves. Behind the usual descriptions of international competitiveness and a flexible labour market, there is a belief in the end of what might be called *collective drifting* into work (Roberts 1995). Work experience, a National Record of Achievement, and the general vocationalizing of the curriculum have to fulfil the requirement that young people know themselves as individuals, their skills and aptitudes, and know the labour market and its needs. But there are only a limited number of things a government can do to fulfil this requirement. It can introduce closer management, control and auditing of work experience, for example, and this is indicated in the White Paper when it talks of 'new national quality standards for work experience placements' (p. 24). However, from reactions of managers and others in our research interviews, employers are likely to see this as a further, unwelcome, development of state bureaucracy. (. . .)

More significant, however, is the whole structure of argument and rhetoric from which these recommendations and policies emerge and which seeks to persuade those concerned with education and employment. Here, it is taken as given that governments can do very little to nourish or protect either working people or national enterprises from what is represented as the hungry, petulant, demanding customers and competitors elsewhere. The resulting flexible labour market, however represented to the young and their parents, might well appear as an alien, unpredictable creation, which, is only accessible by individual action, not by collective drifting. In this political rhetoric, 'learning to compete' sounds too much like being taught a hard lesson. The preparedness of employers to devote much time and money to such policies as work experience, when they themselves are so exposed to the rigours of cost cutting and unrestrained competition, must be open to question.

For those claiming to be national representatives of the employers, the big picture is much the same. For example, in its publication, *Realising the Vision: a Skills Passport* (1995), the CBI follows government descriptions of economic change, based on the contrasts between the old, settled social democratic post-war Britain in a benign world, and the present and future; 'In the past two decades, many of the comfortable certainties of post-war life have disappeared; full employment, a job for life, traditional industries, and the State as a major provider in all our lives' (CBI 1995, p. 6). The 'other' is similarly portrayed – every nation a potential competitor. Of particular concern are Asian countries with a thirst for learning, committed to skills targets beyond ours. (. . .)

But not all discussion or polemic concerning the links between education and industry at the national level includes a 'national' perspective, or starts with a picture of Britain in competition. One publication by Industry in Education (*I in E*), with very explicit implications for work experience, sets the scene in terms of the problems for the employer of 'poor employability' (*I in E* 1996, p. 6). Unlike the CBI publication, it concentrates on the immediate changes in the organization of work and the effects these have on what education should be providing; 'Larger companies are splitting down into smaller units and often removing layers of supervision. Consequently there are fewer unskilled and 'backroom' jobs of the type which were traditionally filled by young people' (p. 9).

The focus here is on the young people's lack of the qualities which make up 'employability' (p. 2) – young people not prepared for work; lacking the broader skills and qualities. The work adjustment period for young workers is too long and expensive (p. 6). This is a more direct approach than either the CBI or government and focuses on a number of factors which we found to be identified by respondents in our research of local employers, e.g. estimating the costs of 'poor employability' (p. 6), including productivity forgone and the need for extra supervision during what is called the 'work adjustment process'.

In a way Industry in Education is also more forthright in its critique of young people arising from research it commissioned into young peoples' ideas about employment. The conclusion is that few had thought about the personal qualities needed for employment:

> There was little appreciation of the concepts of 'customer care' or 'conforming to corporate norms'. Indeed, it seemed to us that a shift towards interaction by contract, rather than by covenant, was a disturbing characteristic of modern youth culture with important implications for social interactions in the workplace.
>
> (Industry in Education 1996, p. 12)

Industry in Education also expresses the more traditional criticisms of the educational system and its inability to prepare the young for work. Its methods are inappropriate (p. 13), teachers lack experience of work and have little conception of the organizational changes in workplaces. (. . .)

It advocates much closer contact between the providers of work experience and the teachers responsible, before, during and after the placement and the use of the NRA to focus on 'personal learning' (p. 19). The CBI has appeared much keener on integrating 'work related learning' into the National Curriculum (CBI *undated*; CBI 1994) although it did express reservations about linking 14–16 work experience directly to the acquisition of units towards NVQs (CBI *undated*, para. 17).

Thus, work experience and related policies concerned with the links between schools and work are promoted at the national level against a background of concerns about the national economy and possible failings in the supply of suitable labour. As a policy it is seen as contributing to the preparation of young people for the world of work. Among the contributions to the debate there are some shared perceptions about the future of work and current changes facing young people which could help argue the case for employer involvement in such schemes.

In a more general sense, the elements of these meta-narratives of social change inform the public sphere and provide a common currency of terminology for thinking about the contemporary context. Through political debate, TV and newspapers, they become the touchstone for collective understandings of 'the way things are today'. Although specialized for the particular purposes of policy promotion, these discourses are in no sense restricted to the sphere of policy formation or the more esoteric domains of adjacent academic debate. Ideas such as 'globalization' and 'flexibilization' can be recovered from the everyday conversation of normally well-informed citizens — especially as the conditions they denote have dramatically impinged upon many lives through the impact of 'delayering' and 'downsizing' and radical changes in services, such as banking, at those crucial points where the public (the 'global economy') transmutes into the private (the intimacy of the household). The rhetoric of policy and the rationale it provides for the promotion of work experience, resonates with the wider discourse of collective understanding. But when it comes down to examining the motivations and activities of those who actually decide on implementing these schemes — whether their enterprise should be involved at all and to what extent — then the 'big picture' may not be shared, or even regarded as relevant.

Trends in education and the youth labour market

As far as work experience is concerned, it is important to recognize that these accounts of change do not simply imply that young people need new skills. They suggest, far more broadly, that not only is the labour market being restructured but also that the kinds of relationships and arrangements that previously sustained a particular pattern of transitions into work are being dissolved. Studying employers reactions to work experience in 1997 raised issues, for us, concerning social, economic and political change and the precarious balance between the individual and social, public and private, short-term and long-term dimensions involved in this area of policy. A simple contrast can be made between youth employment in the 1970s, when the history of work experience began, and the situation in more recent years. Past research on the reactions of employers to this and related educational programmes suggests that they have, at least until very recently, expressed a number of both short-term and longer-term reasons for involvement. As far as short-term instrumental reasons are concerned, Shilling found firms admitting that they welcomed the actual labour provided by the students (Shilling 1989, p. 137) and the belief that providing work experience built a positive image of the enterprise (also, Wellington 1992,

p. 165). However, it was the use of work experience in the *recruitment* of young labour which was most frequently mentioned in the past. Fifteen out of the twenty employers in Shilling's study used it as a screening device (p. 146) and it was clearly a significant part of their 'unofficial agenda'. Watts (1991) mentions the reported savings to firms in recruitment if they used work experience as a means of identifying future employees (p. 140). It is upon the screening device factor that recent changes have had a significant impact – essentially because of the virtual collapse of the recruitment of young people into full-time work.

When the school leaving age was raised in 1972 two-thirds of school pupils left as early as possible, and most of those obtained full-time employment. By 1992, in contrast, only 13% of the equivalent group of 16–17 year-olds had full-time jobs.[5] There are many other ways of presenting the decline in the full-time employment of young people over recent years. Using the New Earnings Survey, for example, one can detect a fall of ¾ of a million of young people under the age of 21, in full-time work from 1990 to 1994. In the under-18 age group there has been a fall of 67% for manual occupations and 78% for non-manual, compared to a fall of 18% of 25-year-olds and over in manual occupations and an increase of 4% in non-manual occupations (Hughes 1995, p. 2). Whilst demographic changes might account for a fall of 20% in young people available for work, the above percentage drops could legitimately be called 'a collapse in employers' demand for young people in full-time employment' (Hughes 1995, p. 7).

This decline in full-time employment for young people is not a simple reflection of the recession. In the period of expansion between 1982 and 1990 there was no growth in youth employment, partly because such growth as there was came in sectors which had not previously employed young people, and both employers and the young themselves had come to adjust to the exclusion of 16 and 17 year-olds from full-time work (Roberts 1995, p. 10). The sectors of the labour market occupied by young school-leavers, it seems, have been particularly vulnerable to recent economic restructuring (Ashton *et al.* 1990). Young males have been progressively concentrated in less skilled jobs in manufacturing, displacing all-age males, but which are, in turn, vulnerable to technological change. For young women, the growth of employment in the service sector made up for their losses in manufacturing, but here they have had to face increasing pressure from older women working part-time (Ashton *et al.* pp. 50–1).

Interrelated changes in the general process of youth transition, such as the extension of education, changes in family structures and what some have termed the process of 'individualization' (Roberts 1995, chapter 5) also have to be considered. Schools now have a vested interest in keeping young people on beyond 16. It is also possible that familial financial pressures to obtain full-time work have reduced with the rise in married women's employment, not necessarily because there is more disposable income but because of changes in patterns of financial allocation which accompany it (Vogler 1994).

As far as work experience is concerned, it is important to stress that what aggregate levels of youth unemployment do not show is the growth in actual part-time employment of the young whilst they are still at school or on other educational courses. Since the birth of work experience as an initiative there have been great changes in attitudes to part-time work by secondary school pupils and by the 1990's probably a majority of young people will have had 'real', formal work experience before leaving school, mostly in retailing (Hutson 1992; Hutson and Cheung 1991; Hobbs *et al.* 1996). Many younger children will also have had less formal work experience (Lavalette 1996). Compared to their Fordist predecessors, not only do more young school students now have access to the world of formal work, but they also have the means to acquire consumption goods individually within their own markets. The significance of this for work experience will be indicated below.

In contrast to the earlier period where the structuring of transitions made work experience attractive as a screening device for the recruitment of young workers, the evolving, contemporary situation appears as follows.

First, as the transition between school and full-time work becomes even more extended, unpredictable and fragmented, the support for formalised, universal policies such as school-based work experience may become more doubtful. In particular, fewer employers are likely to be interested, short term, in the usefulness of links with schools for recruitment purposes. However, we have found that managers in the retail sector and banking were particularly committed to work experience for school pupils and able to provide it. They had also developed many other links with educational institutions. But, significantly, managers in these sectors tend see it as an exercise in general customer relations and do not share the rationales provided by government concerned with national competitiveness, or even the need to improve the school's output. Seeing the pupils as actual or potential customers may be symptomatic of wider changes in the distinction between production and consumption which has accompanied the growth of certain services and changes in forms of management (see Discussion/Conclusion p. 251ff).

Second, as we shall discuss in more detail, those very companies which exhibit the qualities which are politically promoted as representing the way forward for the international competitiveness of the British economy as a whole (flexibility, use of advanced technology, production of high value added goods and services) are often those for whom the organization of school-based work experience is both most difficult and least rewarding as far as recruitment is concerned.

Hence, structural changes have both removed the general traditional practical rationale for work experience involvement by employers and introduced a new type of motivation in certain sectors.

Local employers and the youth labour market

There are major and significant differences between sectors both in relation
to work experience itself and towards the recruitment of young workers.
These differences are reflected in attitudes towards young people and their
schooling. We will examine these contrasts through some comparisons
between different sectors. It is important to stress that such sectoral differences have significant implications for attempts to construct a universal
system of work experience providing consistencies of quality and experience
for all pupils. The translation of national policy into local practice needs
to be fully aware of these implications and the manner in which they construct substantive parameters to what is in fact possible for work experience
in practice.

Services

As far as services were concerned, the local managers, human resource co-
ordinators and others we interviewed made no spontaneous references to a
general national picture and the demands of new economic conditions, etc.
The point which many saw as most relevant, as far as work experience was
concerned, was their lack of any plans to offer full-time employment to
school leavers at 16, although some mentioned the possibility of recruiting
18-year-olds, usually on temporary contracts. However, many companies in
the services recruited young part-time workers who were either still at
school or at college. In the retail sector, the full-time employment of someone
on work experience in the distant future was accepted as a possibility, but
the greatest attraction for a number of managers was that work experience
put them in contact with possible part-time staff. In the case of a clothes
shop, for example, names and addresses were kept and those who proved
useful on work experience were sometimes taken on as 'Saturday girls' when
they reached 16. The recruitment and retention of such staff was seen as
so important that one large department store also made available an 'inter-
store transfer' for those part-time Saturday workers who go on to university
or college in another town. In the case of food retailing where work experience also provided a means of recruiting part-time temporary staff it was
noted that, occasionally, part-time staff have gone on to become full-time.
It was this view of young labour which affected both their motives for
providing work experience placements, and their approach to the young
people on those placements.

Taking two service sectors which had previously been substantial recruiters
of young full-time labour (local banking and building societies and retail)
there is now a general reserve about youth recruitment, but not because of
any major inadequacies in young people's education. In fact, numerous
respondents were impressed at the levels of competence; in keyboard skills,

for example (although some expressed the traditional concern with spelling and the ability to write letters). The major reason employers gave for not offering full-time jobs to school leavers was because other categories of recruit were more suitable, being prepared to work part time, and having a certain closeness to the customers.

Fundamental reorganization of work in banks and building societies over recent years has meant that there are fewer positions which are insulated from direct contact with customers. The barriers between processing tasks and customer contact have been lowered and, for many of the interviewees, this reorganization of work has been problematic for younger workers and, indeed, for work experience placements. It has deprived the young of unexposed places to develop and mature, of a place to hide. There is no protected space for the gauche office junior. These reorganizations favour the mature 'women returners'. In local branches of a building society, it is they who are seen as having, 'the ability to interact with a person on the other side of the counter . . . ' and, 'A much wider perspective of what's going on in the world'. Around the time of the interview, another building society was running a national advertising campaign featuring a picture of a smartly dressed woman of 30+ with the phrase 'Run by people like you, for people like you' (*Daily Telegraph* 1997).

(. . .)

Perhaps ten years ago we could have approached this matter in terms of a fall in demand for young labour, but now, at least in the Cambridge area, there is also a question of the decline in supply. This particular area has tended to be ahead of the national trend in terms of the percentage of young people continuing in education and declining numbers seeking employment at the minimum leaving-age (although, as Figure 12.1 shows, figures suggest that the national trend is converging with the local situation).

Hence, changing conditions of demand for young workers roughly echo changing trends in supply. Obviously there is an interaction between supply and demand (young people being, perhaps, more inclined to stay-on because of a perception of increasing difficulties in obtaining work), but it would be wrong to see this as a simple causal process. For reasons given, it is very likely the case that even if the supply of young people was high, employers would still prefer other categories under current conditions. It is necessary to stress, here, that the exclusion of young people from full-time employment is not based upon a perception of their deficiencies (educational or otherwise), but because they lack, by definition, the kinds of qualities preferred in others. No amount of education can change a 16-year-old school leaver into a 40-year-old woman returning to work after years of child-rearing and home-making. No educational qualification can confer the qualities of the latter upon the former or substitute for them. What became increasingly obvious to us in our interviews in this sector was the very conscious and

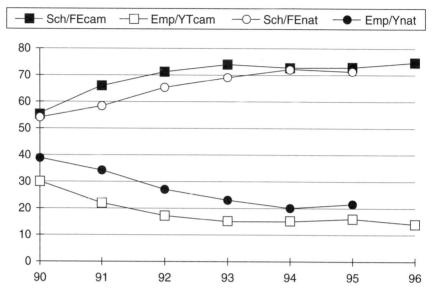

Figure 12.1 Destinations of year 11 school-leavers 1990–1996 in Cambridgeshire and nationally

explicit way in which employers recognized and valued the qualities that mature female returners brought to their workplaces. (. . .)

Manufacturing

The situation, however, in manufacturing, construction and utilities was quite different. A number of contrasts can be identified:

- Many of these companies continued to recruit young labour, often via varying forms of the traditional apprentice system.
- Standard forms of employment contract predominated, even in those companies undergoing substantial reorganization through takeover, difficult market conditions, technological change, or a desire to deliver 'shareholder value'.
- Many places within these companies remained 'distant from the customer', although general customer sensitivity by the companies was promoted.
- It was managers in these sectors who remained the most critical of the schools and their products.

Take, for example, a sub-contract precision engineering company. In many ways this company could be described as innovative and flexible, not in its contracts of employment, but at the level of work practices. The staff here had standard full-time contracts and, as far as the recruitment of young people was concerned, the company continued to take apprentices onto a 4-year scheme each year. We found no enthusiasm in this company, or in the sector as a whole, for the types of short-term conditions favoured by the services. This reflected the amount the company invested in their training. For a company geographically situated in an area of relative high levels of employment and a local economy dominated by the services, there was a definite concern for the problems of skills shortages. This combined with a very critical view of the school system; 'the standards of literacy of the children coming out of schools is appalling . . . I think it's the way they're taught, cos they're not corrected when they do things wrong. Their spellings and all that sort of thing, just aren't corrected at all. When they come out of school they think they're fine, and they're not. It's not fair to the youngster'. Nor were recent attempts to put these things right by central government much appreciated.

We found many of these views repeated by managers whose companies were involved in similar types of production, where full-time permanent contracts were standard and extensive training required. They rejected the educational dominance of a model of work that originated in the service sector where lower demands were made of young workers in exchange for less security and commitment. From their point of view, the schools seem to be more orientated to this *particular* new world of work rather than the realities of their own sector. Unlike those we interviewed in the services, the training manager of one of the largest local engineering companies was unimpressed by the computer skills of the young trainees, as they were mostly related to word processing.[6] (. . .)

Comparisons

Summarizing this situation, one can say that, in the service sectors, those responsible, directly or indirectly, for recruitment were fairly uncritical of young school leavers but rarely offered them full-time, permanent positions. Among banks and building societies, few expressed any interest in using work experience as a means of sifting and recruiting full-time staff. Most did not mention recruitment as a motive and in one case a bank stopped providing work experience placements because the recruitment of young school leavers had ceased. This was the only case in which we found an explicit recognition of the dilemma of providing work experience yet not providing work for school leavers.

In manufacturing the situation was different. Here we found a greater readiness to take on a limited number of school leavers in a more 'settled' form of employment, but greater reservations about their suitability and their preparation for work by the schools. Short- and long-term recruitment was regarded as a major reason for being involved in work experience by many of our interviewees. This was consistent with findings from earlier research (Wellington 1992; Shilling 1989). The personnel managers, training officers and general managers we interviewed in engineering and building, for example, saw work experience and other links with education as a way of improving the image of their sectors as a whole with a view to future recruitment of young people. In such companies we found a direct relationship between recruitment of school leavers onto full-time work and work experience, with a preference expressed for providing work experience placements to schools from which they had recruited school leavers in the past. In the case of the building industry, it was thought that work experience was particularly useful as there was less of a chance of an apprentice dropping out in their first year if they had some introduction to the physical side of the work from a work experience placement beforehand. Clearly, 'the world of work' to which work experience was meant to provide an introduction was seen quite differently by managers in these two sectors and, consequently, the motives for providing placements were significantly different.

The contrast between financial services and manufacturing exposes significant differences in the meaning and implications of economic change between sectors. Flexibilization in the services sector is strongly associated with changed conditions of service represented by part-time and short-term working. This in turn reflects the way in which technical changes, such as the use of computerized systems to inform decisions on credit-worthiness, have radically reduced the amount of discretion open to staff (as used to be exercised by the 'old fashion' branch bank manager). Social and interpersonal skills in customer service come to the fore, but, in reality, staff have little leeway in the decision-making processes. In this sense, the change involves a de-skilling in terms of traditional expertise and judgement and a shift to a different type of skill. In that the new skills are very much characteristics of the individuals themselves (a pleasant manner and appearance, etc.), they are more selected for in initial recruitment than developed by the company through training. It is this, perhaps, that explains why this sector has adopted flexible conditions of service – staff bring these essential qualities with them to work that is routinized by standard procedures. By contrast, manufacturing industry appears to be developing flexible production processes but is still investing considerable amounts in training. On this basis, security of employment remains a priority – workers need extended initial training and frequent retraining and, obviously, employers do not want to risk their considerable investment through insecurity in conditions of employment. One manager in this sector told us that his ideal would be to employ young people straight from school, to train them in-house and support them through further education including degree level and beyond! As noted above, it was the manufacturing sector that was most critical of schools and financial services that was least. Ironically, schools seem to please best those companies least likely to recruit young workers and please least those that are most likely to!

Hi-tech: at the cutting edge

We will conclude this section by considering those companies that in many respects best exemplify the model promoted by contemporary 'big picture' scenarios of economic change. These are 'hi-tech' companies at the cutting edge of technological and product development. They tend to be small-scale but highly innovative in their organization, production processes, work organization and products. In these ways, they might be seen as the 'wave of the future' requiring a new type of flexible, multi-skilled worker and having very clear messages for education. From this point of view, they would be ideal placements for work experience pupils. However, it was particularly noticeable that it was precisely companies of this type that were not involved in work experience. They typically employ a small number of highly qualified, multi-skilled personnel, usually of a graduate and post-graduate level of qualification and frequently utilizing experience gained previously in larger organizations. Companies of this type are a distinctive feature of the Cambridge labour market and reflect the influence of the University within the local economy.

The reasons why they do not involve themselves with work experience are as follows:

- as small companies they are simply too busy and too highly pressured to provide the time,
- by the nature of their work force, the skill levels and combinations utilised are too complex to accommodate school pupils,
- quality control and health and safety issues make work experience placements too much of a risk.

Even where, in rare cases, they may take work experience placements, they are restricted to routine and mundane activities (making tea, posting letters, etc.) separated from the primary work process. The types of work experience that could, by some criteria, be seen as most desirable are, for these reasons, least available. A number of the issues, here (health and safety, in particular) are not restricted to companies of this type.

Discussion/Conclusion

If one of the major, earlier reasons for employer's involvement in work experience (recruitment) is losing its significance, new motives for 'educational' contacts with young people are emerging, but are potentially problematic for the schools and young people themselves. These were motives which could be seen as having more to do with a view of the young people and their families as actual or potential customers than as future employees. The bank which had stopped providing work experience placements because it never recruited school leavers was still keen to pursue the young as customers via other school-based liaison work. Other banks also saw such work in schools as very important. One personnel manager described a programme of school banking as 'trying to attract the under 16s before they start work'. The use of work experience to attract customers was quite explicit. In particular, having young people 'on the inside' was thought to help show banks as welcoming places to take one's custom. One small local building society deliberately provided work experience for schools in areas where they had branches, seeing it as part of their corporate plan to encourage community links.

In a situation where there are large numbers of young people working part-time and having at their disposal sufficiently large amounts of money, educational institutions and programmes such as work experience are bound to be used by producers in the pursuit of young customers. We found that some retail outlets which catered for the youth market were keen to use work experience as a way of maintaining their customer's loyalty. Sometimes the enterprise used pupils on work experience to provide market feedback on the way young people as consumers may see the company. Even in the case of those enterprises which had no interest in the youth consumer market the provision of work experience was seen as useful in enhancing their local image.

It might be thought that this is simply the use of work experience as a marketing ploy, because, in most of the above examples, young people or their parents could be in direct contact with the service as shoppers, savers or borrowers. However, the language of customer-orientation, derived from notions of Total Quality Management, is also to be found in other sectors where the young people are unlikely ever to be the customers in the sense of direct purchasers of goods. The image of the customer–producer relationship here is used to instil discipline and responsibility.

The point is that there have been such changes in the management of work in all sectors, that work experience is bound to be seen and understood in different ways in the late 1990s. Indeed, one could argue that the very bases for the distinctions between 'school-place' and 'work-place' have been undermined, on the one hand, by the restructuring of the former as commercial businesses, oriented towards customers, and, on the other, by the centrality given to self-development and cultural change in the discourse of modern management (du Gay 1996). Many of the reorganizations of companies informed by Total Quality Management have been aimed at turning employees into each others customers within the corporation. (. . .)

Looking back at the rationales for work experience provided by employers' organizations and government, very little in the 'big picture', national agenda was ever expressed by our interviewees. At the level at which we were conducting our interviews no respondents took up the challenge to use work experience as a way of improving the general employability of the young, for example, or redirecting the efforts of schools in accordance with the new conditions of global competitiveness, labour flexibility, or technological change. Given the different perspectives and practices we found between the service and non-service sectors, there was very little agreement within what the DFEE has called the 'employer community' (DFEE 1996, p. 5) on the qualities needed for this new world of work. Ironically perhaps, the only area in which we found some agreement about the usefulness of work experience was over the question of preparing the young for a full day's work – a number implied that the school day was too short and a poor preparation for real work.

The fine detail of local labour market structure and divisions suggests that the kind of universal pattern of work experience aspired to in policy will, in practice, only ever have an approximate relationship to the actual world of work. Whatever the big picture, provision in practice will inevitably be skewed towards particular types of concerns. At least on our sample, it would seem that those concerns (financial services) most happy with educational provision are also most supportive of work experience, but as a means for recruiting custom. They are, however, least likely to recruit young workers into full-time employment. The sector most likely to recruit young workers (manufacturing) is also that least satisfied with education. Lastly, the type of hi-tech concerns that exemplify 'big picture' models of future developments are least likely to provide work experience placements.

Many of the comments of the personnel managers, general managers and others we interviewed were tied to the problems of the local market conditions for labour and had little or nothing to do with the visions of the future of work promoted nationally. As far as they were concerned, the flexible employment policies promoted by their head offices, and heralded by government as a great achievement (the growth of post-compulsory education, and the 'flexible' attitudes to work of young people) were as likely to produce problems in the present as answers for the future (Rainnie and Kraithman 1994). For example, some in banking expressed grave reservations about their ability to recruit any young staff at all unless the policies of short-term contracts were changed.

A number of respondents indicated unease about these developments continuing and a desire to build up the core of the enterprise again, from the bottom, so to speak, though none thought that there would be much growth in the full-time employment of 16 to 18-year-olds. People we spoke to in these companies were perceptively aware of the way in which radical delayering at middle levels in combination with short-termism for new recruits has the potential to create a long-term problem for developing the kind of experience and expertise provided by the previous, more secure, model of long-term, incremental career development. With the exception of those in high-tech companies, most local managers across the sectors perceived the need to build up the size of the core of employees via the recruitment of young workers on standard contracts in the future. Not only was it believed that this would increase the commitment to the company of the younger staff, but the point was also made that the longer the delay of entry into full-time work as a result of extended education the higher were the expectations regarding pay. Hence, at this level, the central components of the 'big picture' promoted at national level are perceived as problematic.

Non-instrumental reasons for continuing with work experience for young people were never couched in terms of future national requirements but were part of helping young people in difficult times. As one respondent who managed training and human resources in a large firm of chartered surveyors and land managers put it; 'We would like it for our own children, and therefore we're happy to provide it for the parents of other children'. This concern for the predicament of young people was often built on reflections about their own families, or, by contrast, with the interviewees own experiences of entry into work. Another manager looked back on how she joined the bank and made much of the contrasts for young people between then and now; 'I mean, you know, when we joined it was, "That's your career for life". But now, OK, that's gone away'. The non-instrumental reasons for providing work experience placements were attached not to a positive vision of a flexible future but one of a more secure and stable past.

Returning to the relationship between national educational policy, local employers and educationalists, sources of new tensions can be detected. Local employers and managers do not seem to share the perspectives of either the government or, in the case of the larger corporations, their head offices. One wonders whether the contradictory aspects of preparing young people for a future world of flexibilized work will cause them to rethink the provision of work experience placements. To the extent that they emphasize the instrumental aspects of their links with schools, and approach young people as customers as opposed to future employees, then opposition from educators is also to be expected. Indeed, the evolving nature of the relationship between production and consumption has not really been taken seriously by those educationalists who have attempted to hitch their wagon to the star of economic change, flexibilization and globalization (viz. Young (1996); Brown and Lauder (1992)).

Work experience is, at least symbolically, very important for those wishing to change the relations between the academic and the vocational, because it is the only initiative which currently applies to all pupils. However, from some of our observations of employers involvement, any further vocation-alizing of the curriculum under the present conditions must come to terms with the 'forces of consumption'.

Notes

1   This project (Work Experience in the 1990s) was undertaken at Homerton College, Cambridge during 1996–7. It was directed by Professor Jean Ruddock and the team consisted of John Ahier, Roland Chaplin, Rachel Linfield, Rob Moore and Jacquetta Williams. It was funded by BP Chemicals. Further information is available from The Research Unit, Homerton College, Hills Road, Cambridge, CB2 2PH.

2   Kumar's (1992) review of these models of change suggests that we have, rather alarmingly, progressed through at least three epochs of industrial development in the last fifty years! A degree of scepticism towards 'post' theories is suggested.

3   Although it is not our intention, here, to review these competing accounts in detail (see Young 1996 and, for a more sceptical view, Hickox and Moore 1992) or assess their validity, it is important to stress that current orthodoxies, such as 'globalization', have been called into question (e.g., Hirst and Thompson 1996, Robinson 1997).

4   It is interesting to note the continuities between Trident's rationale and the rhetoric of the Plowden and Newsom Reports and the way in which they informed school work experience in the ROSLA period (Moore 1984).

5   See the Youth cohort Surveys, referenced in Roberts 1995, p. 7.

6   It is interesting to note, here, that typically computer skills and studies are represented as 'male' and considerable attention has been given to girls pupils' marginalization in the IT area. However, from the point of view of manufacturers, schools typically present a *feminized* model of IT based on word-processors and spreadsheets that has little point of contact with their uses of processors in industrial production. Indeed, it is the case that there is a strong congruence between the school IT model and those service sectors expressing such pronounced enthusiasm for female staff.

References

Ahier, J. (1996) Explaining economic decline and teaching children about industry; some unintended continuities?, in Ahier, J., Cosin, B. and Hales, M. *Diversity and Change, Education, Policy and Selection*, Routledge, London.

Ashton, D, Maguire, M. and Spilsbury, M. (1990) *Restructuring the Labour Market*, Macmillan, Basingstoke.

Bell, D. (1973) *The Coming of Post-industrial Society*, Basic Books, N.Y.

Brown, P. and Lauder, H. (1992) *Education for Economic Survival. From Fordism to Post-Fordism?* Routledge, London.

CBI (1995) *Realising the Vision: a Skills Passport*, CBI, London.

CBI (undated) *CBI input to the DFEE Consultation, Equipping Young People for Working Life*, CBI, London.

CBI (1994) *Creating a Learning Community*, CBI, London.

Daily Telegraph (1997) Chelsea Building Society advertisement, 18 January.

DFEE (1995) *Work Experience, A Guide for Employers*, HMSO, London.

DFEE (1996) *Equipping Young People for Working Life*, a consultative document on improving employability through the 14–16 curriculum, HMSO, London.

du Gay, P. (1996) *Consumption and Identity at Work*, Sage Publications, London.

H M Government (1996) *Learning to Compete: Education and Training for 14–19 Year Olds* (Cm 3486).

Hickox, M. and Moore, R. (1992) Education and Post-Fordism: a new correspondence?, in Brown, P. and Lauder, H. (eds) *Education for Economic Survival: from Fordism to Post-Fordism?*, Routledge, London.

Hickox, M. (1995) The English middle class debate, *British Journal of Sociology*, vol 46 no 2, pp. 311–324.

Hirst, P. Q. and Thompson, G. (1996) *Globalisation in Question*, Polity Press, Cambridge.

Hobbs, S., Lindsay, S. and McKechnie, J. (1996) The extent of child employment in Britain, *B. J. of Education and Work*, 9, 1.

Hughes, J. (1995) *Young Workers in Mr Major's De-regulated Economy*, Trades Union Research Unit Discussion Paper 47.

Hutson, S. (1992) *Saturday Jobs: Part-time Working by Young People 16–18 years in Full-Time Education*, ESRC Report 000231510, ESRC, Swindon.

Hutson, S. and Cheung, W. (1991) Saturday jobs: sixth formers in the labour market and the family, in Marsh, C, and Arber, S. (eds) *Family and Household: Division and Change*, Macmillan, London.

Industry in Education (1996) *Towards Employability*, Industry in Education Trust, London.

Jamieson, I. and Miller, A. (1991), History and policy context, in Miller, A, Watts, A. G. and Jamieson, I. (eds) *Rethinking Work Experience*, Falmer Press, London.

Kumar, K. (1992) New theories of industrial society, in Brown, P. and Lauder, H. (eds) *Education for Economic Survival*, Routledge, London.

Lavalette, M. (1996) Thatcher's working children, in Pilcher, J. and Wagg, S. (eds) *Thatcher's Children?*, Falmer Press, London.

Moore, R. (1984) Schooling and the world of work, in Bates, I., Clarke, J., Cohen, P., Finn, D., Moore, R. and Willis, P. (eds) *Schooling for the Dole*, Macmillan, Basingstoke.

Project Trident (1971) Project Trident: a partnership between education, industry and voluntary organizations, Project Trident, London.

Rainnie, A. and Kraithman, D. (1994) Labour market change and the organisation of work, in Gilbert, N., Burrows, R. and Pollert, A, (eds) *Fordism and Flexibility Divisions and Change*, Macmillan, Basingstoke.

Roberts, K. (1995) *Youth and Employment in Modern Britain*, Oxford University Press, Oxford.

Robinson G. (1997) *Literacy, Numeracy and Economic Performance*, London School of Economics Centre for Economic Performance, September.

Shilling, C. (1989) *Schooling for Work in Capitalist Britain*, Falmer Press, Lewes.

Vogler, C. (1994) Money in the Household, in Anderson, M., Bechhofer, F. and Gershuny, J. (eds) *The Social and Political Economy of the Household*, Oxford University Press, Oxford.

Watts, A. G. (1991) Employers' perspectives, in Miller, A., Watts, A. G. and Jamieson, I. (eds) *Rethinking Work Experience*, Falmer, London.

Wellington, J. (1992) Varying perspectives on work experience: 'there's nowt so queer as folk', *The Vocational Aspect of Education*, 44, 2.

Young, M. (1996) A curriculum for the twenty-first century? Towards a new basis for overcoming academic/vocational divisions, in Ahier, J., Cosin, B. and Hales, M. (eds) *Diversity and Change: Education, Policy and Selection*, Routledge, London.

Index